Feminist ways of knowing

Towards theorising the person
for radical adult education

Anne B Ryan

NIACE
THE NATIONAL ORGANISATION
FOR ADULT LEARNING

Published by the National Institute of Adult Continuing Education
(England and Wales)
21 De Montfort Street, Leicester, LE1 7GE
Company registration no. 2603322
Charity registration no. 1002775
The NIACE website on the Internet is http://www.niace.org.uk

First published 2001
©NIACE

CATALOGUING IN PUBLICATION DATA
A CIP record for this title is available from the British Library
ISBN 1 86201 095 1

Typeset by The Midlands Book Typesetting Co., Loughborough
Cover design by Boldface
Printed in Great Britain by Hobbs

Contents

Acknowledgements

In taking on the work for this book, I have been supported and encouraged by numerous family members, friends and colleagues. I thank my parents, Evelyn Ryan and Brendan Ryan, my sisters, Mary Ryan, Helen Ryan and Joan Ryan, my parents-in-law, Agnes Corway Savino and Vincent Savino, my friends and colleagues, Brid Connolly, Anne Ryan, Linda Connolly, Tom Collins, Derek Walsh, Rosaleen O'Riordan, and Jane Thompson. I owe enormous intellectual debts to the many writers and theorists on whose work I draw, and whom I know only through their publications. I sincerely thank the women who participated in the research, for their time, their openness, and their willingness to allow me to analyse their accounts. I also acknowledge the debt I owe to the women with whom I have worked in personal development education over the years. The Centre for Adult and Community Education at NUI Maynooth part-funded the compilation of the index. Special thanks to Frank Savino, for several years of unqualified endorsement of my attempts to integrate intellectual, physical and personal projects, despite their costs and often unsettling outcomes.

Part One

Part One

1   How this book came to be, and what it is trying to achieve

Introduction

This book offers an account of research on feminist subjectivities and resistance knowledges, and establishes their potential as sources for a politicised practice of women's personal development education. The project is grounded in my recognition, developed over several years' work in adult education in Ireland, that the field has generally accepted definitions of the person taken from mainstream psychology. The book argues that radical adult education – that is, adult education which supports progressive social movements, and which is praxis-oriented – needs to recast the ways that it conceives of the human subject, experience and power, by taking on board recent developments in feminist poststructuralism. The theoretical objective of the book is thus to advance thinking on adult politicisation and the sustainability of radicalised identities, and thereby to add to the resources of adult education for thinking in radical ways about pedagogy and the person.

Praxis-oriented adult education wants to produce critically reflexive people who are capable of shifting social balances towards social justice. How does it try do this? Theoretically stated, how does adult education pedagogy envisage the production of politicised human subjects, capable of successfully resisting oppressive structures and knowledges? For me, a feminist deeply influenced by poststructuralist theory, and with a specific interest in personal development education, the central organising question becomes: under what conditions is self-reflection a politically radical act for women?

I assert throughout this work that, in taking a feminist poststructuralist approach to adult development, there exists the potential for us to know things about the human person, the human subject, or, to use my preferred term, subjectivity. Taking account of poststructuralist developments can help us know more fully who we are and how we and others around us are constructed (*cf* Cherryholmes, 1988: 149). It is a central contention of the book that subjectivity is an arena for political activity. I assert that if radical adult education does not actively theorise subjectivity, then liberal-humanist ideas about the individual will prevail, under a guise of objective knowledge and neutrality.

The concept of subjectivity is developed throughout the book. The language and politics of subjectivity are particularly useful for my project, because they supply ways of talking and thinking about complexities, contradictions and emotional responses that people experience in their engagement with politics and with critical theories. An emphasis on history and context implicit in such an approach minimises the chances of falling into universalist theorising about the human subject. The approach taken to subjectivity also points to the necessity to make conscious the subjectivities of teachers as well as students in settings of emancipatory pedagogy.

Through its study of the construction of subjectivity, the book puts forward a theoretical account of the processes through which adult feminist politicisation and resistance are constituted. In taking subjectivity as a primary focus, I have a pedagogical concern to generate sources and themes for a politicised practice of women's personal development education. I posit that the study of feminist subjectivities helps to understand how individual women are both governed by and, more importantly for a theory of change, resist the different forms of power which structure gender relations. The book presents some pedagogical conditions that enable people (women in particular) to engage in ideology critique and personal and social change (cf Lather, 1986: 266). Thus, the theory which emerges is living, as well as specifically educational, that is, it is distinct from psychological or sociological theory applied to education (cf Lomax, 1994). A focus on subjectivity is appropriate for such a study, because subjectivity is treated as something that is produced and developed throughout adult life.

The first three chapters of the book, which comprise Part One, are devoted to investigating the human subject, and especially the female subject, as it is construed by western academic, liberation movement and pedagogical discourses. In Part One I set out the conceptual and theoretical tools which I consider necessary for my subsequent accounts of feminist subjectivity, in Part Two, by drawing on recent advances in feminist poststructuralist and psychodynamic theory. This chapter, Chapter One, introduces me and my epistemological stance, the social and historical context in which the book has been written, and the questions it explores. Chapter Two is a discussion of the general poststructuralist opposition to the modern, unitary human subject and to essentialist models of the person. Chapter Three examines some other liberation traditions, and discusses what feminist poststructuralism has in common with them, where it has developed their concepts of the person, and where it refutes them. In Chapter Four, I discuss the implications of a feminist poststructuralist stance for liberatory pedagogy and research.

Part Two, which comprises four chapters, begins with a study of the construction of feminist subjectivities in 1990s Ireland, through an analysis of case material from 20 self-defined feminist women. This is undertaken because of my conviction that if we want to produce feminist subjectivities or other kinds of politicised subjectivities in adult education, we need to have some kind of theory of how they are constructed and what they look like. Chapter Five examines the discourses of women and of feminism which form the content of feminist consciousness for the research participants. It also examines feminist subjectivity as a process of relations in the present. In Chapter Six, I examine how psychodynamic concepts can be used for the development of feminist poststructuralist discourses. Chapter Seven 'tests' the usefulness of the theory developed so far in the book for my practice of women's personal development education in a feminist poststructuralist framework. Chapter Seven is in many ways the crux of this book. In it, I attempt to develop feminist praxis which transcends the gap between theory and practical strategies in the classroom. In this chapter, my attempts to create and produce useful feminist knowledge in the course of pedagogical relations with other women are exposed for scrutiny. The final chapter, Chapter Eight, is a discussion of the usefulness of feminist poststructuralism as a tool for developing radical ways in which adult education pedagogy can theorise the person and knowledge.

Subjectivity

Historical conditions, meaning, experience and subjectivity are issues which have concerned certain social scientists and commentators since the 1960s. They have been of concern to movements such as feminism, post-Marxism, poststructuralism and postmodernism. The work of Michel Foucault, in particular, has stimulated interest in history and discourse. Semiotics and similar traditions in theories of language stress that meanings are produced within social and material relations rather than in relation to objects, or to a pre-existing 'reality' (Potter, 1996; Potter and Wetherell, 1987). The third concern, subjectivity and experience, approaches the traditional object of psychology, the individual, from a perspective which stresses power relations, language and meaning and the part played by unconscious forces (Hollway, 1991a: 185).

Language in poststructuralist theory is treated as something which constitutes the social world and subjectivity. It is not seen (as in liberal-humanist theories which underpin modernism) as a transparent reflection of a pre-existing social world or subject. Discourse is a term used to refer to the conceptual repertoires through which we interpret and filter our experiences. The discourses available at any particular period affect the ways that we can think and talk about a phenomenon, or the ways that we can respond to it.

Poststructuralist theorists see the treatment of the subject and the social as separate and different things as characteristic of modernity. This treatment has led to theoretical situations where there is a division of labour between psychology and sociology. To summarise, psychology deals with the individual and its dominant version of the individual is one that is unitary, rational and asocial at its core (the real or true self). It tends to unproblematically view the social as made up of a collection of such individuals (Broughton, 1987a; Fox and Prilleltensky, 1997). Sociology centralises the social and structural aspects of life, but without an adequate theory of individual action and agency in relation to these structures. Mainstream psychology (including human relations and feminist difference psychology) has not satisfactorily resolved problems with concepts like the individual, the self and personality, or with related concepts such as 'self-esteem', yet many sociologists tend to use them unproblematically (see Frith and Kitzinger, 1998). Poststructuralists and critical psychologists have attempted to overcome this dualism through the concept of subjectivity.

Subjectivity is conceptualised throughout this work. To introduce it here, I draw on critical psychology, which uses the term instead of the more usual psychological terms 'identity' and 'self'. Critical psychologists conceptualise subjectivity as an attempt to overcome the dualistic notion that the psychological and social parts of the human person are essentially separate territories: one internal and one external to the person. Instead, I regard both the social and the psychological as being in 'a recursive relationship of mutually advancing production and change' (Mama, 1995: 1). I follow the use of the term developed by Henriques, Hollway, Urwin, Venn and Walkerdine (1984), in their groundbreaking text on poststructuralist psychology and its implications for political struggles. The authors refer to subjectivity as 'individuality and self-awareness – the condition of being a subject' (*ibid*: 3). Weedon also writes (1997: 32):

> The terms subject and subjectivity are central to post-structuralist theory and they mark a crucial break with humanist conceptions of the individual which are still central to western philosophy and political and social organisation. 'Subjectivity' is used to refer to the conscious and unconscious thoughts and emotions of the individual, her sense of herself and her ways of understanding her relation to the world. ... poststructuralism proposes a subjectivity which is precarious, contradictory and in process, constantly being constituted in discourse each time we think or speak.

In this book, I investigate the production of subjectivity at first hand, through examining case material from 20 self-defined feminist women, as they experienced feminism in the particular social context of the second half of the 1990s in Ireland. I examine the historical and social material they draw on and how they process the discourses of feminism, sometimes transforming them, sometimes producing new discourses and sometimes experiencing personal transformation. I work with a theorisation of subjectivity that does not assume a unitary, static subject at its core but instead conceptualises subjectivity as multiple, dynamic and continuously produced in the course of social relations that are themselves changing and often contradictory. I demonstrate the effects of this theorisation on my practice as a facilitator of women's personal development education. However, the theorising is not meant to be a universal theory of human psychic or social development. As Mama (1995) emphasises, any such theorising is a local and specific analysis of adult human subjectivity.

Political and epistemological commitments

The terms feminism, poststructuralism and feminist poststructuralism require qualifiers, in order to avoid universalising very particular concepts. Feminism, as I address it,

> is resistance to invisibility and silencing. It is the recognition that resistance to gendered power relations is both integral to and distinct from all other resistances to global injustice. Feminism is a willingness to reckon with gender disparities as a universal but 'unnatural' power reality, a structural process affecting both male and female, which can be deconstructed through consciousness-raising and social change. Feminist resistance is articulated through women's movements and through individual actions, including refusals and separations. (Faith, 1994: 37)

Feminism is far from being a unified body of thought, as the book as a whole makes clear. Feminist poststructuralists recognise identity difference and power differentials, in common with other 'branches' of feminism, but avoid speaking with authority for 'women' or for 'feminists'. 'Patriarchy' is another term that causes difficulty (Cocks, 1989: 209). The term suggests both centralised and localised male power, unchallenged, and a clearly defined private/public split. The patriarchy as such does not exist (Faith, 1994: 63). Nevertheless, we can speak in various ways of patriarchal relations which structure power, authority and hierarchy and which regulate women's lives.

The term 'poststructuralism' is often used interchangeably with 'postmodernism'. I do not use it in this way, as I do not believe we are in a postmodern era, distinct from a modern one. Modernity is based on Enlightenment ideas and postmodernism is seen as involving the realisation that all knowledge is produced, that there are no fundamental 'truths' (Craib, 1992: 101). We do not live in an age when most people reject the idea of fundamental truths. Nevertheless, I accept the idea that we live in an age with a 'postmodern turn' (Hassan, 1987, cited in Lather, 1991: 4). Following Lather, I use the term 'poststructural' to mean the working out of cultural theory taking the postmodern turn into account.

Feminist poststructuralism, structures and the gender regime

Poststructuralism emerged as a response to structuralism – an epistemological position within modernism which sought to establish the underlying structures which are the foundation of all capitalist societies. Gender (or sex), for example, was seen as an immutable, inherent and generally unproblematic dynamic in all societal forms of capitalism, a dynamic which performed certain functions. In this, we can see structuralism's universalising and historical tendencies and its compliance with essentialist assumptions (Pritchard Hughes, 1995: 221–2). Essentialism and universalism have been problematised by poststructuralists. Postmodernists have done so too, but have dissolved the idea of structures completely. Poststructuralism does not deny the existence of structures, but asks how they have developed and are maintained, and how they can be changed. This project is 'founded on the notion of intervention and resistance and the desire to transform that which is oppressive' (ibid).

Poststructuralism insists on complex understandings, but insists equally on their attachment to political ideals, and a commitment to the construction of a better world. It is important therefore to be able to include a structural analysis in the feminist poststructuralist framework, since there is no doubt that structures have material effects (Connell 1990, 1995; Hollway 1994). How can a concept like structure be used without succumbing to either dualism, determinism, universalism or relativism, all of which are incapable of subverting the gender status quo? Hollway (ibid) has suggested a means to do this, drawing on the work of Connell (1987, 1990).

Connell (1990: 523) defines the term 'gender regime' as 'the historically produced state of play in gender relations within an institution which can be analysed by taking a structural inventory'. He suggests three structures as a preliminary taxonomy of gender relations: a gendered division of labour, a structure of power and a structure of cathexis (Connell, 1987: 96–7; 1990: 523–6; 1995: 74–5).

- *A gendered division of labour, or production.* This includes: organisation of housework and childcare; division between paid and unpaid work; segregation in labour markets (women's and men's jobs); discrimination in training and promotion; unequal wages and unequal exchange.
- *A structure of power.* This includes: hierarchies of state and business; institutional and interpersonal violence; sexual regulation and surveillance; domestic authority and its contestation.
- *A structure of cathexis*, 'or the construction of emotionally charged social relationships' (Connell, 1987: 112). This includes: the patterning of object choice; desire and desirability; the production of heterosexuality and homosexuality and the relationship between them; the socially structured antagonisms of gender, trust and distrust; jealousy and solidarity in marriages and other relationships; the emotional relationships involved in child-rearing.

According to Connell, the first structure is based on the principle of separation and the second on the principle of unequal integration. He does not suggest a principle for the third structure, but Hollway (1994) does. She suggests that it is emotional investments in gender difference. Her suggestion is based on gender analyses that have confronted the question of how subjectivity is fundamentally gendered and how structures and practices are reproduced or modified through subjectivity. The emotional investment in gendered subjectivity reproduces gender-differentiated power relations and this is important for the analysis of structures of cathexis.

Feminist poststructuralist politics

Although feminist poststructuralism is not a unified body of theory, Fuss (1990) is of the opinion that if there is any essentialism in feminist poststructuralism, it is the centrality of politics. Politics for feminist poststructuralism refers to opposing and subverting power relations, by revealing the vested interests and social construction process that lie behind them (*cf* Frosh, 1987: 12). Generating new theoretical perspectives from which the dominant can be criticised and new possibilities envisaged is especially important. Radical feminism in particular has contributed much to the development of concepts that include the personal in the political. The original consciousness-raising approach to politics was deconstructive, in that the personal/political binary was exposed and attempts made to subvert it. Yet, the nature of the personal and of personal experience is problematised for feminist poststructuralism in ways that undermine the humanist assumptions implicit in liberal and radical feminisms. This valuing of women's difference from men is based on a belief that timeless and true differences exist. While it can be strategically useful to emphasise and celebrate these differences from time to time (Kristeva, 1986), the valuing of such essential difference, if misused or misinterpreted, can be used to support the reintroduction of stereotyping (Middleton, 1993: 129). Negotiating diversity, multiplicity and differences is a different but necessary political project.

Feminist poststructuralism sees the categories of female and male as socially constructed and rejects the idea that human beings have essential natures, including essential gendered natures. For example, the idea that men and women are identified as such on the basis of 'transhistorical, eternal, immutable essences' (Fuss, 1990: xi) is rejected, because it cannot account for some people's discomfort with existing arrangements and their desire for change. An essentialist formulation of womanhood, even when made by feminists, binds the individual to her identity as a woman and thus cannot represent a solution to sexism (Alcoff, 1988: 415). This objection to essentialism leads to a rejection of reductionist, monocausal or foundationalist explanations characteristic of liberal-humanist thought and practice. History and genealogy are seen as crucial in the development of ideas, since 'truth' does not exist outside the social formation.

The body of theory pertaining to feminist poststructuralism is capable of analysing the workings of a patriarchal society in all its manifestations – ideological, institutional, organisational, subjective – accounting not only for continuities but also for how changes take place. Through its embracing of the concept of the deconstruction of dualisms, it enables us to think about gender without either simply reversing old hierarchies or confirming them (Scott, 1988). Deconstruction involves examining the ways that meanings are based on oppositions (such as feminine/masculine, public/private, rational/intuitive, nature/ culture) which are constructed, not natural. The work of Derrida has shown that such fixed oppositions conceal the extent to which things presented as oppositional are, in fact, interdependent. Derrida has also shown that the interdependence is hierarchical, with one term dominant. Deconstruction, then, analyses how power operates when such dualisms or oppositions are called into play as rhetorical indicators of a fixed reality (Nicholson, 1999: 7).

Feminist poststructuralism sees women as oppressed by virtue of their sex, but also along other axes of social difference, like age, race, ethnicity, sexual practice, religion, ability, etc. Its anti-essentialism requires that we look on a broad scale at gender identity and at the gendered positions which are available. It recognises the workings of difference, and that women are not a unitary category. It can embrace a variety of feminist, socialist and green politics. It emphasises the constructed, historical and contextual nature of conclusions and knowledge, yet recognises the importance of making choices and taking action for change, however flawed. Strategy becomes important, and this may mean using humanist and essentialist concepts from time to time, drawing on them selectively (Spivak, 1990: 100).

In adopting a feminist poststructuralist politics, I take the epistemological position that all knowledge is socially constructed and socially and historically situated. Therefore there is no value-free or universal social theory. I believe that the goal of intellectual rigour can best be served not by claiming objectivity and ignoring the values underpinning one's intellectual work, but rather by acknowledging the commitments, motivations and conditions that have played a part in its production. Feminist poststructuralism is not the only body of theory that can support political and epistemological positions such as these, but it is through reading and engaging with poststructuralism that I, as a feminist woman, have found the clarifications and insights which seemed most useful to me and the most enabling of my feminist practice.

Much feminist hostility to poststructuralist theories of subjectivity focuses on their anti-humanist tendency. Anti-humanism as a theoretical position is often confused with being anti-woman, especially by feminists whose primary concern is to value and celebrate the experience and culture of women (Weedon, 1997: 71). However, feminist poststructuralism's concern with subjectivity is motivated by a concern with understanding how individual women in society are both governed by and resist the different forms of power which govern social relations, seeing this as necessary for providing the context for a radical politics (Kerfoot and Knights, 1994). Feminist poststructuralism emphasises the importance of making choices and taking action, however flawed or imperfect they may be.

Feminist poststructuralism also realises that, although some concepts may be rejected as inadequate for a radical politics today, they were politically progressive in their time. I want to avoid any kind of teleological implications when I say that feminist poststructuralist theories are the best so far, or the 'one best way' (cf Lather, 1991). Feminist poststructuralism has a principled objection to ideas of progressivism. To accept such a position would imply that the field of critical theory can make repeated incremental advances as a function of specific discoveries, methodological innovations and clarifications of terminology, in a progressive process of construction independent of political motive or aim (Broughton, 1987b: 2).

One difficulty of working within a feminist poststructuralist framework has been mentioned: that many people see its anti-humanism as anti-women. Another difficulty is that it is perceived as currently fashionable in academia, but of little practical use in 'the real world' (Wilkinson, 1997). Poststructuralism and feminist appropriations of it have been criticised for removing feminism and feminist theory from the lives of most feminists and from 'ordinary' women, into a closed academic realm (see, for example, Gill, 1996; McNeil, 1993; Ransom, 1993). In this realm, it is claimed, feminist poststructuralists use feminism as a means to advance their professional careers. They also offer it only as negative critique, with no practical value for political action. While this particular use of feminist poststructuralism may be happening, it does not diminish what I see as its practical value. Authors such as Lather (1991); Kenway, Willis, Blackmore and Rennie (1994); Lewis (1993) and Middleton (1993) have shown in their work how they have used it in practical ways to construct feminist change. It is one of the aims of this book also to show its practical value.

Power, resistance and agency

Power, resistance and agency are issues central to this book as a whole. Resistance is the antithesis of the victim identity often associated with the position of women (Faith, 1994: 56). But it needs to be accompanied by 'success' (cf Walzer, 1986, cited in ibid: 58). 'Success' is what I conceptualise as agency throughout this work. The concern with agency has been identified as one of the most important areas of work for feminist sociologists (Roseneil, 1995: 200, 201) and, I assert, for psychologists and educators also, in coming years. As yet, it remains undertheorised (*ibid*).

In the traditional or agonistic definition of agency in sociological theory, to act is necessarily to be the agent who carries out various acts (Davies, 1990a). Agency is an individual matter in which any individual conceives of a line of action, knows how to achieve it and has the power, authority and right to execute it. In this model, which coincides with what has largely become the common-sense view of the person in the social world, there is an agonistic relationship between self and other and self and society. The individual, along with other individuals, does not collaboratively construct the social world. Rather, the individual is conceived as being in relation to 'society', which acts forcefully upon the individual and against which any individual can pit themselves.

Davies (*ibid*) develops a model of the person and of agency which stands in sharp contrast to the agonistic one. Following a poststructuralist model of language and discourse (which will be elaborated in the following chapters), she asserts that persons are persons, by virtue of the fact that they use the discursive practices of the collectives of which they are members. Such collectives might include children, girls, boys, a group of friends, a study group, a classroom, or one's family. Each person can speak only from the positions made available within those collectives. A child, for example, may know how to speak as an adult, but is not allowed to and may not want to. A feminist may choose not to speak as such in certain situations, or if s/he does speak as such, may not be understood. One's desires are formulated in the terms that make sense in each of the discourses, or frames of reference available. Embedded in the discursive practices of one's collective is an understanding that each person is one who has an obligation to take themselves up as a knowable, recognisable identity, part of the collective, but recognisably separate from it. In this separateness from the collective, one can be said to have agency.

There are discursive practices which make it not thinkable or do-able for certain persons or categories of persons to take themselves up as agents, that is, for their actions to influence the way the 'ball-game' (Smith, 1987: 32) develops. This is frequently women's experience. Davies uses as an illustration of this point Busfield's (1989) example of the way problematic female behaviour is often viewed as illness, and male as active wrongdoing. Agency can be denied to women and others, depending on the particular discursive practices in use and the positioning of the person in those practices. It becomes clear, then, that it is not a necessary element of human existence to be agentic, but a contingent element. This is in marked contrast to the agonistic model, where simply acting confers agency.

The discursive approach to agency has important political implications relating to the possibility for change. As Henriques *et al* (1984: 223, 224) demonstrate, roles and stereotypes are social impositions on a pre-existent subject. One implication of such a 'role' approach is that change is possible through the production and reinforcement of positive images for women (*cf* Coward, 1984: introduction). However, this approach prompts a simplistic view of the relation between social 'oppression' and individual 'repression'.

Personal development education examined in the context of the position of women in Ireland

In the past three decades in Ireland, there have been significant changes in family structures, lifestyles, and in work and leisure patterns. Legislation has also been introduced such as the removal of the marriage ban in the civil service in 1972, the Equal Employment Act 1977, the changed definition of dependency in 1986 and the introduction of divorce in 1996. Such changes have affected women's lives. Equality, contraception, divorce/separation and domestic violence have become issues of public debate. The contemporary Irish feminist movement experienced a resurgence in 1970 and has made an impact in challenging the status of women in Irish society (Connolly, 2001). Women are participating in the paid labour force as never before.

Nevertheless, economic inequalities persist. Despite the growth of the 'Celtic Tiger' economy in the late 1990s, low-paid, part-time and temporary jobs and lack of childcare facilities act as barriers to the economic equality of women. The Irish Constitution portrays a narrow role for women, equating them with motherhood and work in the home, perpetuating beliefs that women should be the main carers in society. Recent childcare debates have been constrained by the assumption that women are the only sex properly suited to childcare, and by the silence of most men on the issue.

In parliamentary political life, since the most recent general election women make up 20 of 166 TDs in Dail Eireann and 8 women senators out of 60. There is no woman secretary of any government department and women in top jobs in the judiciary and other areas are still in a minority. Daly (1989: 17) asserts that three main factors account for women's lack of formal power within government and state agencies: women's limited role in the economy; attitudes towards women and the roles they should play; and access to resources. She argues that 'women must actively develop an understanding of power itself, of the institutions of power and how power is exercised' (ibid). This call is echoed by Mulvey (1995). However, it seems that these calls to analyse power are rooted in a liberal-humanist understanding of where power resides and how it operates. The liberal view 'claims that power resides in legal and governmental institutions' (Young, 1998: 5), and does not recognise discursive power or cathectic structures. This is an understanding of power as juridical, and one of the things this book wishes to do is to broaden understandings of power, in order to take its discursive, and less obvious, forms into account.

During the late 1980s and 1990s the women's movement in Ireland has been most evident in the 'mushrooming' of community-based women's groups, the consolidation of Women's Studies in Irish universities and growth in women's publishing (Connolly, 1996: 68). In the community women's groups, new forms of structure and organisation are emerging, emphasising non-hierarchical relations, participation and autonomy. Collins (1992) considers that these groups resemble the small-group, consciousness-raising radical women's sector of the 1970s, although this view is disputed by O'Donovan and Ward (1996, 1999). Some of these groups are autonomous, some are highly interconnected and networked with the generic community group's movement and others are connected to the state through its various funding programmes (Connolly, 1996: 68) and through the Home-School-Community Links Scheme of the Department of Education and Science. This growth co-exists with the growth in the last decade of widespread interest in personal power, spirituality, counselling, psychotherapy and the life of the emotions, which form part of what Giddens (1991) describes as projects of personal reflexivity.

A strong anti-feminist climate also exists (Spray, 1997; Connolly, 1999). Inglis (1994) highlights the role of the Roman Catholic Church in the backlash, as does Byrne (1995: 13). Wilcox (1991, cited in O'Donovan and Ward, 1996: 16) concludes that Catholicism is a determining factor in people's attitudes to greater gender equality in family roles. O'Dovonan and Ward (*ibid*) point out that Galligan (1993) has developed this by arguing that while there is a great demand for equality in all aspects of what she terms public life in Ireland, social attitudes and values indicate that there is considerable public pressure on women to achieve equality, while retaining their traditional family roles. O'Donovan and Ward (1996: 17) conclude that 'to argue that women's groups per se are inherently part of the feminist movement is akin to arguing that woman, by definition, is feminist'.

For the most part the women's groups have concentrated their activities on personal development courses (Ryan and Connolly, 2000). The criticism has been made that the energy invested in these courses has not gone on to tackle structural changes (Daly, 1989; Mulvey, 1991, 1995). Inglis (1994) on the other hand, while acknowledging these criticisms and also having a central concern with power, concludes that the groups' concentration on personal development courses is based on felt needs and interests. The next section examines the content of such courses, but for the moment I wish to concentrate on some of the debates surrounding personal development education in Ireland.

In the analyses and commentaries on these issues and on personal development, and in the assertions that women need to 'move beyond' personal development, there is an assumption that structures are the 'root causes' of oppression. This is emphasised especially in Mulvey's (1995) report on women's power, which arises out of a conference of women's networks in Ireland, entitled *Women's Power for a Change*. This document provides an overview of current dominant feminist attitudes to women's power and personal development education in Ireland, as the conference was attended by influential activists, policy makers, academics and community leaders. The report documents frustration at the lack of structural change and lack of participation and representation by women in community, regional and state development. It exhibits a belief that a concentration on personal development is preventing women from engaging in structural analysis. The reluctance of women to accept the label feminist is noted, as is the view that the priorities of funders mean that women's work is acceptable only if it is 'poverty work' (*ibid*: 17). The role of the Roman Catholic Church and religious personnel in facilitating personal development courses is also noted and identified with the failure to address feminist issues in personal development.

Clancy (1995), in a large-scale survey, found that the majority of personal development courses in Ireland are run either by religious personnel or by people with a primary interest in counselling and/or psychology. While several writers and commentators have already identified religion with the maintenance of the gender status quo, there is little published work on the Irish context which makes links between the maintenance of the gender status quo and the predominance of a psychological view of women as essentially different from men. Gardiner (1997: 42) points to the existence of a 'dual culture' or a 'female culture' mentality in Irish political life as evidence of the continued existence of patriarchal social relations. Feminist writing from Britain and the USA (which I explore in Chapters Two and Three) has demonstrated the role of psychology (both mainstream and feminist 'difference') and beliefs in a female nature and culture in maintaining the gender status quo (see also Oakley, 1998), but such writing has had little influence on published feminist work in Ireland.

Psychological approaches to women's personal development and education are usually seen as a secular challenge to religious perspectives on women's nature. This is particularly so in Ireland, where traditional, old-style Roman Catholicism is widely seen as having contributed to women's oppression. Both religion and psychology, however, share a view of 'woman' that does nothing to challenge existing power arrangements. Mednick (1989: 1122) describes the problem as follows:

> It is my view that the different voice/maximalist view, even though professed by feminists who are not in agreement with the rightwing agenda, nevertheless attained its popularity because it meshed so easily with the pro-family women's nature ideology that has become the dominant public rhetoric ... arguments for women's intrinsic difference, whether innate or deeply socialised, support conservative policies that, in fact, could do little else but maintain the status quo *vis à vis* gender politics.

Given the dominance of religious and counselling-based facilitators, there is little feminist personal development being carried out in Ireland. It is a mistake, therefore, for Irish feminists concerned with power to call for women to 'move beyond' personal development, as the conference organisers did (Mulvey, 1995: 19). The personal should not be regarded as constituting merely a 'first step' which is less important than structures. This is reductionist thinking which ignores cathectic structures and which recent feminist theorising has shown to be inadequate for transformative politics.

Mulvey's report, which forms the basis for this discussion, does, indeed, draw attention to the strengths which women can bring from personal development into other areas of political activity. But what both the report and the conference fail to do is to distinguish different types of personal development. Courses in personal development in this country are facilitated from a feminist perspective in only a tiny minority of cases. This is borne out by Clancy's (1995) survey, which found that counselling is the main training undertaken for facilitators. Clancy argues, correctly in my view, that counselling training is capable of treating the symptoms, but not the causes, of women's oppression and diverts attention away from inequalities to focus on individuals. This is not a fault of personal development *per se*. It is a result of the dominance of mainstream psychology practices, an issue to which I return in more detail in Chapters Two and Three.

Mulvey (1995: 19) reports that the conference on power concluded with a number of questions for the participants, one of which was 'What is needed for women to move beyond personal development?' This question would have addressed the issue much better, if it had asked what is needed to politicise personal development education for women and prevent it becoming an exercise focused *solely* on personal symptoms, spirituality and individual healing. My immediate answer to this question, shared by Clancy (1995) in her research conclusions, is that we need feminist/politicised facilitators who are able to incorporate social analysis, radical politics and feminism into course content which is also capable of meeting the felt and expressed needs of many women for a focus on their personal lives.

Martin and Mohanty (1988) ask, 'What has home got to do with it?' The answer must be that patriarchy and patriarchal relations are at their most naturalised and normalised in family life and in heterosexual relations. In the particular point in history where we live now in Ireland, and given the strong climate of anti-feminism which co-exists with religious and liberal-humanist ideological views of women, home has an awful lot to do with it. We live in a formally egalitarian liberal democracy, where it is acceptable for women to take on roles outside their homes, in paid work, sport, party politics and many other arenas. But through discourses that position them as essentially domestic and maternal they are still widely considered to be the only sex properly suited to primary childcare. Issues of domesticity and maternity surface time and again in the personal development courses of my experience (*cf* Clancy, 1995). Dealing with them is a major challenge to contemporary feminism (Coward, 1993; Hochschild, 1990). 'Moving beyond' personal development is not the solution. Politicising personal development by taking feminist poststructuralism and the existence of cathectic structures into account is one of the necessary responses to this many-faceted challenge.

What does a personal development course look like?

There is no set content for personal development courses. However, a typical Stage One course runs for eight to ten weeks for two to two and a half hours one morning a week, for the number of weeks decided on by the facilitator. Topics covered include: reasons for coming to the course and hopes and concerns about it; ground rules; life stories; human rights; feelings; relationships; guided relaxation and visualisation; managing stress; assertiveness; communication skills; setting goals; social analysis; women's health and nutrition; sexuality; education; envisioning 'my ideal world'; affirmation of self and acceptance of praise (Aontas Women's Education Group, 1991; Clancy, 1995; Clark and Prendiville, 1992; Hayes, 1990).

There is usually a check-in with each woman at the beginning of a session, to see how she has been feeling and what has been going on in her life since the last session. Games, icebreakers and energisers are used. 'Homework' is usually set, in the form of giving oneself a treat during the week between sessions. Self-help is emphasised. The methodology is highly participative and women are encouraged to share only as much information about themselves as they feel comfortable with. A typical group starts off with 12 to 14 women. Invariably, a few drop out after a week or two. Clancy (1995) also found that some groups are run on an 'open' basis, with different members attending each week. This was found to be a problem for the development of a sense of collectivity in a group (*ibid*). When I refer to personal development education from here on in this work, especially in Chapter Five, I assume closed groups, running for eight to ten weeks, with the same facilitator or co-facilitators throughout.

Women come to personal development courses because they feel a need to make some changes in their lives, usually starting with family life and with a desire to 'get out of the house more'. This was Clancy's (*ibid*) finding and is my experience. Courtney (1992) interprets the act of participation in most adult education courses as evidence of a desire for change and West's (1996: 25, 26) findings bear out this interpretation. Fagan (1991: 67) describes the community women who attended her social analysis classes as 'searching for an unspecified development'. Personal development courses are part of the distinct process that is adult learning. Adult learning is seen as voluntary, self-directed, practical, participatory, with sharing of experiences and resources, related to individuals' self-concept or self-esteem, and possibly anxiety-provoking for the learners. It also attempts to take cognisance of different learning styles (Cranton, 1992: 5–7). Of themselves, these qualities do not necessarily make for politicisation of the participants (Kiely, Leane and Meade, 1999). However, the processes which they involve are widely seen as essential for radical pedagogies which are also providing new or radical content (McDonald, 1989).

How this book came to be

The study and practice on which this book is based are situated deep in the tensions, contradictions and flawed resolutions of Irish feminist life and social relations, in my everyday working life and in my home life (*cf* Middleton, 1993: 65). The conditions of my work as a teacher of young people from 1979 to 1991 were often in conflict with the feminism I had been constructing for myself from the mid-1970s, when I finished second-level schooling. Sexist and other regulatory discourses filter experience in schools and the difficulty of sharing and promoting muted discourses, such as feminism and other discourses of egalitarianism, in a schooling context often led me into conflict with authorities and peers. The power of hegemonic practices frustrated and depressed me. I was also aware of my cultural and economic capital (Bourdieu, 1986) and my privileged status, conferred on me by the institutions of the schools where I worked, and of the power related to that status. As time went on, I also became aware that schooling is not always successful in socialising pupils into hegemonic discourses (see also Connell, 1995: 37). There is room in schooling for contestation and resistance, although it appeared to me that the forms of contestation taken almost always reproduced dominant discourses of sexuality and gender relations.

My later work as a home-school-community liaison teacher (1991–5) centred on parents, which, in practice, meant mothers. This sort of work bolstered certain dominant assumptions about families and the functions of mothers, which I considered ideological, and which I wanted to resist. Westwood (1988: 80) comments:

> Ultimately, adult education worked with a notion of the incompetent woman in need of upgrading through adult education. For all its contradictions, feminism was in direct opposition to this. The woman of feminist discourse was competent, active and struggling in and against the state, and the discourses that defined her personal and public world. Those struggles are ongoing.

Westwood is writing about the late nineteenth and early twentieth centuries. But this is how I felt the Home-School-Community (HSL) scheme constructed women, as well as assuming that the function of these 'upgraded' women would be to socialise their children and to produce them as the kind of self-regulating subjects on which the existence of the bourgeois state relies. The tensions with my feminism were great.

Yet, the existence of an ideological scheme such as HSL allowed me to have contact with women which, as a classroom teacher, I would not otherwise have had. In my contacts with the women, I attempted to play a subversive role whenever I saw a space to do this. I participated in and later facilitated personal development courses with many of the women in the area where I worked and saw evidence of consciousness raising and of some radical personal changes. However, my subversive desires were not obvious within the school where I was employed. There, it was generally assumed that I shared dominant assumptions. So whenever I tried to operate in a different discourse and persuade the institution as a whole that it needed to examine assumptions about class, gender and ability, these discourses were alien to many (although by no means all) of my colleagues, and led to my marginalisation.

While I was marginal to mainstream schooling discourses, this was not obvious to most of the parents I met. (Those who were aware that I felt marginalised were the women with whom I took part in the personal development courses. They know me well and this colours our ongoing relations.) For most of the parents, I embodied the power of the school as institution, as well as the power and privilege of the middle classes. Even though I have engaged in a critique of my class positioning, I am aware that privilege, once bestowed, cannot be undone (Mantel, 1994: 44). Yet the existence of my critique and my awareness of the regulatory nature of many schooling practices marginalised me within the school as institution. So I was positioned within and outside dominant discourses of education. This is not unusual for educators who want to challenge the status quo:

> I tried to distance myself from my institution, both ideologically and physically. Nevertheless, I had to acknowledge and live with the authority they bestowed on me and the resources it provided me with. (Johnston, 1993: 81)

In personal and social relations, I am positioned and I position myself as both feminist and feminine, with all the different relations attached to those discourses. In all my relations, I perceive myself as partly on the margins. I do not recognise myself in dominant texts, even within feminism. It is from the margins that political resistances are often formed (Faith, 1994: 39), although we should not romanticise the idea of marginality. Moreover, along with my marginality, I possess cultural capital which positions me powerfully.

For a long time, the experience of marginality was a source of disablement for me. However, the productive personal work which I have done on my experience of contradiction and the attendant loss of certainty has had the outcome of enabling me to construct feminist knowledge useful to me. It is the product of interweaving my own life history with theoretical knowledge and it leads me to the postmodern challenge of revealing the personal history of one's work (Greene, 1993). I discuss some of my story here because it shows my personal affinities in what could seem otherwise to be abstract theory. It is my belief that there are always personal, biographical affinities in theory.

Having called myself a feminist, and having been influenced by socialist feminism and radical feminist theory since I finished school in 1975, I entered 1993 in a state of crisis. I felt irrevocably 'stuck' in my political agency. I had just completed a thesis (Ryan, 1992) which mapped the oppression of young women. I had adopted a feminist poststructuralist theoretical framework for the thesis and had spent three years engaging intensely with the theory. The theory refined my feminist identity and ideas and I felt passionate about its value for 'making hope practical' (Kenway *et al*, 1994), but the research had failed to investigate successful acts of resistance and change, and I was unable to use the work I did for the thesis to overcome the crisis of 'stuckness' I was experiencing. Strong feelings dominated my life: of anger, rage, depression, paralysis and fear. Added to this was a dreadful bitterness that I, who had identified my politics as feminist for so long, was ineffective. Eventually, I was persuaded to seek counselling. This was something I had always scorned, because of my belief that it bolsters the status quo. But I liked the counsellor and decided to give it a try, as we concentrated on the strong feelings I was experiencing. What I had not anticipated was the way that my work on my emotional life would interact with the feminist poststructuralist theory I had been reading and engaging with intellectually, to produce transformation and feminist agency.

It was an enormous challenge for me to work on my feelings and emotional investments. I arrived at a great deal of the 'really useful knowledge' (Thompson, 1996) alone, between sessions with my counsellor. I think that taking the space and time to acknowledge the feelings allowed me to do the other work in between sessions. I came to acknowledge the construction of my subjectivity in discourses that were not feminist and I found this difficult, because being a feminist had been so important to me for so long. But while it was painful, it was also productive of new feminist ways of being for me. It also made it possible for me to undertake this present work in the way I do. In Chapters Five and Six, where I analyse accounts from other feminist women, I draw attention at several points to my own role in producing their accounts and to where my self-knowledge illuminates similarities and differences between us.

Hollway (1989: 39) points out that psychic defences operate against formulating different accounts of oneself, because of the self-threatening implications. For some women, feminism is a threat. For me, femininity operated in the same way. I felt threatened by the possibility of recognising that my subjectivity had been produced in discourses of femininity. But by ceasing to suppress their productive forces in creating meaning in my subjectivity and in my heterosexual couple relationship, I came to an understanding of parts of my power in that relationship and in other relationships also. One of the ways structural gender difference is reproduced recursively is in the minutiae of heterosexual couple relationships (Hollway, 1982; 1984a), and in relationships between women and men in work organisations also (Hollway, 1994). This, then, was of major importance in helping me to have agency in creating structural changes, as well as, and distinct from, having the potential to improve interpersonal relations.

I no longer felt fraudulent as an individual in my intimate relationships and this seemed to free me to make progress on work relationships also. That is, I no longer felt that the political convictions which I held and expressed were 'invisible' in my actions. I was able to centralise rather than marginalise feminism in my moment-to-moment actions, with a sense of agency. The structures of many organisations and job settings, while often formally based on equality policies, reproduce sexist and classist discourses similar to those operating in heterosexual relations (Hollway, *ibid*). Strategies developed in my domestic life became inspirations for strategies taken at work. While not always successful in the ways that I envisaged, they disrupted patterns of work relationships with often interesting effects. Working out these and similar issues for myself, using a combination of my intellectual theoretical background and the counselling process, was immensely satisfying. None of the issues I have mentioned here was the subject of counselling sessions, yet the attention to emotionality within those sessions facilitated the broader process which I describe here.

Attention to the emotions carries with it the danger of being dominated by liberal-humanist discourses, with their individualising effects. Intellectually, I had been aware of this from my engagement with feminist poststructuralist theory. As Kenway, Willis and Nevard (1990) remind us, any process that attends to personal growth is on tricky ideological ground. Avoiding emotional issues is not the way to go about change, but the dominant discourses or intellectual repertoires (whether consciously articulated or not) which provide resources for reflecting on the emotions are dominated either by religion or by human relations psychologies. For reasons which I explore in Chapters Two and Three of this book, these theories of the self are not sufficient to sustain a disruption of the gender status quo. Yet, crucially, they are the theories on which adult education in Ireland has relied for the most part, either explicitly or implicitly.

Attending to my emotional life was the crucial missing piece for me in developing a practical theory of myself, within a feminist poststructuralist framework. Most importantly, I had a discourse outside the dominant ones within which to reflect on myself and filter my experiences. This is one of the reasons why I place an emphasis in Chapters Two and Three on reviewing theories of the person which refute liberal-humanist accounts. I also assert in those chapters that recent radical feminist theory, while it is critical of liberal humanism, falls into an account of the human subject which is highly deterministic, in such a way that it cannot provide a theory of agency.

Before I developed a theory of myself, I related to feminist poststructuralist theory in an analytic and rationalising manner. This is not to say that I was not passionate about what I believed. But because I perceived myself as ineffective, the passion was not allowed to express itself in productive ways. It showed itself most often in anger, self-pity or frustration. My inability to act was in conflict with my political analysis and a contradiction of feminism's insistence on action. Conventionally, I could have been labelled 'burnt out'. Through the politicised personal development and self-reflection process, I was able to 'reclaim conflict and contradiction as knowledge' (Walicki, 1983, cited in Selby, 1984: 348).

Following my individual work with the counsellor, I changed my attitude to personal development education, in my work as home-school-community liaison teacher. I organised and participated in two personal development courses with another facilitator and began to theorise about the possibilities for them to be facilitated from a specifically feminist perspective. Under supervision, I facilitated several courses and I became convinced of their potential for politicisation, if facilitated by a politicised facilitator. The other factor that convinced me I should become involved in personal development course facilitation was that women were and are attending them in very large numbers in Ireland. They provide a forum where feminism can reach women who are looking for names for their experiences of power and resistance. If feminists distance themselves from personal development education, it is open to colonisation by right wing forces, without even a struggle.

My own personal development work has been valuable to me. It has helped me to formulate a personal radical feminist politics, taking into account the poststructuralist knowledge which I like so much. It has also helped me to feel more agentic in this political sense, in the adult education arena, which I see as one forum for feminist activism. However, I am also acutely aware of the regulatory potential of personal development courses, when the areas of enquiry that are generally repressed are left that way. This leads me to a point where I am more accurately able to set out what I am trying to achieve by writing this book.

What this book is trying to achieve

Radical adult education is part of a tradition of radical praxis-oriented pedagogy which wishes to link education with social justice, and which wishes to act, politically and culturally, to change history. It is interested in the pedagogical and epistemological conditions that can facilitate learners and educators to push forward this aim. One of the ways to understand these conditions is by studying politicised adult subjectivities. Feminists provide strong examples of politicised adults, about whom we can ask the following questions:

- What forms do feminist subjectivities take? How are they constructed?
- Under what conditions can women do personal development and self-reflection work in ways that construct politicised and agentic feminist subjectivities?

Related to these central questions are the following:

- The personal change which people often experience as a result of personal development work can just as easily ally itself with the status quo as with a desire to challenge the status quo. What makes the difference?

- How, in practical terms, does a feminist politics help women to make powerful changes in their adult social relations, and to successfully take up subject positions which are capable of disrupting the gender status quo?

The questions are important because feminist women's experiences of politicisation and resistance in Irish society have not yet been identified, or adequately researched. The task at hand is not only a matter of their inclusion, but also of the generation of new theory about the person for adult education, which requires the study of resistance ways of knowing, and the taking into account of cathectic structures and discursive forms of power.

2 Feminist poststructuralism and the modern subject

Introduction

Radical adult education is underpinned by the idea that change is possible. Critically thinking people are the agents of change. Thus, as adult educators, we need theories that help people to move and act in ways that challenge dominant discourses and construct more liberating ones. Theory is implicit in all human action. People interested in radical politics, radical pedagogies and social change need to develop theories of the person, of meaning and behaviour which take into account the complexities of the late modern age in which we live. This chapter examines how assumptions about the person as unitary, rational and possessing an asocial core are implicated in many theories and practices, including those which seek to improve the human condition. Having examined what feminist poststructuralism refutes, the chapter goes on to examine the concepts taken up by feminist poststructuralist theorists.

The concept of subjectivity is avowedly social, in contrast to the theorisation of the self implicit in mainstream psychology, human relations and self-help psychology, and feminist 'difference' psychology. Most pedagogical approaches, including critical pedagogies, tend to share dominant psychological assumptions about the self and thus tend to be reductionist and essentialist, assuming that the individual consists of an asocial core and a social outer part. Such assumptions are inadequate for any liberatory attempts in a late modern era. The individual essence inherent in the notion of an asocial core, or real self, inevitably reduces to biology and information-processing mechanisms (Henriques *et al*, 1984; Hollway, 1989). A dualism between the individual and society remains in, for instance, the work of Habermas (1983a,b) on the 'ideal speech situation' and in Giddens' (1994, 1999) notion of 'dialogic democracy'. All of these perspectives on change, on which adult education draws, retain essentialist models of the human subject. The notion of the autonomy of the self and the autonomy of individual desires is a liberal individualist one, inadequate for supporting radical change.

Much feminist thought has fallen prey to dualistic tendencies, by uncritically taking up mainstream psychology's models of the person (Hollway, 1991b). In doing so, it has posited an essential difference model of masculinity and femininity, and a universal feeling female subject, in opposition to the universal rational male subject proposed by Enlightenment thinking. This move is often portrayed as a paradigm shift, but actually constitutes an inversion of the dualism rather than a subversion, and buys into the very paradox that it protests about (Oakley, 1998: 725). As Oakley (*ibid*: 724) points out, 'a basic requirement of patriarchal societies … is the rule of a clear opposition between men and women'.

The modern subject

Disparate as the 'grand theorists' of poststructuralism are, their 'common theme is that the self-contained, authentic subject conceived by humanism to be discoverable below a veneer of cultural and ideological overlay is in reality a construct of that very humanist discourse' (Alcoff, 1988: 415). The modern subject combines two identities. On the one hand, there is the subject of reason, which was born with modern science and the new social order that replaced feudalism (Easlea, 1980). On the other hand, there is the abstract legal subject, the subject of general 'rights of man'. The first is represented in Descartes' dictum, 'I think, therefore I am'. The second refers to a new conception of the individual that in theory equalises the subject with regard to law, to contractual obligations and to property (Venn, 1984). However, for a long time, women, children, non-white people and the propertyless were excluded from this definition on the grounds of lesser rational ability, for the most part. This demonstrates the relationship between the two notions of the individual subject (*ibid*).

Following the Copernican revolution, which decentred the earth in the cosmos, the work of Galileo is a symbolic turning point in the development of western thought, because it makes dependence on rationality a necessity (Clavelin, 1974, cited in Venn, 1984: 134; Bhaskar, 1979: 145). Another principle of this rational framework is one of order founded in mathematics (Foucault, 1966; Walkerdine, 1989a). Together, they are in opposition to the previously dominant Aristotelian–Thomist doctrines and to the teachings of the Church (Easlea, 1980). Gradually, rationality and logic came to be regarded as primary, even if ultimately underwritten by a divine creation. In the seventeenth century, there began with Descartes in *Meditation* (1641) and *Discourse* (1637) the search for a new certainty, a new reason and a new explanatory structure for the world (Venn, 1984).

Many analyses of ideas about reason and reasoning cannot be understood historically outside considerations of gender (Walkerdine, 1989a: 27). The modern certainties that emerged about the development of reasoning and reason included 'truths' about girls and women. Fisher and Todd (1988: 227) point out how the construction of subjectivity (that is, the condition of being a subject) in the sexes leads to separate, well-defined gender identities. These gender identities are very much taken for granted in western thought. To investigate these 'truths' about women, we need to understand something of the history of modern ideas about the female body and mind, in the context of a 'history of the present'. This is Foucault's term for an examination of taken-for-granted practices, which have come to seem obvious and unchallengeable facts (Walkerdine, 1989a: 20).

In the development of modern ideas, reason alone becomes the source of knowledge and of truth, viewed in the western philosophical tradition as that which is universal, transcending the idiosyncrasies of partial, individual perspectives (Benhabib and Cornell, 1987: 7). Young (1987) characterises this concept of reason as deontological and locates its pitfalls in the inability to deal with difference and particularity, without reducing them to irrationality. The cognitive and affective domains are split. Knowledge is seen as produced by individuals through the application of thought or reason, and its social and developmental nature is denied (Layder, 1994: 117). Layder cites Elias (1978: 122), who points out that the self-perception of individuals as self-contained entities separate from the rest of society first developed between the fourteenth and fifteenth centuries in Europe (that is, from the late Middle Ages to the early Renaissance). Modern sociology and psychology reinforce this idea. For example, role theory simply endorses it, providing a bridge between the individual and society, when the idea of a bridge is false, because no distinction exists between 'inner self' and 'outside world' (Layder, 1994: 115). History and social anthropology have both complemented sociology's perspective and have remained descriptive (*ibid*). Venn (1984) points out that the emergence of the dominant concept of reason did not go uncontested: the writings of Porta (1650), Paracelsus (in Koyre, 1933) and others portray a struggle for a different conception of the world, which asserts a fundamental symbiotic relationship between all things, including humans, and which does not split the cognitive and affective domains.

Social change and humanist models of the subject

By the 1960s, the unitary rational model of the human subject which dominated the positivist social sciences was being challenged by human relations or humanistic models, which emphasised feelings as part of an approach to the whole individual (Hollway, 1989: 26). However, this did not overcome the problem of individual/ society dualism. As Hollway (1989) points out, once the individual and the social are assumed to be different things, the central problem becomes the manner in which they are related (the bridge referred to by Elias, above). On the one (liberal-humanist) hand, the individual enters freely into relations with the social world, and can just as easily change these relations, through individual agency. On the other hand, in the structuralist way of seeing things, the individual is determined by social forces, which must change before individual change is possible. Social psychology, for example, has depended on the idea of 'interaction' (Broughton, 1987b; Riley, 1978) and has developed theories of socialisation, social cognition, sex roles and stereotyping. In each case, the idea of the subject involved is an individual with an asocial core, with the social parts contained in the other half of the dualism (Hollway, 1989).

Roles and a real self

The idea of role as a technical concept for bridging the gap between individual and society in the social sciences, and as a serious way of explaining social behaviour generally, dates only from the 1930s, although the metaphor of human life as a drama is an old one (Connell, 1995: 22). It provides a way of linking the idea of a place in social structure with the idea of cultural norms. The most common way of applying the concept of role to gender is that in which being a woman or a man entails enacting a general set of expectations, which are attached to one's sex – the sex role. Masculinity and femininity are interpreted as internalised sex roles, the products of social learning or socialisation. Most often, sex roles are seen as the cultural elaboration of biological sex differences, to the extent that research findings of sex differences (which are usually slight) are simply called 'sex roles' (*ibid*). The idea that masculinity and femininity are internalised sex roles allows for social change, and that was seen by earlier feminists and others interested in social change as role theory's advantage over psychoanalysis (for example, Friedan, 1965) Since the role norms are social facts, they can be changed by social processes. This will happen whenever the agencies of socialisation such as family, school, mass media and church transmit new expectations. However, for the most part, the first generation of sex role theorists assumed that the roles were well defined, that socialisation went ahead harmoniously and that sex role learning was a good thing, contributing to social stability, mental health and the performance of necessary social functions.

Feminism in the 1970s contested the political complacency of this framework, rather than the concept of sex roles. Sex role research bloomed with the growth of academic feminism (Connell, 1995). It was generally assumed that the female sex role was oppressive and that role internalisation through socialisation was a means of fixing girls and women in a subordinate position. Research became a political tool, defining problems and suggesting strategies for reform, which included changing expectations in classrooms and setting up new role models

Stimulated by feminism, by the mid-1970s many authors were also painting a picture of the traditional male sex role as placing pressures on the self. The American psychologist Joseph Pleck contrasted a traditional with a 'modern' male role. A great deal of writing of the time encouraged men towards the modern version, using therapy, consciousness raising, political discussion, role-sharing in marriage and self-help (Connell, 1995: 24). Connell points out that many of the writers remained sympathetic to feminism and tried to include connections with hierarchies of power in their work (for example, Pleck, 1977 and Snodgrass, 1977). Others, however, equated the oppression of men with the oppression of women and denied that there was any hierarchy of oppressions (for example, Goldberg, 1976).

Inherent in sex role theory is the idea that the two roles are complementary and reciprocal; therefore polarisation is a necessary part of the concept (Davies, 1990b). There is nothing that requires an analysis of power, because roles are defined by expectations and norms that are attached to biological status. To the extent that oppression appears in a role system, then, it appears as the constricting pressure placed on the self by the role. This can happen in the male role as readily as in the female. It precludes an analysis of issues of power in social relations. It does not have a way of understanding change as a dialectic within dynamic gender relations (Connell, 1995: 27).

Human relations psychology

The idea of an autonomous, real, asocial self hidden behind social roles or masks has also been facilitated by the growth of counselling and therapy, much of which is inspired by the work of the major theorists of humanistic psychology, Carl

Rogers and, especially, Abraham Maslow. Friedan (1965) and Daly (1973) both used Maslow's conception of self-realisation and self-actualisation as the basis of what they wanted to see as a realisable goal for women. A great deal of feminist psychology since then has used their work as inspiration, with consequences that many commentators consider to ultimately defeat feminist aims (see Grimshaw, 1986). The focus shifts away from the social domain and its importance in the construction of the self in a way which complements role theory and which shares its difficulty with a power analysis. It is important to point out that I am distinguishing here between Maslow's and Roger's theories and their therapeutic practices.

While humanistic or human relations psychology has many different manifestations, it does have a consistent theoretical view of the self. This view is drawn largely from the work of Rogers and, especially, Maslow. The major concept in Maslow's theories is that of 'self-actualisation'. He sees human needs as existing in a hierarchy, starting at the bottom with needs for food and shelter and progressing through security and self-esteem. Once these are gratified adequately, the 'higher' needs like self-actualisation can come into play. Two of the central characteristics that he identifies are those of autonomy and of not needing others. Those who have not yet reached the 'highest' level of human motivation still need others. But, 'far from needing other people, growth-motivated people may actually be hampered by them' (Maslow, 1970: 34). They like solitude and privacy and can remain detached from other people. Maslow constantly contrasts such people with 'ordinary' people. Ordinary people need others, self-actualising people do not (*ibid*: 161).

There are also people who are autonomous or self-determined and those who are not. Self-actualising people are autonomous, and their actions and decisions come from within:

> My subjects make up their own minds, come to their own decisions, are responsible for themselves and their own destinies. ... They taught me to see as profoundly sick, abnormal or weak what I had always taken for granted as humanly normal: namely, that many people do not make up their own minds, but have their minds made up for them, by salesmen, advertisers, parents, propagandists, TV, newspapers and so on. They are pawns to be moved by others, rather than self-moving, self-determining individuals. Therefore they are apt to feel helpless, weak and totally determined: they are prey for predators, flabby whiners rather than self-determining persons. (*ibid*)

What Maslow calls self-actualisation, Rogers (1961) calls 'becoming a person'. He sees 'being a person' as involving emotional self-sufficiency and the determination to pursue one's own individually defined goals. Like Maslow, he draws a sharp distinction between those people whose focus of evaluation is external and those in whom it is internal, those who are, as he puts it, pawns rather than persons (Rogers, 1978). These ideas imply that a process of personal change or individual effort will lead by itself to individual liberation and fulfilment, and the ultimate abolition of things like poverty or racial and sexual oppression (Henriques *et al*, 1984). It is a notion endemic to humanist psychology that the only route to personal and social change is through working on one's feelings, individually or in groups (see Hollway, 1994). Rogers, for example, posited that the problems of Northern Ireland might be solved if only sufficient trained humanistic counsellors were to go there and hold encounter groups on every street corner (cited in Grimshaw, 1986: 149).

Grimshaw (*ibid*) demonstrates that, despite the veneer of egalitarianism in Maslow's work, with its emphasis on the self-actualisation of every human being, it is hierarchical, not egalitarian. In his studies of self-actualisation, he talks of 'higher' levels of motivation and of 'superior' human beings. He believed that an elite of self-actualisers should be legitimate leaders. One of their characteristics is 'their relative independence of the physical and social environment' (1970: 162).

> Could these self-actualising people be more human, more revealing of the original nature of the species, closer to the species type in the taxonomical sense? Ought a biological species to be judged by its crippled, warped, only partially developed specimens, or by examples that have been overdomesticated, caged, trained? (*ibid*: 159)

Consistently, Maslow identifies self-actualisation with superiority, dominance, success, and winning (Grimshaw, 1986: 151). He equates strength with dominance also (1939, 1942, cited in *ibid*). In addition, he posits that high-dominance women (that is, women with high self-esteem) need even more dominant men, to whom they would enjoy being forced to submit sexually. His elites are socially empowered, but nowhere does he acknowledge this (Grimshaw, 1986: 151).

This critique of Maslow and Rogers is not to say that the techniques of humanistic psychology should all be disposed of, but to assert that it is a far from neutral body of thought. If used in a supposedly asocial framework, without regard to social conditions and without a philosophy of egalitarianism, people with 'learning deficits' will be left out of the picture. They will become further marginalised, while those who experience the 'superiority of the higher self' will continue to justify such marginalisation as the consequence of personal deficiencies in the socially excluded.

The feeling subject

Human relations perspectives replaced the rational subject with the feeling subject as the essence of individuality. However, as Hollway points out, this apparent reversal was not as straightforward a challenge as it seemed. 'Human relations appeared a relevant, personal caring psychology which valued change and liberation ... [but] its challenge was never on the content of psychological theory, rather on the dehumanising effects of scientific method' (Hollway, 1989: 95). There remained 'the therapeutic rationale that if feelings were spoken, the non-rational would be exorcised and action would be governed by rationality once again' (*ibid*). In this case, rationality is not displaced at all.

In the human relations model, the idea remains of a core individual, a 'natural' essence that exists prior to socialisation (Maslow, 1968; Rogers, 1961). Feelings are seen as the indicators of this essence, although the feelings are often hidden under layers of culture and/or socialisation. Gradually, human relations groups interested in change moved towards the idea that radical change comes from within the individual and that social change follows individual change. Such an approach to social and personal change is voluntaristic and is evident in liberal feminist thought, as well as strands of cultural feminism. Both of these varieties of feminism depend on the humanist premise that the individual agent initiates change and that it depends on the individual's freely made choice. It is in direct contrast to the position that change (including individual change) is achieved by a change in structures (the orthodox Marxist position, and similar to that adopted by many radical feminists).

Socialisation theory

Liberal feminists have largely adopted socialisation theory in their approach to gendered subjectivity and change. Socialisation in one or other set of gender attributes is considered to start from birth, with different messages being given to boys and girls, through toys, games, communications media and education. Socialisation theory opposes the notion that gender differences are biological, and traces the processes through which gender is acquired. However, few socialisation theorists take into account the variety that exists within the categories male and female, especially within different social classes, ethnic groups and societies (Connell, 1995; Davies, 1990c). As such, socialisation theory tends towards a universalism. It also tends to assume that people are passive in their acquisition of gender, indeed that women are socialised into a 'false consciousness' (Walby, 1990: 93). It fails to account for people's psychological investments in their roles and for their interests in maintaining structures and power relationships. Neither does socialisation theory problematise the content of gender nor study its construction (Jones, 1993). It studies the process of gender acquisition through a perception of the individual as an 'information processing system' (Walkerdine, 1984), a perception owing much to the developmental psychology of Piaget. In this context, the categories available to the child play an important part in the process (Weinreich, 1978). This approach sees no path of 'normal' development and is thus avowedly anti-biologistic. But Henriques et al (1984: 21) argue that, ultimately, the opposite is the case, because the capacity of the individual to process information is reduced to the biological capacities of the human system. The socialisation model of interaction between society and the individual means that the focus is on the way that the individual assimilates available information. Overcoming issues like sexism and racism becomes a matter of providing education and information, of making more possibilities available, not a matter of politics and economics, bound up with power, exploitation and psychological investments (ibid). As with the issue of violence and change, the focus is on the individual, not the social context.

A theoretical reliance (whether implicit or explicit) on socialisation has further pitfalls. When attempts to socialise children in families and in schools into 'gender equal' ways of behaving fail to have the desired effects, people often have recourse to the notion of an essential human nature, to explain attachments to femininity and masculinity. This lapse into a 'nature/nurture' dualism results from a lack of scrutiny of the nature of power and its part in the construction of subjectivity. If gender is acquired through social relations or interaction, or through family dynamics, if it is relational, rather than determined by nature, then we must try to understand the social relations themselves, which socialisation theory fails to do.

Object-relations theory and Chodorovian psychoanalysis

Within feminism, there are varied attitudes to psychoanalytic theory and practice. Although Freudian, Lacanian and Kleinian thought has given productive ideas to feminist poststructuralism (see Chapter Three), radical second-wave feminism tends to be hostile towards Freudian psychoanalysis. Freud privileges the role of the father and gives little importance to the role of the mother in the formation of identity. One psychoanalytic approach which has detoured Freud and has had enormous influence with radical and cultural feminists is the work of Nancy Chodorow (1978).

Chodorow has been the principal theorist (see also Balbus, 1982; Dinnerstein, 1976; Flax, 1978) in a branch of feminist psychoanalysis drawing on non-Kleinian object-relations theories. Her theories form the theoretical basis for the practice of "feminist 'therapy' (Eichenbaum and Orbach, 1982, 1984). This work has attempted to situate psychoanalytic theories of the psychic construction of gender within an historically specific social environment. Chodorow's work has also been used to develop a theory of lesbian sexuality (Rich, 1980; Ryan, 1990). Chodorow does not address the issue of lesbianism, but her theories have lent themselves to an idea of the 'woman-related' woman (Rich, 1980). Although Chodorow (1980, 1994) herself cautions against the notion of fixed gender identities, her work has also been used in the theories of 'difference feminism' of Bordo (1987), Keller (1985) and Gilligan (1982).

Chodorow uses the object-relations theory of Winnicott (1956) to explain how women's child-caring role is perpetuated through the earliest relationship between a mother and her child. She develops a theory of gendered relations centring on early childhood experiences (Chodorow, 1978). This leads her to a demand for a fundamental change in how childcare is organised between women and men in our culture. She examines the reproduction of mothering, rather than gender identity *per se*, arguing that women develop a greater desire to be mothers than men do to be fathers. For her, the cause of differences between the genders is that, while all girl children continue to identify with the mother, boy children have to make a serious break and identify with the more distant father, in order to become masculine. This is a wrench for boys and develops a different type of personality, which is less nurturing. The process is embedded in the unconscious and is not amenable to simple conscious resolution. Consequently, girls grow into nurturing adults, while boys do not (*ibid*: 43, 44). Women and men have different experiences of relationships and issues of dependency. Masculinity is defined through separation and is threatened by intimacy, while female gender identity is threatened by separation.

Instead of privileging the Oedipus and castration complexes, as Freud does, Chodorow focuses on the psychic effects of the pre-Oedipal mother-daughter relationship, over the mother-son and father-son relationships emphasised by Freud. The girl is seen as struggling with her likeness and unlikeness to the mother, before her entrance into and her inscription within the law of the father (Michie, 1989). The problematic bond between mother and daughter is what produces language, identity and a provisional notion of 'self' in the little girl. Chodorow's historical and relational positioning of the production of feminine identity initially contrasts favourably with Freud's theorisation of the construction of sexual difference around 'the phallic economy' (Harris, 1989: 131).

> The identification of the girl is more informed by process and becomes problematic only when she realises that she identifies with a negatively valued gender category, and an ambivalently experienced maternal figure, ... accessible but devalued. Conflicts here arise from questions of relative power and social and cultural value. (Eisenstein and Jardine, 1985: 14)

Chodorow (1978: 208, 9) stresses 'the fact that women universally are largely responsible for early childcare and for (at least) later female socialisation'. Working in a North American context, she uses psychoanalysis to dispute biological and social theories of gender acquisition, which deny the significance of important mental processes. What in Freud and Lacan are abstract positions with which the child identifies, for example the position of the father, become real people in Chodorow's work. This has led Rose (1990) and Kurzweil (1989) to describe Chodorow's work as part of socialisation theory, rather than as a truly psychoanalytic approach. As Hochschild (1990: 155, 156) points out, 'all women come out pretty much alike' in Chodorow's theory, as do all men. The approach is descriptive, detailing the successful internalisation of patriarchal ideology. It is also reductionist (Segal, 1987: 140, 141), suggesting that ideology could be changed by changes in childcare arrangements. It does not address changes from generation to generation, or the contradictory nature of women's experiences and expectations, which have often been the impetus for feminism (Ryan, 1990: 253).

Chodorow values mothering highly. She argues that gender is reproduced through mothering and that no change is possible until one is part of a family where men mother, as well as women. Her analysis recognises the strength of the social processes and suggests that the social changes could change the organisation of the psyche and the formation of subjectivity. But she does not analyse the social processes which give low rewards to motherhood. Mothering is not highly socially valued, apart from its role in socialisation and regulation, as propounded in the work of Winnicott (1956, 1957). Chodorow's solution to gender inequality, for men to parent, ignores wider social issues which devalue women in society (Walby, 1990).

In her attempt to make pre-Oedipal relations social-familial, rather than ahistorically psychosexual, Chodorow acknowledges that women's social role as mother is always historically and culturally specific in its organisation and meanings. She thinks that changes in family structures can affect individual change and thus social change. But, on the other hand, in her privileging of mothering, she theorises it and its psychosexual and social implications as universal (Segal, 1987). In doing this, in common with all psychoanalysis, Chodorow reduces subjectivity to sexual identity and the constitution of this identity to the first five years of childhood (Weedon, 1997: 60). And, at the same time, 'she loses sight of Freud's radical deconstruction of the ego, replacing it with a stable gendered subjectivity, founded on gender roles learnt in the context of the unconscious structuring of femininity and masculinity which reinforces them' (*ibid*).

Change, for Chodorow, is located at a single point, the point of origin of gender. As Hollway (1982: 104, 5) points out, we must use psychoanalytic concepts in a way that does not reduce gender to a single, unchangeable, originary moment. The incorporation of social content through language and the unconscious makes this possible, as does the incorporation of contradiction. Taking as a starting point the formation of a feminist subjectivity in the context of adult social relations, as this book does, implies that there are no origins, not even complex ones. 'Rather, any starting point is relatively arbitrary and depends on tracing the recursive (Giddens, 1979) relations which have produced the subject *at that time*' (Hollway, 1982: 105, emphasis added).

The tools of feminist poststructuralism

Feminist poststructuralism is not a unified, closed body of thought, nor does it claim to have all the answers about how gender, meaning and experience are constructed in social relations. There are, however, certain basic assumptions which feminist poststructuralists make and which are evident in their 'contingent and revisable' conclusions (Alcoff, 1988: 431). For that reason, I now outline those assumptions.

Language

Following the work of structuralist linguistics, which built on the semiology of Saussure (1974), language has become a central focus of poststructuralist analysis. Saussure sees language as a system of signs. Each sign is made up of a signifier (the sound-image, or its graphic equivalent) and a signified (a concept of meaning). The relationship between the signified and the signifier is arbitrary – there is no necessary reason for one concept rather than another to be attached to a given signifier. Therefore, there is no defining property or essence which the concept or essence must retain in order to count as the proper signified of a particular signifier (Culler, 1976: 23). This arbitrary relation between signifier and signified means that there are no fixed universal concepts. Each sign in a system has meaning only by virtue of its difference from others, and in its relations with other signs. Only when articulated with other elements do individual elements acquire a positive or a negative value (Silverman, 1985: 173). It is not assumed to be a representation of ideas or material relations which exist outside language itself and which language merely represents. The analysis of language provides a starting point for understanding how social relations are conceived, how institutions are organised, how relations of production are experienced, and how collective identity is established (Scott, 1988: 34). In particular, subjectivity can be seen as self-signification, without a fixed meaning or essence.

A further dimension to the issue of meaning is that of its extension in time. Derrida (1973) has coined a concept for this aspect of meaning – *différence* –

which refers to the fact that meaning is always deferred. While structuralist linguistics grasped the capacity of meaning to extend infinitely in space (difference), at one instant, Derrida points to the extension of meaning in time (Hollway, 1989: 40). Poststructuralists insist that words and texts have no fixed or intrinsic meanings and that there is no basic or ultimate correspondence between language and the world, between meaning and the world. Language, for feminist poststructuralists, is a means of finding out how meaning is acquired, how meanings change, how some meanings become normative and others muted and/or pathologised.

Discourse

The relationship between language and meaning is addressed in the concept of discourse, particularly as Foucault has developed it. A discourse is not a language or a text, but a historically, socially and institutionally specific structure of statements, categories and beliefs, habits and practices. Discourse is used to filter and interpret experience (Holland and Eisenhart, 1990: 95). It is responsible for reality, not just a reflection of it. Foucault suggests that the elaboration of meaning involves conflict and power and that the power to control meaning in a particular field resides in claims to (scientific) knowledge. Discourse is thus contained or expressed in organisations and institutions as well as in words. The discourses in circulation determine how we are able to talk or think about, or respond to, or act on various events and issues. Discourse appeals to 'truth' for authority and legitimation and different discursive fields overlap, influence and compete with each other (Scott, 1988: 35).

> The brilliance of so much of Foucault's work has been to illuminate the shared assumptions of what seemed to be sharply different arguments, thus exposing the limits of radical criticism and the extent of the power of dominant ideologies or epistemologies. (*ibid*)

Blackman (1996: 366) points out that Foucault (1972a, b, 1973a, 1980) maintains a distinction between veridical and vernacular discourses. Veridical discourses are those knowledges such as psychology and psychiatry which 'function in truth'. They are organised around norms of truth and falsehood, maintaining the ability and status to divide the normal from the abnormal. They are embedded in and organise specific discursive practices, for example schooling (see Walkerdine, 1988, 1990). They provide the techniques and understandings through which behaviours, conduct and thought are classified, administered and managed.

Vernacular discourse is a conception of the ways that power and the norm-producing effects of the veridical discourses (science, psychology, psychiatry) are implicated in the production of knowledge. Foucault uses the power/knowledge couplet to highlight this distinction (1980). This couplet refuses to reduce knowledge to an effect of power, as analytic concepts of ideology, social control and social interest tend to do. 'These are the concepts utilised by many where history is viewed as a play of dominations and those resistances against them' (Blackmann, 1996: 367). Foucault develops his idea of a 'history of the present' to re-pose questions concerning the relation between truth and power, asking under what conditions certain discourses and practices emerge (1972a). The specific sites, which he identifies, and terms 'surfaces of emergence' (*ibid*) were the family, the streets and other institutions, such as the prison and the asylum. These ideas inspire one of the central questions of this work: under what conditions can a politicised and agentic practice of women's personal development education emerge?

Foucault shows knowledge and discourse to be political, material products that represent a privileged way of seeing things, reflected in power, position and tradition (1972a, 1980). Meaning, situated in the power/knowledge nexus, cannot be separated from time and place, culture and history, politics and society. Foucault argues that underlying power relations shape a discursive practice. Its rules are rarely explicit or subject to criticism, but those who participate must speak in accordance with them. Discursive practice is 'a body of anonymous, historical rules, always determined in the time and space that have defined a given period, and for a given social, economic, geographical or linguistic area, the conditions of operation of the enunciative function' (Foucault, 1972a: 117).

Discourse is thus institutional, and truth is politically produced. The effects of power and knowledge are interwoven in communicative interactions. Institutionalisation can occur at the level of a discipline, a politics, a culture, or a small group. Discourses can compete with each other, or they can create distinct and incompatible versions of reality (Davies and Harre, 1990). When we speak, we have less autonomy than we think or claim, because we always use the categories, argumentative strategies, metaphors, modes of composition and rules of evidence that precede us and which, in turn, have no single, identifiable author. Thus, discourse is anonymous (Foucault, 1980: 113–138).

> Truth is a thing of this world. It is produced only by virtue of multiple forms of constraint. And it induces regular effects of power. Each society has its regime of truth, its 'general politics' of truth: that is, the types of discourse which it accepts and makes function as true; the mechanisms and instances which enable one to distinguish true and false statements, the means by which each is sanctioned; the techniques and procedure accorded value in the acquisition of truth; the status of those who are charged with saying what counts as true. (*ibid*: 131)

For Foucault, the meaning of what is spoken, understood, experienced, or asserted cannot be separated from time and place, culture and history, politics and society. The situation of meaning in a power-knowledge nexus arises out of his focus on the political production of truth, which is beyond our immediate control. Discourses represent political interests and, in consequence, are constantly vying for status and power. The site of this battle for power is the subjectivity of the individual (Weedon, 1997: 40).

Power and gender

In opposition to Marxist theory, Foucault denies that capitalism and class are the means by which power is structured. Feminist poststructuralism does not refute Marxist theory in the way that Foucault does (see Chapter Three), but also sees value in Foucault's assertion that power is highly dispersed. Instead of a simple equation of power with blatant oppression and negativity, power is seen as productive, neither inherently positive nor negative. It is both an enabling and a constraining force (Foucault, 1980). It produces knowledges, meanings, values and practices in specific ways. Neither is it static: it is a process that is always in play. It exists in all forms of social life. This differs from the view that power is always oppressive and negative and can be got rid of only by revolution. This is a valuable theorisation of power but there is a problem in Foucault's failure to distinguish between different forms of power. In the words of Fraser (1989: 32), he 'calls too many things power and leaves it at that'. He writes 'as though he were oblivious to the existence of the whole body of Weberian social theory with its careful distinctions between such notions as authority, force, violence, domination, and legitimation. Phenomena that are capable of being distinguished through such concepts are simply lumped together under his catchall concept of power' (*ibid*).

Neither is Foucault's gender blindness to be underestimated (Braidotti, 1991; Connell, 1985; Ramazanoglu, 1993; Walby, 1990). Despite his concern with power, he fails to consider the implications of gender inequality for sexual discourses. He discusses whether the bourgeoisie is controlled by or controls the new discourses of sexuality, without considering that one gender within the bourgeoisie might be using sexuality to control the other. He analyses only the most powerful discourses (male, bourgeois) and, according to some of his critics, omits discourses of resistance in the cases of both class and gender (see, for example, Beckwith, 1999). Others, however, have not seen 'discourse determinism' as a necessary outcome of a theory of discourse. They have focused on Foucault's assertion that power is best examined in terms of resistance to it (Faith, 1994; Weedon, 1999). Faith (1994: 46, 47) points out that, while Foucault does not examine specific resistances, he

> ... rather, again and again, stresses in passing the importance of resistance as a conjunct of power. In discussing Foucault's view of resistance, Dreyfus and Rabinow summarize as follows:

> 'Foucault holds that power needs resistance as one of its fundamental conditions of operation. It is through the articulation of points of resistance that power spreads through the social field. But it is also, of course, through resistance that power is disrupted. Resistance is both an element of the functioning of power and a source of its perpetual disorder (1982: 147)'.

Because so much of Foucault's work is concerned with the conditions that make discourses possible and the conditions of their emergence and disappearance, one can see possibilities for change. For example, an active feminist politics could create conditions where some discourses were no longer possible (or at least not as widely determining of practices) and where other new discourses were possible and/or recognised. This has happened, particularly in the case of rape, once seen as purely a sex crime, now widely seen as involving an abuse of power.

Subject positions and positioning within discourses

The concept of positioning within discourse is used by feminist poststructuralists (for example, Davies,1990a; Davies and Harre, 1990; Hollway, 1984 a, b, 1989, 1994; Mama, 1995; Walkerdine, 1989a) to replace the static concept of socialisation into roles. The poststructuralist paradigm recognises the constitutive force of discourse and discursive practices and, at the same time, recognises that people are capable of exercising choice in relation to those practices (Davies and Harre, 1990). The constitutive force of discursive practices lies in their provision of subject positions. A subject position incorporates both a conceptual repertoire and a location for persons within the structure of rights for those that use that repertoire. Once having taken up a particular position as one's own, a person sees the world from the vantage point of that position and uses the images, metaphors and concepts that are made relevant within the particular discursive practice in which they are positioned. At least a possibility of notional choice is involved, since there are many and contradictory discursive practices that each person could engage in (*ibid*: 46).

Positioning is the discursive process whereby subjects are located in conversations and other discursive practices, as recognisable participants in a narrative or repertoire. Whenever we speak, we are positioning and being positioned, and we move from one discursive practice to another, one audience to another, and one conceptual repertoire to another. As a feminist, if I invoke feminist discourse of some kind, I may, depending on who the hearers are, be positioned as one who should be listened to, or one who is marginal (Davies, 1990a). There can be interactive positioning in which one person positions another, and there can be reflexive positioning, where one positions oneself. Positioning is not necessarily intentional, although it can be. Different positions in discourse are available to people on the basis of categories of social discourse, which are historically generated out of collective experience (Mama, 1995: 82). People's accounts reproduce whatever discourses they are using to position themselves or others at a particular time. A central idea in all of this is the differential power associated with different positions (Hollway, 1989).

Difference and deconstruction

In western philosophical thought, the essentialism rejected by feminist poststructuralism is especially manifest in the notion that timeless and true differences exist, such as man/woman, or culture/nature. Feminist poststructuralist analysis of difference is based on Derrida's reworking of Saussure's linguistic insight that meaning is made through implicit or explicit opposition or contrast, that positive definition rests on the negation or repression of something represented as antithetical to it. Instead of framing analyses and strategies as if such binary pairs were 'real', deconstruction involves examining the ways meanings are based on oppositions that are constructed and interdependent, not natural.

Derrida's deconstruction of binaries can be broken down into three steps:

a) identify the binaries, the oppositions that structure an argument

b) reverse or displace the dependent term from its negative position to a place that locates it as the very condition of the positive term

c) create a more fluid and less coercive conceptual organisation of terms which transcends a binary logic by simultaneously being both and neither of the binary terms (Grosz, 1989, xv, cited in Lather, 1991: 5)

This process means that concepts can be exposed as ideological, or culturally constructed, rather than a natural or a simple reflection of reality (Alcoff, 1988: 415).

According to Derrida, philosophy's notion of a mastery of ideas rests on a profound misunderstanding of the linguistic sign. The 'meaning' of a text is not definitively available, there can be no fixed signifieds. Signifiers, that is, sound or written images, have identity only in their difference from each other and are subject to an endless process of deferral. This means that the effect of a 'true' representation is only retrospective and temporary (Weedon, 1997: 25). What a particular signifier means at any given moment depends on the discursive relations within which it is located, and it is open to constant reinterpretation.

Dominant liberal-humanist discourse relies on the philosophical notion of ideas as something outside ourselves, of difference as self-evident and transcendent, to be discovered through experience. Yet, Derrida shows the structure, coherence and stability of meaning and of knowledge to be a fiction, always open to challenge. For liberal humanism, experience is what we think and feel in any particular situation and it is expressed in language. Experience is seen as authentic in this perspective, because it is guaranteed by the full weight of the individual's unitary subjectivity, a real self at the pre-social core of the person. It relies on what Derrida calls a metaphysics of presence, that is, the conviction that words are only signs of a real substance that is elsewhere (*ibid*: 85). But Derrida places meaning in a radically different position to this metaphysical illusion of presence. Philosophy must give up the futile attempt to manipulate meaning that exists 'out there' and must return to considering the never-ending play of signs (Goodsin, 1990).

Attempts by social theories outside a poststructuralist framework to deal with the problem of binaries and their associated hierarchies have largely inverted the binaries, rather than subverting them, as deconstruction tries to do. Cultural and separatist feminisms have tended to invert the man/woman hierarchy by extolling all that is female, but without challenging the symbolic order that sets male and female in opposition to each other in the first place. In the case of individual/society or agency/structure dualisms, structuralists have emphasised the social and the structural in the construction of the human subject, in a scenario where individual agents have little or no ability to bring about social change. Liberal-humanists have emphasised the idea of a core individual, a natural essence that exists prior to socialisation, with change initiated by the individual agent and depending on the individual's freely made choices. Poststructuralists see binaries as existing in a mutually dependent relationship, and try to subvert them, rather than inverting them.

The French feminist Cixous has drawn heavily on Derrida's work and developed a discussion of 'death dealing' binary thought. She identifies the following oppositions:

activity/passivity
sun/moon
culture/nature
father/mother
head/emotions
intelligible/sensitive
logos/pathos
(Cixous and Clement, 1975: 115)

These oppositions correspond in all cases to the underlying man/woman opposition and can be analysed in each case as a hierarchy, where the 'feminine' side is seen as negative and powerless. Thus, nature and passion, associated with women, become opposed to culture, as represented in art, mind, history and action (*ibid*: 116). Cixous' project then becomes one of proclaiming woman as the source of life, power and energy (Moi, 1985). To enclose maleness and femaleness in opposition to each other is to force them to enter a death-dealing power struggle. For Cixous, like Derrida, meaning is not achieved in the static closure of the binary opposition, but is achieved through the endless possibilities of the signifier. Following this logic, the feminist task becomes the deconstruction of patriarchal metaphysics (that is, the belief in an inherent, present meaning in the sign). If we are all contaminated by metaphysics, as Derrida has argued, then we should not attempt to propose a new definition of female identity, because we would necessarily fall back into the metaphysical trap. Woman's identity should be that which escapes definition.

The linguist and psychoanalyst Kristeva refuses to define 'femininity' at all, preferring to see it as a position constructed by patriarchal thought and marginalised by the patriarchal symbolic order, as defined by Lacan (Moi, 1985). This is a relational approach to the problem of what it is to be 'feminine' and allows Kristeva (1986) to argue that men can also be constructed as marginal to the symbolic order. Her emphasis enables feminists to counter biologistic definitions of femininity. Cixous shows that femininity is defined as lack, darkness, irrationality and chaos. Kristeva, while recognising the dichotomy between masculine and feminine as metaphysical, approaches the notion of women as positional marginality, rather than as essential definition. Where Cixous tries to develop a new feminine language which will subvert the binary schemes that silence women, Kristeva shows that what is perceived as marginal at any one time depends on the position one occupies. If patriarchy sees women as occupying a marginal position in the symbolic order, then it can construe them as the limit of that order, representing the frontier between man and chaos, but also merging with the chaos outside. Women are neither completely inside or completely outside the symbolic order – they can thus be vilified or venerated. Patriarchal thought has vilified women as Lilith, or the Whore of Babylon, as well as elevating them to a position of Virgin and Mother of God, where they protect men from chaos (Moi, 1985).

Kristeva's position is that one must reject the notion of identity. This is different from Cixous' project of developing a positive feminine identity and an *écriture feminine*, emphasising the power and energy of women. Although Cixous emphasises the multiple identities and heterogeneous differences among women, in opposition to any scheme of binary thought, her project eventually falls into a form of essentialism, where everything to do with women is glorified (Moi, 1985; Walby, 1990).

Identity politics

Kristeva (1986), in advocating a deconstructive approach to sexual difference, wants to create a new theoretical and scientific space, a signifying space (Davies, 1990c: 502), where the very notion of identity is challenged. Her perception of women's historical and political struggle is as follows:

1. In a liberal feminist framework, women demand equality and equal access to the symbolic order.
2. With radical feminism, women reject the male symbolic order in the name of difference and glorify femininity.
3. Women reject the dichotomy between masculine and feminine.

There is some debate about whether this scheme would represent a feminist version of Hegel's philosophy of history, where position three would be exclusive of positions one and two, or whether they should be simultaneous and non-exclusive positions in contemporary feminism (Jardine, 1985; Moi, 1985, 1990).

As Moi (*ibid*) sees it, the problem in adopting position three exclusively is that, in deconstructing patriarchal metaphysics, we also risk deconstructing the logic that sustains the first two forms of feminism (*cf* Segal, 1999: Chapter One). As long as patriarchy remains dominant, it remains politically essential for feminists to defend women as women, in order to counteract the patriarchal thought that despises them as women. We must continue to pay attention to 'social *structures*, *relations* and *practices* which an earlier feminist project prioritised in pursuit of political-economic restructuring, and the transformation of public life and welfare' (Segal, 1997: 7, original emphases). But an unreconstructed form of stage two feminism runs the risk of becoming an inverted form of sexism, unaware as it is of the metaphysical nature of gender identities. It runs this risk by uncritically taking over metaphysical categories created by patriarchy, which have led to women's oppression, in spite of feminists' attempts to attach new worth to the old categories (*cf* Cocks, 1989).

If feminists exclusively adopt Kristeva's third space of deconstructed identities, there is one sense in which it changes nothing, because it rejects the notion of identity on which so much of the feminist political struggle is based. In another sense, however, the deconstruction of identity radically changes our perception of the political struggle. A feminist appropriation of a deconstruction like Kristeva's, which can show the notion of a feminine identity to be incomplete or contradictory, is useful if it incorporates the first two of her stages also. Situating attempts at deconstruction in specific political contexts is important in avoiding ahistoricism and in recognising the significance of interests and investments in operative factors which structure relations between men and women. Kristeva's deconstruction, however, has shown the contradictory nature of such a project. A commitment to equal rights for women must assert the value of women as they are, before equal rights have been won (that is, in their difference from men, in their femininity as it is currently and varyingly constructed). But a commitment to equal rights for this constructed femininity risks glorifying women in their essential difference, a difference from men that is metaphysically and patriarchally constructed. Because we actually live in a system of patriarchal relations, however, feminists have to take positions that assert the value of women as women, in order to counter structural devaluation of them. In this context, equality and difference are not easily compatible. In isolation, a feminist theory of women's difference comes disturbingly close to echoing patriarchy's conception of them as different. Yet, the same is true of the isolated articulation of a feminism that values women as a unified category. Given this logic, the feminist influenced by poststructuralism cannot settle for either equality or difference. But even if we are aiming for Kristeva's deconstructed world, it does not exist now, we cannot live in it. Patriarchal forms are constantly shifting and changing and one of the tasks of any kind of feminism must be to expose these forms. Because we live in patriarchal, metaphysical space, we have to try to hold all three of Kristeva's positions simultaneously (*cf* Moi, 1990). This is a far from easy task. As Fraser (1989: 6) writes,

> ... you can't get a politics straight out of epistemology, even when the
> epistemology is a radical antiepistemology, like historicism, pragmatism,
> or deconstruction. On the contrary, I argue repeatedly that politics
> requires a genre of critical theorising that blends normative argument and
> empirical sociocultural analysis in a 'diagnosis of the times'.

Alcoff (1988) considers this dilemma by drawing on the work of Lauretis (1984, 1988) and Riley (1983). She develops the idea of an identity politics, combined with the notion of the subject as positionality and construction. Subjectivity and identity must be recognised as always a construction, yet also a necessary point of departure. The concept of identity politics problematises the relationship between this constructed identity and political theory or analysis. In doing so, it departs from the mainstream methodology of western political theory.

> According to the latter, the approach to political theory must be through
> a 'veil of ignorance' where the theorist's personal interests and needs are
> hypothetically set aside. The goal is a theory of universal scope to which
> all ideally rational, disinterested agents would acquiesce if given
> sufficient information. Stripped of their particularities, these rational
> agents are considered to be potentially equally persuadable. Identity
> politics provides a materialist response to this and, in so doing, sides with
> Marxist class analysis. The best political theory will not be one
> ascertained through a veil of ignorance, a veil that is impossible to
> construct. Rather, political theory must base itself on the initial premise
> that all persons, including the theorist, have a fleshy, material identity
> that will influence and pass judgement on all political claims. Indeed, the
> best political theory for the theorist herself will be one that acknowledges
> this fact. (Alcoff, 1988: 432, 3)

The essentialist definition of woman makes her identity independent of her external situation and denies her ability to construct and take responsibility for gendered identity, politics and choices. The positional definition, on the other hand, makes her identity relative to a constantly shifting context, to a situation that includes a network of elements involving other people and economic, social, cultural and political conditions. If women can be identified by position in this network, then feminist arguments from women can claim the need for radical change, not because some innate essence is being stunted, but because women's position within the network lacks power and mobility. Added to this must be the belief that women's subjectivity is not solely determined by the external elements of this network, but by her engagement with it, her interpretation and reconstruction of her history, as mediated through the cultural discursive context to which she has access (Lauretis, 1988: 8, 9). Feminist discourses must be circulated so that women have the opportunity to do this interpretation and reconstruction in ways that are different from the dominant discourses. As Alcoff (1988: 434), points out, when women become feminists, the crucial thing that has occurred is not that they have learned any new facts about the world but that they come to view those facts from a different position, from their own position as subjects. A political change in perspective means that the framework for assessment has changed, not that the facts have changed, although new facts may come into view.

In this analysis, one can make concrete demands on behalf of women, without entailing a commitment to essentialism. Recognition of the fact that, now, many women need childcare 'in no way commits you to supposing that the care of children is fixed eternally as female' (Riley, 1983: 194). However, as things stand now, invoking the needs of women with children also invokes the accompanying belief in our cultural conception of essentialised motherhood. We need to constantly problematise universalising concepts like 'women's needs', while ensuring that political strategies are developed to ensure that no woman's current needs go unmet. We can do this, for example, by meeting the needs of women with children, while rejecting and challenging 'the idealised institution of motherhood as women's privileged vocation or the embodiment of an authentic or natural female practice' (Alcoff, 1988: 428). Segal (1999: 54) cites Snitow (1990: 510) on this issue:

> From moment to moment we perform subtle psychological and social negotiations about just how gendered we choose to be. ... One can be recalled to 'woman' any time – by things as terrible as rape, as trivial as a rude shout in the street – but one can never stay inside 'woman', because it keeps moving. We constantly find ourselves beyond its familiar cover.

These circumstances mean that we must make political choices. We cannot avoid them, simply because poststructuralist theory has uncovered chinks in the formulation of key concepts of earlier feminist thought. These choices are often difficult and unsatisfactory, since every choice closes off some other possibility. In making a choice and taking up a position, one runs the risk of being wrong, or making oneself vulnerable by revealing one's hand. But we have to engage with the dominant thought structures of our day, while constantly being aware that our choices are limited by our specific material positions in society and history.

People change from generation to generation and do not just reproduce oppression – the factors that make us desire change and the ways that we can produce change must be examined. It is not impossible, though not simple either, to simultaneously challenge and make use of the rules of Enlightenment rationality, which is where we get the notion of emancipation from, after all (Moi, 1990: 375). We must not forget that it is the humanist paradigm that gives critical force to a commitment to the modern ideals of autonomy, dignity and human rights (*cf* Fraser, 1989: 57). What we can do is to give up the quest for metaphysical truth, while not overlooking the truth of women's oppression (*ibid*). As Weedon (1999: 82) writes, 'to subscribe to a theory of the provisionality of meaning, does not mean that meaning does not have real effects'. Feminist poststructuralism's emphasis on meaning is part of the Women's Liberation tradition, and shares its passionate goal of transforming all of society. It is part of a social movement, not a break with the past (Ryan and Connolly, 2000; Young, 1998). It insists that social movements must take into account discursive power, as well as material and structural oppressions, rather than setting up a dualism between discourse and culture on the one hand, and material issues on the other.

Conclusion

This chapter has attempted to demonstrate that feminist poststructuralism uses all the theoretical tools of poststructuralism, while remaining grounded in the politics of everyday life. It has examined the emergence of the modern subject and approaches to subjectivity, along with feminist poststructuralist objections to humanism, human relations psychology, Chodorovian psychoanalysis and role theory. It has also examined how feminist poststructuralist theorists have developed ideas about language, discourse, power, deconstruction and politics, in a drive to theorise and push forward social change. All of the ideas discussed here are used in the analyses of feminist subjectivity in Part Two of the book. The next chapter (Chapter Three) includes a discussion of how feminist poststructuralism relates to other approaches to the subject, manifest in radical, Marxist and dual-systems feminisms, and in structuralism. It also leads into a discussion of the relation of feminist poststructuralism to Lacanian psychoanalysis and developments of psychodynamic theories of the person.

3 The human subject in other radical political traditions

Introduction

In this chapter, I examine some other liberatory traditions on which feminist poststructuralism has drawn. Inevitably, I read these movements through my own concerns and my own position as one who finds that feminist poststructuralism provides really useful knowledge for me. There is always a danger in categorising and labelling different movements, especially in the case of feminism, when one talks of 'stages', 'generations' or types of feminism (Segal, 1999, Chapter 1). Differences between types are never as clear-cut in practice as they may seem when described in writing. In writing them in such terms, there is always the danger that one type will be seen as a pure break with other types. In Chapter One, when discussing how this book came about, and in the conclusion of Chapter Two, through a discussion of the stages of feminism and identity politics, I have been at pains to portray feminist poststructuralist knowledge as part of a vibrant Women's Liberation movement, since that is how I have experienced it. My project in this book is to examine how a consideration of subjectivity is essential for progressive social movements such as those supported by radical adult education. In this chapter, therefore, I examine the ways that other radical movements have construed the human subject, either implicitly, as in the case of early radical feminism, or more explicitly, as with later social constructionist radical feminism, structuralism, and psychoanalysis. I do not want to be teleological, or to imply that feminist poststructuralist theorisations of the subject occur at the end of a series of incremental developments in knowledge about the subject, representing the 'one best way'. Nevertheless, I accept that it is difficult to avoid such teleological readings.

Radical feminism and the subject

In radical feminist analysis of gender inequality, men as a group are seen to dominate women as a group and to benefit from women's subordination. The forms of radical feminism from the 1960s to the present took feminism as a universal struggle of women against men's power (Bell and Klein, 1996; Rowland and Klein, 1996). The system of domination of women by men is called patriarchy and is independent of other systems of social inequality – for instance, it is not a by-product of capitalism. With the work of Brownmiller (1976), Firestone (1974),

Millett (1971) and Rich (1980), radical feminism broadened the scope of the social sciences, politics and the consideration of subjectivity by introducing issues not conventionally considered relevant to an analysis of social inequality. This radical feminist reworking of the term 'politics' is among the most revolutionary and useful ideas for challenging the mainstream of western political theory, and not just in the interests of women (Abrahams, 1992; Segal, 1997).

In consciousness-raising groups and explorations of the personal as political, women came to see their problems not as private misfortunes, but as public issues. In this approach, everything is political (Walby, 1990): sexuality (Millett, 1971), conversation (Spender, 1980), housework (Mainardi, 1970), motherhood (Luker, 1984; Rowland and Thomas, 1996), abortion (Petchevsky, 1988). In its strongest form, this argument implies that nothing is not political. Subjective experience is thus socially formed (Richardson, 1996a). In breaching the public/private split, early radical feminism introduced elements of deconstruction of binaries consistent with feminist poststructuralism. Yet in its insistence on universal differences between men's and women's experiences (whether essential differences or constructed differences), it reinforces binary thinking.

Radical feminists take the view that sexuality is not a private matter to be explained in terms of individual preferences or psychological processes fixed in infancy (in this respect, radical feminism is hostile to psychoanalytic theory). In this perspective, sexuality is socially organised and critically structured by gender inequality. Society is seen as preceding sexuality, giving structure and content to the individual experience of it (Barry, 1995). The institution of heterosexual sexuality is a central pillar of patriarchy for many radical feminists who reverse the traditional practice of setting up lesbianism and male homosexuality as unusual and in need of explanation (Brownmiller, 1976; Kitzinger, 1990; Millett, 1971; Rich, 1980). Intimate relations between women are to be expected, given what women share under male oppression. If sexual partners are chosen on the basis of sharing, liking and loving, as is generally supposed, then the prevalence of heterosexuality (that is, intimate relations with an oppressor) is seen to be in need of explanation. The Leeds Revolutionary Feminist Group (1981) argues that heterosexuality has important political implications in the ways that it divides women from each other, uniting each one with her own special oppressor. To survive the situation, women adopt, at least partially, the viewpoint of men. This suggests that women suffer from a false consciousness in heterosexual relationships. The group suggests that women who are independent from men are more likely to combine politically to resist patriarchy. Lesbianism is an integral aspect of radical feminist practice and the degree to which heterosexually active women can be independent of patriarchy is a source of debate (Ferguson, Zita and Addelson, 1981; Kitzinger and Wilkinson, 1993, 1994; Richardson, 1996b). More recently, this has developed into discussion of whether heterosex can be conducted in a framework of equality (for example, Hollway, 1995), or whether heterosexual desire is predicated on inequality and domination and the eroticisation of power differentials (Kitzinger, 1993).

The problematisation of heterosexuality is connected with the perceived need to create a separate culture of women, in order to develop non-patriarchal thinking, as a prelude to rebuilding society (Daly, 1973, 1978, 1984). Daly's work seeks to embrace, as essence, the devalued characteristics associated in western culture with women and to revalue them. In order to effect this revaluation, opposing patriarchal values are devalued. For Daly, feminists must assume and enjoy their essential female nature or continue as men's pawns, victims and dupes of patriarchy (Bailey, 1993: 120). Connections have also been made between women's nature and the environment (Mies and Shiva, 1993, 1997), with spirituality (Starhawk, 1989) and with peace (Ruddick, 1984).

Critics (Barrett, 1980; Cocks, 1989; Segal, 1987; Rowbotham, 1981) accuse early radical feminism of a tendency to essentialism, to implicit or explicit biological reductionism, which is necessarily universalistic and ahistoric. It is argued that, by setting all men up as exploiters of the female essence that all women possess, radical feminists create an account which, by definition, cannot change. At best, the solution to this problem is to set up feminist free-space and a woman-centred culture. But because differences between men and women are seen as innate, there is no point in feminist activists trying to change mainstream culture. Richardson (1996a:193) notes the variety of radical feminist theorising about sexuality, and its critics' tendency to focus on a narrow range of earlier works in defence of their claims that it is essentialist. Hollway (1995) argues that later radical feminist work (for example, Kitzinger, 1987, 1994; Barry, 1995) is strongly social constructionist and deterministic, and does not allow for a theory of social change.

Echols gives the name 'cultural feminism' to a trend for using radical feminist theory to equate 'women's liberation with the development and preservation of a female counter-culture' (Echols, 1983, cited in Alcoff, 1988: 412). The political effects of cultural/radical feminism have been positive, in insisting on viewing traditional feminine characteristics from a different, affirmative point of view (Eisenstein, 1984; Alcoff, 1988; Weedon, 1999). This kind of thinking reproduces dominant cultural assumptions about women, although giving them new, positive value. But it is difficult to see how it can provide a useful strategy for change in the long term, since it reproduces the categories male and female unchanged. Moi (1985) has charged it with voluntarism, where rational decisions are made and acted on, without attention to emotional investments. Moreover, its development has led to a constraining feminist ideology for some (Gallop, 1988), since not all women recognise themselves in the ideal of womanhood which cultural feminism posits. It fails to represent the variety of differences between women, as well as between women and men. For example, 'caring, which is represented as a fundamental female quality, can be better understood in relational terms as a way of negotiating from a position of low power' (Hare-Mustin, 1991: 70).

Marxist feminism

Marxist feminist analysis considers that gender identity and inequality in gender relations result from capitalism, where men's domination of women is a by-product of the domination of capital over labour. Class relations and the economic exploitation of one class by another are the central features of social structure and these determine the nature of gender relations (Benhabib and Cornell, 1987; Hartmann, 1981; Jagger, 1983; Walby, 1990).

Nicholson (1999: 30) argues that feminist theory has in Marx both a strong ally and a serious opponent. In common with Hartmann (1981: 10), she points out that Marxism enables us to understand many aspects of capitalist societies, such as structures of production, generation of occupational structures and the nature of dominant ideologies, but that its categories, like capital itself, are sex-blind. Nicholson goes on to argue that the concept of production (narrowly understood as the producing and formation of an object), which is central to orthodox Marxist approaches, is also inadequate for comprehending the complex, intersubjective nature of traditional female activities like caring and nurturing and, therefore, inadequate as an analytic tool for feminists (Nicholson, 1999: 30). Walby (1990: 73) considers the strengths and weaknesses of Marxist feminism and radical feminism to mirror each other, in that the former overstates the household labour argument at the expense of gender relations, while radical feminism provides, in isolation from other systems, an important analysis of gender relations.

Dual-systems theory (for example, Delphy, 1984; Eisenstein, 1979; Hartmann, 1979; and Mitchell, 1975), is an attempt to synthesise radical feminism and Marxist feminism. It was one of the first feminist efforts to avoid 'single variable' models, by theorising the intersection of gender with class (and, in some cases, with race). As such, it foreshadows the feminist poststructuralist project of theorising the intersection of different social variables as the ground for differential treatment. But, as Fraser (1989: 8) comments, 'despite this laudable aim, it soon reached an impasse: having begun by supposing the fundamental distinctness of capitalism and patriarchy, class and gender, it was never clear how to put them together again'.

Structuralism's account of the relationship between ideology and the subject

Marx was one of the early theorists who broke with the humanist notion of society as formed by individuals, and showed how individual experience was formed by social structures. The Marxist tradition, mostly via Althusser and his use of Lacanian psychoanalytic concepts, has made sophisticated attempts to theorise the relationship between the individual and the social domain, outside humanist rationalist theory [1]. Feminist poststructuralism, where it draws on Marxism, draws largely but not solely on Althusserian Marxism [2]. Since Althusser's reworking of Marxist theory has been taken as most representative of the structuralist outlook, I concentrate on it in this section.

In general, structuralism is an attempt to apply the linguistic theory of Saussure to activities other than language (Eagleton, 1983: 106). This approach concentrates on isolating the underlying set of laws (structures), under which signs are combined into 'meanings'. The structuralism of the anthropologist Levi-Strauss, for example, meant that, in studying a body of myth, he was looking less at its narrative content than at the mental operations that structure it. As Eagleton puts it, 'like Freud, he exposes the shocking truth that our most intimate experience is the effect of a structure' (ibid: 107). The structuralist approach is also anti-humanist in that, in establishing cultural elements and their rules of combination, it shows the inseparability of cognitive systems and social structures. However, a problem arises in that, in claiming to isolate laws of the mind, structuralism is 'hair-raisingly unhistorical' (Eagleton, *ibid*: 109) and is as guilty as humanism of conceptualising the human subject in universal terms. In taking an anti-humanist stance, structuralism privileges a system of rules and a universal mind. But it does not give an account of human subjects and their intentions, probably out of a desire to avoid reintroducing the Cartesian subject 'through the back door' (Henriques *et al*, 1984: 95). The elimination of the human subject and subjectivity from analysis means that the structures themselves form the framework of a new metanarrative, replacing the 'god' of religion and the 'man' of humanism.

Althusser (1971a,b), like Gramsci (1971), links common sense with ideology [3]. This differs from the widespread classical perception of ideology as a set of doctrines or a coherent system of beliefs deliberately adopted by self-conscious individuals. Althusser considers that ideology is the very condition of our experience of the world, unconscious precisely in the fact that it is unquestioned and taken for granted. As already outlined, in Althusser's use of the term, ideology works in conjunction with political and economic practice, to constitute what he calls the 'social formation'. He sees as ideological things which are widely considered natural or obvious. In this way, he develops the notion of ideology as common sense. Ideology is not seen as a separate package of ideas, or an 'optional extra' (Belsey, 1980: 5). It is seen as a way of thinking, speaking and experiencing and, as such, it is inscribed in discourses, in the sense that it is expressed in them, in writing, speech, thinking and practice.

Althusser (1971a: 153, 155) posits two theses on the nature of ideology:

1. Ideology represents the imaginary relations of individuals to their real conditions of existence.
2. Ideology has a material existence.

In the second thesis, which corresponds to the poststructuralist notion of discourse, Althusser describes ideology as a structure of social relations which can be further described through the ideological state apparatuses (ISAs) of church, state and school. The ISAs are one 'instance' of the social formation. Althussser goes on to describe its relation to other 'instances', notably the economic, which is determinate of social relations, but not necessarily dominant, because the 'lonely hour' of the last instance never comes (Henriques *et al*, 1984: 96, 97). In Althusser's stipulation of relations, he develops the notion of conjuncture to express the idea of the co-existence of necessarily uneven instances at any given moment. Thus, he attempts to break with the determinism of the original base—superstructure model by seeing the 'instances' of the social formation at any given time as having a different capacity to determine other instances. This is what he means by their 'effectivity' (Hollway, 1982: 120).

In Althusser's early work, the agent of change was class struggle, represented in the revolutionary party. Henriques *et al* (1984: 96) point out that his later work responds to the events of 1968 in Paris, when the party failed to deliver the revolution, by developing this different understanding of the relation between ideology and the subject. Thus he formed his ideas on the material nature of ideology. In addition, he was working in a climate in which many activists were questioning the effectiveness of the voluntarism of the liberation movements of the time. Ideology, and the ISAs of church, family and school were seen to produce individuals as subjects, in such a way that they participated in reproducing capitalism (*ibid*). Althusser concluded that the fundamental task of ideological practice, over and above the reproduction of particular ideologies, is the 'interpellation' of individual human beings as subjects, within the place assigned them in the social order. It is thus that individuals acquire and assent to their social identity.

Althusser also stresses the class structure of society and the integral relationship between theory and practice. However, he assumes that social relations, discourses and the social power legitimised by discourses are reducible to economic, that is, capital—labour relations, in the last instance (Althusser, 1971a). Feminist poststructuralists Urwin (1985), Walkerdine (1985) and Weedon (1997) have, however, pointed out that in any one historically specific example, relations may ultimately be reducible to the economic, but that this should not be treated as a universal principle. Other forms of power relations, for example those manifest around gender, race, ethnicity, age and ability, must be allowed and must not be subordinated to the economic in considerations of subjectivity and power.

Useful as Marxist traditions are to the development of a feminist poststructuralist framework for examining the subject, a problem arises with Marxist use of the terms 'real' and 'false'. Marxism has a concept of historical—materialist 'science', which can offer a true explanation of capitalism, guaranteed by the ultimate determining power of the relations of production (Henriques *et al*, 1984: 98, 99). As such, it can offer the notions of 'false consciousness' and of alienation from a true, unrepressed self, as expressed in the Freudo-Marxism of Reich, Marcuse and Fromm (Mitchell, 1975, Part Two). An application of Marxist scientific analysis can lift the 'veil of ideology' which blinds people to the true nature of things (Foster, 1984). While there may have been some ambivalence about the status and meaning of the word 'science' at the time when Marx was writing, Westwood (1988) points out that he uses the word to mean both a method and a real consciousness or truth. Althusser was writing at a different point in history, where the meaning of the word science was unambiguous (*ibid*). Thus, Marxism falls back into the individual/society dualism which feminist poststructuralism is concerned to avoid. The Althusserian notion of ideology problematically places the source of 'ideas' in subjects, such as the ruling class, and does not challenge existing ideas of the role of the individual subject as agent.

Feminist poststructuralism sees ideology as having a material existence, in discourse, not as representative of something else. This differs from the Marxist view of ideology as 'false' and Marxist science as 'true', a view demonstrated in Althusser's first thesis on ideology, that it represents the imaginary relations of individuals to their real conditions of existence. So while Althusser's second thesis on ideology, that it has a material existence, is useful for the feminist poststructuralist project, its usefulness is lessened by the existence of the first thesis, with its implicit reductionism of a search for origins (the 'real' conditions of existence). As Norris (1982: 84) puts it, 'Althusserian Marxism is a form of deconstruction but one that seeks to halt the process at a point where science can extract the hidden message of ideology'.

Both humanism and structuralism share a conception of the human subject that is essentialist: characterised 'as a condition of its creative activity in the one case, and of its subjection to its position in the structure, in the other' (Hindness, 1986: 120). Both perspectives are also reductionist, because they propose to reduce diverse social conditions to other conditions which are considered more basic: either to structures or to the creative actions of individuals (Hirst, 1979).

The strengths of structuralism are many, and they provide resources for the feminist poststructuralist project of theorising a dynamic and multiple subjectivity. A particular strength is the recognition that meaning never resides in a single term, that everything depends on how the constituent elements are articulated. There is an implicit questioning of the possibility of a unique 'correct' set of ideas about the subject, which acquire privileged status. Structuralism has pointed out the value-laden nature of common sense and has shown how whole social ideologies may be present in an apparently 'neutral' approach. It has also partly enabled the critique of liberalism (Grimshaw, 1986; Kitzinger, 1987). Althusserian Marxism also assumes that meaning and consciousness do not exist independently of language, that language and our inscription in discourse through language, are what construct meaning. This is a primary assumption of feminist poststructuralism also, although the notion of language as 'text' extends to habit and practice (Alcoff, 1988: 43).

To see society as primarily determined by structures is more useful for radical adult education than a perspective that sees society as the expression of the individual mind, even if structuralism does not take human subjects and their intentions into full account. However, structuralist premises emphasise what is static and universal, not accounting for history and change. Poststructuralism is not opposed to structuralism, in the way it is fundamentally opposed to humanism. Feminist poststructuralism attempts the dialectical treatment of structure and subject, by combining the insights of structuralism with Foucauldian discourse theory and with psychoanalytic theory about the nature of desire and intention.

Psychoanalysis and feminist poststructuralism

The widespread engagement with Althusserian theories of ideology among Marxist feminists in Britain in the 1970s paved the way for a reassessment of Freud and psychoanalysis, through attention to Lacan's reworking of Freudian theory. Classical Marxism could not supply an equivalent to the sociological concept of socialisation, but an Althusserian approach did (Mitchell, 1971). Althusser used the Lacanian concept of 'interpellation' to examine how human subjects submit themselves to the dominant ideologies of their societies. Althusser draws on the work of Lacan (1977, 1981) for his account of the process of an infant's simultaneous entry into language and social life.

Psychoanalysis has frequently been dismissed as bourgeois, as highly culturally specific while purporting to be universal, and as anti-feminist. Some of the accusations against it are indisputable. For example, Freud privileges the position of the father in the family and his explanation of characteristics of female psychology rests heavily on the concepts of 'penis envy'. Psychological differences between women and men are thus too easily reduced to biological differences, with the implication that women's subordination is natural and inevitable.

> Moreover, the poststructuralists Foucault and Donzelot have cited psychoanalysis in the production of particular sites for intervention and social regulation; for instance, in the prescription of sexual norms (Foucault, 1979) and in the management of child-care and what constitutes the role and responsibilities of parents within the family (Donzelot, 1980). (Henriques *et al*, 1984: 206)

Other normative applications have been noted. Walkerdine (1996: 151), for instance, points out how, from the 1930s onwards in Britain, psychoanalytic practices joined forces with, and were shaped by and in turn shaped, concerns about the presence of the mother in the production of the bourgeois democratic citizen. 'Deprivation' came to be something that could result not just from maternal absence, but also from inappropriate and inadequate mothering (Bowlby, 1971). Anti-social behaviour and delinquency were also laid at the door of the mother by Winnicott (1957).

Feminist poststructuralism, however, insists that we need a radical theory of psychodynamic processes, in theorising subjectivity. The discursive approach and the accompanying decentring of the individual, as based on the work of Foucault, has many advantages over preceding theories of the subject. It succeeds in conceptualising subjectivity and the human subject as multiple, dynamic and as historically and socially (discursively) produced (*cf* Mama, 1995: 124). Nevertheless, it leaves certain areas untheorised:

> ... we are left with a number of unresolved problems. First, in this view the subject is composed of, or exists, as a set of multiple and contradictory positionings or subjectivities. But how are such fragments held together? Are we to assume, as some applications of post-structuralism have implied, that the individual subject is simply the sum total of all positions in discourses since birth? If this is the case, what accounts for the predictability of people's actions, as they repeatedly position themselves within particular discourses? Can people's wishes and desires be encompassed in an account of discursive relations? (Henriques *et al*, 1984: 204)

Given the theoretical lack in both traditional left liberation theory and in Foucauldian theory, it is productive to make a critical and selective use of psychoanalysis and its account of subjective processes which resist change, as well as accounts of failure of identity, which make change and resistance possible. It is important to take into account that contemporary psychoanalysis, like contemporary feminism, is not a single entity. The aspects of psychoanalysis on which feminist poststructuralism draws in its theorisation of subjectivity are principally the theories of Freud and Lacan and, more recently, the feminist object relations theories of Klein (Coward, 1993; Hollway, 1989; Mama, 1995).

Henriques *et al* describe well the aspects of psychoanalysis which need to be addressed:

First, if the attempt to appropriate psychoanalysis is to have politically progressive implications it must obviously utilise the potentially subversive aspects of the theory. There is a marked tendency for these to be suppressed in favour of therapeutic techniques which in effect focus on fostering the individual's adjustment to his or her environment. ... Second, such an approach must also recognise explicitly the historical specificity of the psychic phenomena and reading of unconscious life which psychoanalysis produces. This is recognised in most feminist appropriations of psychoanalysis. ... Unless its appropriation enables us to envisage the possibility that things can be otherwise, and to move towards a theorisation of the possibilities of change, psychoanalysis will lock us into a closed circle. (Henriques *et al*, 1984: 207, 8)

The concept of the unconscious can help conceive of ideology as a contradictory construct, full of inconsistencies. It can also, as Moi (1985: 26) points out, explain how, throughout history, some women have resisted patriarchal ideology, because of a failure of the dominant feminine identities (*cf* Rose, 1990). In this, it is a challenge to the self-evidence and common-sense ideological character of everyday life. These have also been the targets of different feminist approaches which have challenged the 'natural' and pre-given qualities ascribed to women's social position. The Freudian subject, then, is non-rational and multiple, subject to forces that are not always under the control of the conscious mind (Mama, 1995: 128). Furthermore, Freud's ideas on the development of human sexuality are subversive, in that his theory takes neither masculinity nor femininity for granted. 'Instead, the Freudian infant starts out as sexually undifferentiated (polymorphously perverse) with the potential to develop in any number of different directions, and only later develops masculinity or femininity after a complex struggle between contradictory forces' (*ibid*). Mama points out that psychoanalytic theory is also a truly relational and social account of the history of the individual, because in it, the person is constructed in the course of relationships with other people. In Freud's culture, this is the nuclear family (*ibid*).

Lacan

Many of the challenges to Freud, from analysts with whom he engaged in debate, ended by producing an account of femininity which had more normative effects than his own (Rose, 1990: 234; Henriques *et al*, 1984: 212). From the 1930s, Lacan challenged all of these therapeutic practices, particularly that of ego-psychology in the USA. He saw ego-psychology as a misuse of psychoanalysis for purposes of social adaptation and control and singled out for particular criticism its notion of a strong ego as the rational monitor of consciousness. He also argues that the notion of rational self-determination is an illusion produced through the social conditions of bourgeois society. He seizes on the deconstruction of the ego and the unitary subject, developing an account of a subjectivity fundamentally decentred from consciousness. 'The ego is necessarily *not* coherent' (Wilson, 1982, cited in Rose, 1990: 234, original emphasis), but always and persistently divided against itself. An ideological world conceals this division, this splitting of the subject, and the conscious part of the subject is '... supposed to feel whole and certain of a sexual identity. Psychoanalysis should aim at a deconstruction of this concealment and a reconstruction of the subject's construction in all its aspects' (Mitchell and Rose, 1982: 26).

For Lacan, not only is the subject split, but its very production depends on the use of language. The entry into language is the pre-condition for becoming aware of oneself as a distinct entity (distinct from the mother), within the conditions laid down by already-existing social relations and cultural laws. In addition, the process of entry into language founds the unconscious. This brings us to Lacan's theory of the imaginary and symbolic orders.

The imaginary corresponds to the pre-Oedipal period when the child believes itself to be part of the mother and perceives no separation between itself and the world. At this stage, the child is neither feminine nor masculine and has yet to acquire language (Lacan, 1949). Between the ages of six and eight months, the child enters the 'mirror stage' (still part of the imaginary). This stage allows for dual relationships, where the child identifies with the Other (usually a parental figure) and misrecognises itself as the source of meaning and power over this Other (the mirror stage). This development is inserted by Lacan into Freud's account of narcissism, which asserts that a period of self-love precedes object-love and the resolution of the Oedipus complex (Freud, 1914).

In the Oedipal crisis, the father splits up the dyadic unity of mother and child and forbids the child further access to the mother's body. The phallus, representing the Law of the Father (or the threat of castration), thus comes to signify separation and loss to the child. The loss is that of the maternal body and, from now on, desire for unity with this body must be repressed. With this repression, the child enters what Lacan calls the symbolic order, which is the social and cultural order in which we live our lives as conscious, gendered subjects. To speak as one of these conscious subjects is to represent the existence of repressed desire for the imaginary order, where there is no loss or lack. This is how Lacan can claim that the speaking subject *is* lack. When the child takes up its place in the symbolic order and learns to say 'I am', to identify 'me', distinguished from other people, this is the equivalent of the subject saying 'I am s/he who has lost something', the loss being the identification with the mother and the world which existed in the imaginary.

The entry into language and repression of the imaginary simultaneously form the unconscious. Since language is a social system, Lacan is able to assert that the social enters into the formation of the unconscious. The primary repression involved in entering the symbolic opens up the unconscious, which is always connected with lack. In the imaginary, there is no unconscious, since there is no lack. The speaking subject comes into being through the repression of desire for the mother, and Lacan asserts that 'the unconscious is structured like a language'.

Contrary to popular appropriations of psychoanalysis, for Freud and Lacan, the unconscious is not the seat of drives or instincts, but of traces of repressed ideas, signs or memories. These can become linked to words and find psychic expression. Thus, language is doubly attached to the expression of the unconscious. Freud (1900) addressed the relation between symbolic processes and the working of the unconscious, in his work on the interpretation of dreams. In this work, he also deals with the difference between needs and desires. The distinction is also important in Lacan.

Desire

For Freud, needs can be fulfilled, since they arise from a state of internal tensions. For example, hunger can be satisfied by food. Wishes and desires, on the other hand, are based on 'needs' that have once known satisfaction. Through memory traces, this satisfaction is remembered and sought again (Freud, 1973). In so far as desires can be fulfilled, it is through the reproduction in fantasy of perceptions and/or states which have become *signs* of this satisfaction. In trying to fulfil desire, we try to reproduce states that signify satisfaction for ourselves.

Lacan looks to Saussure's linguistic theory, in his own theorising of the sign. He stresses processes of selection and combination as fundamental to the organisation of meaning in language, but modifies the Saussurean account of the relationship between signifier and signified. Saussure's account privileges denotative meaning (Culler, 1976), that is, something real in the world which is referred to, so the signifier and signified can be 'harmoniously united' (Eagleton, 1983: 166) when real meaning is grasped. In Saussure's account, fixed *a priori* signifiers exist. For Lacan, the speaking subject is produced through the entry into the symbolic, which is itself made up of signifiers. But in Lacan's departure from Saussurean theory, these signifiers are not linked to fixed *a priori* signifieds or concepts. Language is seen as 'a constant stream of signifiers which achieve temporary meaning for a speaking subject retrospectively through their difference from one another' (Weedon, 1997: 51). The unconscious consists of chains of signifiers, or the relationships between them. One term finds its meaning only by excluding the other.

Possession of the object of desire, the Other, means the satisfaction of desire. The child learns that language stands in for objects, becoming a substitute for some direct, wordless possession of the object itself (Eagleton, 1983: 166). But as it is learning these lessons of language, the child is also learning them in the world of sexuality. The father, symbolised by the phallus, breaks up the dyadic unity of mother and child, teaching the child that it takes up a place in the family which is 'defined by sexual difference, by exclusion (it cannot be its parent's lover) and by absence (it must relinquish its earlier bonds to the mother's body) (*ibid*: 167). In accepting this, the child is negotiating the Oedipus complex, to use Freud's term. In Lacan's terms, it is moving from the unity of the imaginary, where there is no desire because there is no lack, to the symbolic order of pre-given social and sexual roles. The lack, or loss, present in the symbolic order presents itself as 'the unbridgeable gap between signifier and signified' (Cornell and Thurschwell, 1987: 146).

Lacan's theory of language resembles Derrida's critique of rationalist theories of language and the metaphysics of presence, which presuppose that the meaning of concepts is fixed before their expression through language. Derrida also transforms the relationship between signifier and signified. For both Derrida and Lacan, meaning can occur only in a specific context and in a relation of difference from other contexts. For Derrida, the principle of *différence*, discussed in Chapter

Two, prevents a final fixing of meaning. For Lacan, it is the mechanisms of desire that prevent it.

However, for Lacan, there is one *a priori* signifier. This is the signifier of sexual difference, which he calls the phallus. The control of satisfaction of desire is the primary source of power within psychoanalytic theory and the phallus signifies power, in the symbolic order. Desire, for Lacan, is the motivating principle of human life. The desire for control of objects through possession becomes the primary motivating force of the psyche and control is identified with the position of the father, which is symbolically represented by the phallus. Thus, Lacan's appropriation of the symbolic order is ultimately structural (Walkerdine, 1985: 227). Although he privileges the *sign* of difference (the phallus) and not biological difference, the phallus still stands for ultimate difference, which fixes meaning in language (Cornell and Thurschwell, 1987: 146; Mitchell and Rose, 1982: 42). Language in turn is regulated through the power systems of society. The child becomes a subject according to the cultural laws which pre-ordain it. Lacan is, ultimately, a structuralist.

Some problems with Lacan's account

A feminist poststructuralist point of view rejects transcendental, *a priori* explanations. The phallus as the 'signifier of signifiers' is unacceptable, because it produces a simple, deterministic reductionism. The inbuilt phallocentrism and universalism of the signifier is incompatible with theorising the production of subjectivity in a way which accounts not only for how the processes may occur under patriarchy, but also how things could be otherwise (Urwin, 1984: 278). Men, by virtue of their possession of a penis, can aspire to a position of power and control within the symbolic order, whereas women have no access to it in their own right and cannot be represented in it. 'There is no woman, but excluded from the value of words' (Lacan, cited in Irigaray, 1985: 87). This aspect of Lacan can be seen to openly disclose the reality of male power instead of hiding it under a guise of 'neutrality' or 'impartiality' (Gallop, 1982: 36–8). The theme of women's exclusion from the symbolic order has been the starting point for the work of the French feminist psychoanalysts and deconstructionists Cixous and Kristeva (see Chapter Two).

A second problem with Lacan's work is that desire, in his account, is inevitably unfulfillable, to be governed by or subordinated to fantasy (Henriques *et al*, 1984: 216). For Lacan, desire works in the same way as language, moving from object to object or from signifier to signifier and 'it will never find full and present satisfaction, just as meaning can never be seized as full presence' (Moi, 1985: 101). Urwin (1984) points to Lacan's emphasis of narcissism in his reading of Freud and his insistence on the unfulfillability of desire [4]. Urwin (*ibid*: 279) points out that some desires can be fulfilled and this is why people cling to practices which give a feeling of control and consequent fulfilment, however fleeting. She recommends an investigation of *how* desires are fulfilled and how people are capable of satisfaction – a necessary consideration if we are to accept the possibility of change.

A third problem in Lacan's account is the precise sense in which the unconscious is structured like a language. This poses two problems for feminist poststructuralism. First, as we have seen, Lacan draws heavily on structural linguistics, with its acceptance of *a priori* signifiers. Second, Thom (1981), Urwin (1984, 1985) and others have questioned the implication that the unconscious is therefore to be comprehended entirely through the rules of language, particularly if these rules are provided by structural linguistics.

> As in all structuralist accounts, there is an inbuilt tendency for the specificity of content and process to be subordinated to a universalist mode of explanation ... one of the implications of using a structuralist paradigm is that Lacan's theory tends to collapse into an account of a universal, albeit contradictory, subject who is not situated historically, who is tied and bound by pre-existing language, and is incapable of change because of this. This, of course, is precisely the position which we wish to avoid. (Henriques *et al*, 1984: 217)

Despite these problems, it is Freudian and Lacanian psychoanalysis which has provided a theory of the dynamic unconscious, radically challenging the unitary rational subject. 'This is one of the sources of the subversive impact of psychoanalysis: it overturns the western view that the distinguishing mark of humanity is reason and rationality' (Frosh, 1987: 25). It is not that rationality does not exist, rather that it is always being contested by forces of the unconscious, where repressed ideas, feelings, desires and fantasies lie. 'The forces governing subjectivity and action are therefore not derived from a single source' (Hollway, 1989: 29). There is no currently available substitute for psychoanalysis, or more broadly, psychodynamic accounts (Hollway, 1995: 95) of these symptoms which indicate the existence of the unconscious.

Using Kleinian concepts

A further problem with psychoanalysis, applicable to any work that examines the production of adult subjectivities, as this work does, is that most psychoanalytic accounts of human psychic development focus on processes occurring in early infancy. Feminist poststructuralist theorists take the view that subjectivity is not only dynamically formed, but also continually changing and being constituted from one instant to another, as well as over long periods of time (Mama, 1995: 129). This means that subjectivity can be studied at any point in the life cycle, an approach particularly important for adult education that wishes to support political change. Subjectivity is treated as located in history, with specific content, and not as an abstract idea which can be treated as if it were devoid of that content. Even if similar psychodynamic processes occur in all people, the cultural and discursive content will be group specific and historically located (*ibid*). Treating entry to the symbolic as a moment in childhood which is the effect of a structure, as Lacan does, means that the theory is static (Hollway, 1989: 84). This static point of entry of the subject into the symbolic order also denies the 'continuous, everyday defensive negotiation of intersubjective relationships within the field of effects of power/knowledge relations' (*ibid*).

Hollway's (1982, 1984a, b, 1989, 1994, 1995) work has used psychoanalytic and Foucauldian theory to address a crucial question for feminism: if we accept that subjectivity is constructed, how do we explain why people take up subject positions in one discourse rather than another? If the process is not a mechanical one, why, for example, do some men position themselves as subject in the discourse of aggressive male sexuality (1984a: 231)? What do they gain from it and why don't all men position themselves in this way (cf Wetherell, 1986: 136)? According to Hollway, we must pay attention to the histories of individuals and also to the question of a subject's investment in a particular position in discourse. By claiming that people have investments in taking up certain positions in discourses, and consequently in relation to each other, she means that there is some satisfaction involved for people through these actions. The feeling of satisfaction may not be conscious or rational and may also be in contradiction with other resultant feelings (Hollway, 1984a: 238). Her concept of investment is a re-theorisation of the concept of desire and is connected to power and the way it is historically inserted into the subjectivity of individuals. Desire comes from a lack of a feeling of control over and oneness with the other, as experienced in Lacan's imaginary. If people's individual histories have taught them that a certain subject position in a particular discourse can, even fleetingly, reproduce a feeling of fulfilment of desire, then they may make an investment in that position.

Power is thus more than material or economic. If discourses alone are examined in relation to power, then the examination is confined to material structures and practices. Material inequalities between men and women need to be addressed, but Hollway's (1989) work also points to the importance of the construction of subjectivity in power relations which are not a direct or immediate effect of material structures. Power is always 'dynamic and two-way and tied to the extra-rational forces' (ibid: 85, 86) of the unconscious, which she conceptualises through the notion of anxiety and intersubjective defence mechanisms.

Hollway argues (1995: 98) that the interconnection between power and desire is overemphasised in Lacanian accounts, resulting in a psychic determinism which is not useful for theorising change. She emphasises therefore the connections between power and anxiety, based on an understanding of pre-Oedipal relations, derived from Kleinian object-relations psychoanalysis. Although this work was developed on the basis of work with young infants, Kleinian theory asserts that primal processes pave the way for processes that continue throughout adult psychic life (ibid; Mama, 1995: 130). Klein privileges the defence mechanisms which work between people rather than within a person, so that intersubjective relations become the location for the negotiation of meaning and its effects, through power, on subjectivity.

> These relationships are always the product of two or more people's unique histories, the contradictions between meanings (suppressed and expressed), differentiated positions in available discourses, the flux of their continuously renegotiated power relations and the effect of their defence mechanisms. Thus, they are never simply determined, either by the intentions of those involved, or by language/discourse. (Hollway, 1989: 84, 85)

Although the relationships and their effects on subjectivity are not determined, neither are they arbitrary. Hollway (*ibid*) posits that the principle motivating the taking up of positions and the mobilising of defences is the vulnerability of what psychoanalysis calls the ego. According to Klein, vulnerability is an unavoidable effect of human nature; anxiety is its original state. Hollway accepts the importance of vulnerability, but without resorting to human nature as its cause, through an examination of the ways that the infant is positioned by adults: adults, as a result of their anxieties, defence mechanisms and power relations, as well as their access to differentiated positions in discourses, create a situation of cultural anxiety for human infants, rather than a naturally occurring state of anxiety. The continuous attempt to manage anxiety and to protect oneself is never finally accomplished, although in mature adulthood, people can achieve relative stability and a state of apparent peace with anxiety. Anxiety thus provides a continuous, more or less driven motive for the negotiation of power in relations (*ibid*).

The subject's main defence against anxiety is the process of splitting, a projective process which involves separating an object into good and bad. According to Klein, the primordial experience of good and bad occurs at the breast which is experienced as either benevolent and nurturing, or as rejecting and frustrating. When splitting occurs, the good object is incorporated into the ego – that is to say, it is introjected. The bad object on the other hand is projected – directed outward and away from the ego, on to other people or objects (Mama, 1995: 131). For Klein, these projective processes are intimately bound up with idealisation and denial:

> Idealisation is bound up with the splitting of the object, for the good aspects of the breast are exaggerated as a safeguard against the fear of the persecuting breast. While the idealisation is thus the corollary of persecutory fear, it also springs from the power of the instinctual desires which aim at unlimited gratification and therefore create the picture of an inexhaustible and always bountiful breast – an ideal breast. (Klein, 1986: 182, cited in Mama, 1995: 131)

The idealisation of the breast and the corollary fear of it produce ambivalence. The baby in its state of dependency is both gratified and enraged. In its rage, it has fantasies of striking back at the breast and hence at the mother (Coward, 1993: 114). These hostile fantasies are followed by fear of retaliation by the mother. These feelings and destructive thoughts are a source of guilt, which, theoretically at least, is experienced no differently by boy and girl children. Human beings of either sex experience rage and grief against the mother for loss of oneness. Yet, some clinical experience has shown women to be far more susceptible to guilt than men (*ibid*: 116).

Coward (*ibid*) posits that the different responses of the sexes have to do with their different abilities to tolerate ambivalence and the expression of destructive, aggressive feelings. In particular, guilt has much to do with the ability to tolerate ambivalence. In Klein's – and in most psychoanalytic accounts – the 'healthy' individual is the individual who can most easily tolerate ambivalence, who can integrate hostility and aggression with love and reparation. Dealing with ambivalence is a possibly universal process which is culturally exacerbated for women by the fact that women have made and continue to make themselves responsible for their families' well-being, at considerable personal cost and sacrifice (*ibid*). It means that, for women, the unconscious fantasies of having possibly destroyed the mother are overlaid with more immediate and real fears. In a culture where women are always at risk of being devalued or rendered invisible or insignificant, as opposed to the importance of men, a daughter's destructive fantasies can appear to have a basis in fact (*ibid*).

Mama and Hollway both take up the experience of contradiction as indicative of anxiety and this can be joined to Coward's identification of the importance of feelings of ambivalence and associated guilt, which are experienced by women when they make changes in their lives. Feminists have long identified the experience of contradiction as indicative of the need for change and for the possibility of change, in 'traditional' women. Feminist women too experience contradiction and ambivalence when they make changes in the gender status quo, despite a rational conviction of and commitment to feminist change (*cf* Davies, 1990c). In seeking to address the anxiety which arises from contradiction and/or ambivalence, feminist poststructuralism uses and needs theories of the unconscious.

For the feminist poststructuralist theorists cited, then, the experiences of contradiction, anxiety, ambivalence and guilt are major forces in the dynamics of subjectivity. Discursive changes which accompany politicisation are, at the same time, psychodynamic movements which involve splitting (*cf* Mama, 1995: 133). Individual women frequently separate off certain qualities which they find unacceptable in their own sex, such as ambition, ruthlessness and aggression, and project them onto men (Coward, 1993: 132). Essentialist feminist discourses do this on a collective basis with men as a group, in the process idealising the feminine.

Conclusion

This chapter has posited that all social movements for change rely on theories of the human subject, whether these are explicit or otherwise. The theories of such movements, such as feminism, need sophisticated theories of the human agent, or subject. Social constructionism has emphasised, often using discourse theory, how people's social positions construct how they are, and it has been criticised for being too deterministic. The theorisation of subjectivity arrived at by feminist poststructuralist theorists implies that discursive movements are accompanied by psychodynamic processes within the individual and *vice versa*: psychodynamic processes have discursive (social, historical and cultural) content.

> In other words, there is a constant resonance between psychodynamics and social experience in the construction and reproduction of the individual's subjectivity. This means that both discourses (theorised as conveyors of history, culture and social meaning) and individual subjects are produced in a continuous dialectic, out of reverberations between historical—cultural and psychological conditions. Here we have a theory which transcends dualism because it conceptualises the individual and the social as being produced simultaneously. This is not to say that every individual change generates new discourses but that when individual

changes are provoked by conditions that are widely experienced – such as those of race and gender – then these are more likely to become widespread, to gain social power and become discourses that convey culture and social meaning, or collective knowledge. (Mama, 1995: 133)

When the possibility of social change arises, therefore, it demands the tackling of feelings and needs and of the contradictions and difficulties of the situations which arise in tandem with discursive movements. At least some answers lie in looking at the social conditions which produce these feelings (cf. Coward, 1993: 198). Desire and the concept of the unconscious are given a social basis through theorising their historical development in relation to meaning and discourse (Hollway, 1995: 94), not simply as something universal and inevitable which will pull us back into essential ways of being. We have to take into account the power relations that construct systems of desire (Frosh, 1987).

In taking an approach like this, we can hold on to the importance of the unconscious, but also see a route past Lacan's failure to deal with the material conditions of people's lives (Henriques *et al*, 1984). Such reworkings can produce a more historically specific reading of desire and the unconscious which will, by implication, be less universalistic and less pessimistic (with regard to the unfulfillability of desire) than Lacan's. Foucauldian discourse theory is also drawn on in accomplishing this reading, but at the same time, the discourse determinism of Foucault has been addressed, by acknowledging that individual history plays an important part in the reproduction or change of social relations. All of these issues are relevant for the analysis of feminist subjectivities and ways of knowing undertaken in Part Two.

Part Two

Part Two

4   Subjectivity, pedagogy
and research

Introduction

This chapter reviews how knowledge about subjectivity has shaped different educational and research practices. I start by examining how both religion and science have been envisaged as educational tools for both regulation and liberation, and how a rejection of science and religion brought a turn to psychology, especially human relations psychology. I examine the popularity of the idea that women have special female ways of knowing, and link this to the dominance of the psychological model of the person in the Western world. I further link these developments to a problematisation of the concept of experience, in research and education. I finish the chapter by describing how I approached research on subjectivity, experience, knowledge and identity for this book.

How did the aspects of pedagogy and research that I single out for examination come to be what they are? Approaches to pedagogy, research and knowledge are social, that is, they are embedded in the dominant discourses and theoretical perspectives of their time. For example, adult education methodologies in Ireland have been produced partly in opposition to schooling methodologies (see Kiely *et al*, 1999). They have also emerged in conditions where psychological perspectives (both mainstream and human relations) have shaped (since the 1960s) the dominant discourses through which people in the western world interpret themselves and their behaviour. It is important to bear in mind the historical place of different educational and research discourses concerning the person, or subject, and the progressive political positions often associated with them. Nevertheless, I will go on to argue that the theorisations of the person implicit in many progressive educational discourses are not adequate for the kinds of change called for by feminist poststructuralism, because of their reliance on dualistic thinking and the assumption of a unitary subject.

The emergence of the subject of pedagogy

Walkerdine (1984) asserts that many educational practices have been concerned with the search for a pedagogy which could provide the desired forms of individuality of the authorities of the day (or of the revolutionaries). These have ranged from Adam Smith's overt desire to produce people capable of working in the factories of the English industrial revolution (*ibid*), to the formation of correct moral attitudes in Sweden (Gee, 1988), to the desire of the Owenite movement to develop a rational means for working-class children to be freed from the pre-conceptions of existing society (Stewart, 1972), to the desire of the British administration to regulate education in Ireland and thus prevent nationalists or insurgents from fomenting revolution (Coolahan, 1981), to the less overt concern with producing the self-regulating individual which is characteristic of the modern bourgeois state (Walkerdine, 1988, 1989a,b; Walkerdine and Lucey, 1989).

Certain tendencies in educational practices have been introduced into public education and administration by individuals and groups from outside public education (cf Hollway, 1991a). These introductions were originally linked with a belief in science and the supremacy of the rational which began with the Enlightenment of the eighteenth century. The idea of scientific legitimacy adopted by forward and progressive thinkers was seen as modernism. In some cases, science was adopted to replace religion (for example, Marxism) and in other cases (for example, public educational systems in Sweden, Ireland and England), scientific rationality was adopted, but continued to be underwritten by religion.

Forms of power thus emerged which allowed techniques of producing knowledge and knowing about human beings to be used. These techniques had regulatory effects. But it is not the case that they were produced by one monolithic group for the domination of another group. On the contrary, it was often liberals and radicals who proposed the new forms of scientific administration and pushed for them as preferable to the forces of religion. This tendency characterised the work of Marx. His belief in the science of history and the scientific basis of historical materialism has to be understood as part of the rise of the scientific and rational movements (Walkerdine, 1984: 165). As Walkerdine (ibid) points out, if so subversive a figure as Marx opted for the legitimation of science this points to how scientific forms of knowledge and administration were privileged. Science, by its naturalisation, became a tool for normalisation and regulation, even when used by those who envisaged it as a tool for liberation.

The late eighteenth and early nineteenth centuries saw significant initiatives in state involvement in education in many European countries such as Switzerland, Holland, Prussia, France, Spain, Greece, Italy, Denmark, Sweden and Norway (Coolahan, 1981; Gee, 1988). England was influenced by a prevailing political philosophy of laissez-faire and state involvement in education came much later, with an Education Act in 1870 and compulsory education established about 1880. The Act of Union of 1800, which brought Ireland under the direct control of the government and parliament and Westminster, sought to bind Ireland more closely to Britain by a policy of cultural assimilation. But as Coolahan (1981: 3, 4) points out, Ireland was frequently used to try out various policy initiatives before introducing them in England, such as an organised police force, improved health services, a Board of Works. Thus, Ireland got a state-supported primary school system, under the control of a state board of commissioners, in 1831.

State legislation on education in Ireland developed in response to various commissions which recommended that school systems be supervised for purposes of politicising and socialising goals, for cultivation of attitudes of political loyalty and cultural assimilation. In addition, after Catholic emancipation in 1829, Catholic demands for fair treatment could not be suppressed any longer and the national school system under state control seemed to the government the best way of directing educational provision (*ibid*: 4, 5).

These were among the arguments used for the provision of schooling in Ireland at that time. Jones and Williamson (1979, cited in Walkerdine, 1984) point out that all popular texts of the time of the introduction of (at first popular and later compulsory) schooling in England show that the goals of education were to provide a solution to crime and pauperism. The principles and habits of the population were to be changed through schooling. Popular education thus came to be seen as a possible solution to the nation's ills, by the inculcation of good habits, notably of reading, especially reading the Bible. Gee (1988) points to similar developments in Sweden, where the popular literacy movement was directed towards Bible reading, the development of rational powers of mind, and consequent moral development. Gee (*ibid*: 202), citing Graff (1987a, b), also points out that the Catholic countries of Europe had very low rates of literacy, due to the way the Bible was interpreted by Catholic church authorities, who then tried to standardise interpretation through illustrations. Ireland, though predominantly Catholic, was also a colony and so received the literacy teaching of the coloniser.

The form of pedagogy advocated to achieve such understanding was to be carried out through class instruction and a curriculum based on the study of natural phenomena. Such methods had been pioneered as early as 1813 by the Scottish philanthropist Robert Owen, following the philosophy of Rousseau and others (Harrison, 1969). Owen had at first admired monitorialism, but later denounced the system which could render a child 'irrational for life' (Owen, 1813, cited in Walkerdine, 1984: 167). A radical who supported the French Revolution, Owen had introduced his methods with an emancipatory intent. He provided schools for the children of workers in his mills. Owen too made the assumption that, given the right conditions, achieving understanding would mean that children would make the correct, rational choices which would ensure their liberation. He moved away from the constant surveillance of monitorialism to love as a basis for education. This love, however, was to be rational and hygienic, without passion. Passion was not scientific and therefore not a basis for progress.

Those with an interest in the regulation, containment and civilisation of the working-class child based their pedagogy on the assumption that if people made rational choices based on understanding, they would 'do the right thing'. Walkerdine (1984: 168 ff) points out that it was not a smooth transition from monitorialism to class teaching. Both approaches were defended and contested. Eventually, though, class teaching, based on groups of same-age children, became widespread. This was the first time it was assumed that children of the same age should be grouped together for instruction. Walkerdine also points out that this understanding of class in a school context came about at the same historical moment that class as a social concept emerged. She places both developments in a context of increasing classification and measurement aimed at the working class. She also asserts that all these practices in education which depended on reason and science were first developed with working-class children and only later came to be used with all children, as statements of scientific fact (*ibid*: 198).

The idea that those who possessed understanding would choose to behave correctly and be good citizens was possible because of developments in ideas of normal development which were emerging around the same time. The techniques which Owen developed claimed to be based on an amplification of the natural and, therefore, of the normal (Stewart, 1972: 47). Owen insisted that knowledge of the natural world was a means by which the mind could be freed from the preconceptions of society. The utilitarians called for understanding to be taught and encouraged, so that the children of the labouring classes, recognising the 'order of things', would be capable of being gainfully employed.

By the beginning of the twentieth century there were two parallel developments going on, both of which related to the scientific classification of children: child study and mental measurement (Walkerdine, 1984: 169). At this time, the work of Darwin and other developments in evolutionary biology were inspiring surveys of populations which included histories of family 'pathologies'. Characteristics, including those of children, were recorded with a view to establishing what environmental conditions might produce physical illness, immoral and criminal behaviour. Children came to be singled out as a class, to be classified in their own right (Rose, 1979). It was seen as important to give heredity the best chance. This is an important shift in emphasis from the degeneracy of the population being a moral problem to one amenable to scientific solutions. Again, it is symptomatic of the shift away from religion towards science.

The individual (and in the case of schooling, the individual child) became a legitimate focus of concern and study. As Henriques *et al* (1984: 119–52) point out, certain forms of social problems were located as an object of science. Therefore science could provide techniques of detection by establishing population statistics and providing tools for establishing the scientific basis of the normal, that is, in respect to a normal curve of characteristics in the population (Hacking, 1981; Gardner, 1983). Normal individuals could be produced and the abnormal cured through some form of institutional provision (Walkerdine, 1984: 170). All of these social events provided the conditions for the emergence of a scientific pedagogy based on the model of naturally occurring development which could be observed, measured, normalised and regulated. The new science of child-development psychology was involved in all of these happenings from the start (*ibid*).

The psychologisation of pedagogy

Early in the twentieth century, straddling the colonial and independent administrations, and later, in the 1960s and 1970s, Irish elementary education was affected by all of the emerging practices, although Ireland was not industrialised and did not have the kind of working-class population with which many of the earlier practices were developed. In the late 1960s the introduction of what was popularly known as the 'New Curriculum' for primary schools was influenced by the structure of the disciplines approach (An Roinn Oideachas, 1971). Developments in human relations psychologies in the 1970s were also influential in their approach to the individual (for example, Holland, 1979). The growth in social sciences and psychology and the emergence of a social psychology provided the conditions for these changes. The school, family and individual emerged as legitimate sites of intervention, with the aims of changing human behaviour and ensuring that children developed properly and became socially fit adults.

Acker (1988: 315) traces the development of three ideologies in this context: ideologies about child-centred learning; about the determining role of factors outside school on educational achievement; and about the political neutrality of the school. These ideologies assumed that if children (or people in general) are truly treated as individuals, it is impossible to discriminate against a social group. This stance, in practice, rules out positive action as well as negative discrimination. To be individual, personal or child-centred can have important feminist effects (*ibid*; see also Middleton, 1993). However, in practice, such beliefs can also obscure sex-differentiated practice (Clark, 1989). Comments like 'he's naturally boisterous' or 'she's naturally quiet' can support and promote gendered practices in relation to work and behaviour. As Gill (1987: 6) suggests, 'treating them as individuals can lead teachers unconsciously to a perception of individual male and individual female appropriate behaviour and attitudes'. Even a comment like 'it's his family background' about a troublesome and boisterous boy can be seen as appealing to a socially produced effect on behaviour, which conforms to appropriate male behaviour in the face of home difficulties.

The focus on the individual led to increased psychometric testing and the development of IQ scales. Where children did not meet the standard set by psychologists, deficit models and remediation programmes were employed to remedy the deficits. Mainstream psychology has been severely criticised for this approach (Drudy and Lynch, 1993; Gardner, 1983), for its inaccuracy and inhumanity. Intelligence has been shown by Gardner and others to be multiple and culturally based. The inhumanity of mainstream psychology has been attacked by the human relations school of psychology, especially influenced by Rogers. Human relations approaches have concentrated on raising self-esteem and confidence as a prerequisite for learning. But as Kenway and Willis (1990: 16, 17) point out, raising self-esteem within the terms of the educational status quo may have the effect of underscoring the dominant sex, class and ethnic groups in society.

The effects of power in a social system become less visible, the more integrated the social system is. This theme is central to the work of Foucault. In the context of human relations practices of pedagogy which emphasise individuality, this is particularly evident. There is less an overt controlling, than an underlying conviction that it is possible to educate the individual in a way that makes her/ him 'want' to make the 'correct' choices. The power of reason can legitimately and recognisably be called on to displace conflicts. In this view, attempts within pedagogy to construct a rationally ordered and controllable child are deeply bound up with the modern form of bourgeois government and the emergence of the modern state (Walkerdine, 1987, 1988; Walkerdine and Lucey, 1989).

Thus pedagogy inspired by human relations is implicated in the production of compliant forms of individuality, by means of 'natural development' towards maturity (Burman, 1994) rather than by compulsion or coercion. These regulatory pedagogies produce and have produced knowledge about human beings which are often presented as 'discoveries' (*cf* Henriques *et al*, 1984). Human relations psychology is, by the fact of its naturalisation in schools through self-esteem programmes, becoming the very basis of the production of normalisation. The same danger exists in adult education through personal development, if not firmly enmeshed in a political and structural framework.

Psychology has constructed for itself a power base in the places where pedagogies are created: in pre-schools, schools, universities, colleges and communities. While mainstream psychology is being challenged by human relations perspectives, both rely on a preconception of the human subject as unitary and rational. The adoption of human relations perspectives (including a democratising of the processes of pedagogy) has allowed feelings and intuitive knowledge to be accepted as valid ways of knowing, but only insofar as they allow access to the core individual, untrammelled by social forces.

The appeal of the human relations self-esteem discourse to policy makers and teachers has been theorised by, for example, Renshaw (1990), Kenway *et al* (1990) and Gilbert (1989, 1990). They show that the 'self' literature, as it arose out of social psychology, emerged in various guises in many fields in, and associated with, education. It has informed a wide range of 'progressive' attempts to humanise the curriculum and engineer educational change which might militate against educational and social 'disadvantage'. In a sense, the 'progressive' educational movements of the 1970s, in their various manifestations, provided a complementary body of thought to help facilitate the acceptance of the schooling and self-esteem literature. Both pinned their hopes for educational and social progress on micro-politics and individual change. In so doing they paint an educational and social reform scenario in which the teacher is central. Enlightened and humane teachers are to be the driving force of a movement in which all individuals develop their full potential together, in an atmosphere of unconditional positive regard. Social change is made possible by change at the 'chalk face'.

A great deal of adult education practice in Ireland places emphasis on interpersonal skills and personal development. It doing so, it defines itself in opposition to behavioural psychology and psychometric testing and emphasises the need to deal with the whole person. Where it differs from the schooling use of interpersonal skills is that it attempts to help people understand how the transfer of these skills into the social world, for its transformation, is possible. In its focus on the person, with this objective, it draws on liberal-humanist and human relations discourses, which cannot be divorced from the content of their assumptions about the human subject. It attempts to combine these assumptions with social analysis. However, these models do not have the radical content necessary for social change in social relations in general, because of their reliance on a core, rational and unitary subject, nor in gender relations, because of their reliance on the notion of male/female essential differences and dual cultures (Ryan and Connolly, 2000). Despite their good intentions, they maintain the gender status quo.

Liberatory pedagogies

Education, knowledge and pedagogy were for a long time typically conceptualised as institutional practices associated with schools. This began to change when new agendas concerned with social justice began with the publication of Freire's work in 1969. These agendas sought, in the words of Weiler (1988: 50), to discover 'how the human ability to create meaning and resist an imposed ideology can be turned to praxis and social transformation'. Freire sought to do this with his notion of conscientisation. He questioned the role and authority of the teacher, recognised personal experience as a source of knowledge and took into account the perspectives of people of different races, classes and cultures. Underlying Freire's theories is a vision of social justice which was influential in the critical and liberatory movements that emerged in the 1960s and 1970s, and has been influential in Ireland in recent times. However, as Weiler (1991) points out, Freire's claims to universal truths and his assumptions of a collective experience of oppression do not adequately address the realities and complexities of students' lives.

Freire's still most widely read and classic text is his first book to be published in English, *Pedagogy of the Oppressed* (1970). In this work, Freire organises his approach to liberatory pedagogy in terms of a dualism between the oppressed and the oppressors and between humanisation and dehumanisation. This organisation of thought in terms of opposing forces reflects Freire's own experiences of literacy work with the poor in Brazil, a situation in which the lines between oppressor and oppressed were clear (Weiler, 1991: 452). Freire's thought is, like all other thought, historically and socially situated. For Freire, humanisation is the goal of liberation. Simply reversing the relations between oppressor and oppressed will not create liberation. Liberation and humanisation are possible only if new relationships between human beings are created. This is to be achieved by naming and analysing existing structures of oppression (denunciation) and by the creation of new relationships and ways of being as a result of mutual struggle against oppression (annunciation).

The main problem for feminists in Freire's thought is the ideal of humanisation and the assumption that all forms of oppression are uniform (*ibid*: 453). The assumption of the work is that in struggling against oppression, the oppressed will move toward true humanity. But this leaves unaddressed the form of true humanity and implicitly accepts the existence of a real, true self which poststructuralist thought has shown to be both a fiction and a central tenet of liberal humanism. In his usage of the concept of oppression, what is not addressed is the possibility of simultaneous contradictory positions of oppression and dominance: the man oppressed by his boss could at the same time oppress his wife, for example, or the White woman oppressed by sexism could exploit the Black woman. By framing his discussion in such abstract terms, Freire slides over the contradictions and tensions within social settings in which overlapping forms of oppression exist (*ibid*).

> There is too much universalism in Freirean thought to satisfy feminist poststructuralist needs for situated teaching, learning and generation of knowledge. This is not to say that Freirean pedagogy should be rejected, but it is to say that we need to add to it what we know about subjectivity and the nature of oppression. (*ibid*)

Freire, like Marx, also works with a concept of false consciousness, and sees conscientisation as the solution to its transformation. However, Cocks (1989: 15) shows Freire's magical consciousness to be equated with medieval superstition. This implies a reliance on rationality in Freirean concepts of the knowing subject and conscientisation.

Freire (1970: 47) importantly ties transformation of consciousness to the idea of praxis: transformation of perspectives is not a purely intellectual action. It must involve action for change; only then can it be termed praxis. 'Knowledge is praxis, a constant interplay between theory, ideas and the actions that derive from them and in turn influence their development' (Maher, 1987: 94). This idea of praxis has been taken up by many feminist theorists and is crucial to any politicised poststructuralist viewpoint.

Adult education shares with all other pedagogies the production of particular types of subjects. The core goal of adult education practice which strives for social justice in recent decades has been to produce critical thinkers, who will mobilise to resist oppression (Tennant and Pogson, 1995: 199). A key thinker in the field of critical thinking is Mezirow (1978, 1981, 1991), whose concept of transformative learning is implicit in the idea of critical thinking. Mezirow has been influenced by the work of Freire and Habermas (1971a,b, 1983a,b) and has in turn influenced many other thinkers in adult education and critical pedagogy.

Mezirow's (1991, 1996) theory of transformative learning has developed over nearly two decades into a comprehensive and complex description of how learners construe, validate and reformulate the meaning of their experiences. Mezirow sees Freire's (1970) work on conscientisation as parallel to his own work on perspective transformation. Perspective transformation is intended for emancipatory purposes: 'The intent of education for emancipatory action – or ... perspective transformation – would be seen by Habermas as the providing of the learner with an accurate in-depth understanding of his or her historical situation' (Mezirow, 1981: 6, cited in Cranton, 1992: 24). The core of transformative learning in Mezirow's (1991) view is the uncovering of distorted assumptions – errors in learning – in each of the three domains of meaning perspectives: psychological, sociolinguistic and epistemic perspectives. A learner can be advanced in the development of reflective judgement or the intellect and still hold distorted assumptions (*ibid*: 43).

The main problems with Mezirow's work, from a feminist poststructuralist point of view, are first, that of distortion and, second, the assumption that accurate information exists. Distortions are similar to false consciousness, whose problems I have discussed already in relation to structuralist Marxism (see Chapter Three) and to Freirean thought. Distortions, in a feminist poststructuralist framework, are as real as the 'accurate information'. They do not represent a false consciousness, since no such false consciousness exists.

A reliance on this notion of distortion betrays an assumption that accurate information and rational understanding alone can lead to transformation. The assumption that accurate information exists and that consensus can be reached on the basis of access to such information is a legacy from Habermas. The danger with consensus and trying to achieve it through what Habermas calls the 'ideal speech situation' (1983b) is twofold. First, it does not allow for the investments that people make in certain positions or in certain kinds of knowledge, based on how these investments give access to power or positions of power. Second, the idea of consensus is based on rational talk (Young, 1987: 67–73) and too often such talk reflects dominant discourses, because of the power associated with such discourses and the fact that muted discourses have little currency and therefore cannot be made sense of, even by people with the best will in the world. Rational talk and the idea of rationality again betray assumptions that the human subject is unitary and rational, all other things being equal (*ibid*).

In this approach to critical pedagogy, there is a trend towards ensuring that students are given the chance to arrive logically at a consensus that it is universally valid that all people have a right to freedom from oppression (Alcoff, 1988). Habermas (1983a: 19) insists that impartial reason will emerge from dialogue, as long as the dialogue takes place under conditions of co-operatively seeking the truth, where all motives are neutralised. As long as all perspectives are heard and taken into account, there is a possibility of consensus. Having deconstructed the assumptions of accepted consensus, he reconstructs a presumption of impartiality in his ideal of rational consensus (Young, 1987: 69). In Mezirow's theory, the concept of perspective transformation has as its foundation this concept of the unified self and a belief in the decisive power of human agency (Mezirow and Associates, 1990: 14). He also emphasises the importance of content, process and premise reflection. However, he uses them to serve primarily a critical function of revealing theoretical obfuscations and injustice. The self, for Mezirow, exists apart from structure; it is essentially disengaged, disembodied, dehistoricised. 'Mezirow may in fact have reified the masculinist ideal of the "unencumbered subject"' (Welton, 1990, cited in Clark and Wilson, 1991).

A universal female subject? A critique of 'women's ways of knowing'

A major influence in feminism is the idea that women have special 'female' ways of knowing which coincide with essentially female ways of being. This is also perhaps the most visible and influential face of feminism in the mainstream of everyday life, in the media and in adult education in Ireland. I agree with Brookes (1992) that it is important to connect being and knowing through a model of education which draws on the everyday experiences of women, but that it will not challenge the gender status quo if it bases itself on a difference mode. The Harvard Project on Women's Psychology and Girls' Development, from which a great deal of this difference work emanates, is a project which represents one of the most influential strands of feminist social psychology today (Wilkinson, 1996: 13). Such educational work has been influenced by the work of Chodorow (1978), Gilligan (1982), Brown and Gilligan (1992, 1993) and Taylor, Gilligan and Sullivan (1995). Much of the research emanating from this project deduces sex differences between women and men on the basis of research carried out with women and girls (Crawford, 1997). Its most popular manifestation with reference to education is in Belenky, Clinchy, Goldberger and Tarule's (1986) book, *Women's Ways of Knowing*.

Drawing on the work of Perry (1970) and positioning themselves against it, Belenky *et al* use the findings of a study of 135 women learners to reformulate five stages of women's knowing, from silence, through received knowledge, subjective knowledge, procedural knowledge to, finally, constructed knowledge. Perry's work is a study of developmental theory derived from his analysis of male students attending Harvard University and the ideas in it are still influential.

Perry assumes that it is not problematic to use his research to indiscriminately chart the epistemological development of both female and male students, despite the fact that his work originates in male experience. He assumes that students move in a linear way, from a basic dualism where the world is viewed in terms of black/white, right/wrong, through to increasingly advanced stages. In the last stage, one is presumed to know that all knowledge is relative and socially constructed. Perry assumes that 'dualists are rare at Harvard' (1970: 63, cited in Brookes, 1992: 41).

Belenky *et al* are critical of Perry's assumptions that people learn in a linear manner. They argue that 'women's thinking did not fit so neatly into his categories' (1986: 14), particularly women's experiences of male authority (*ibid*: 23, 24). However, they build on Perry's scheme when they argue that women's learning can be grouped into 'five major epistemological categories' (*ibid*: 150). Also problematic is their assumption that women learn differently from men and therefore require a woman-centred education (*ibid*: 214–29).

As Brookes (1992: 41) points out, any pedagogy that suggests that women should be isolated in a woman-centred environment is problematic. Theoretically, it is unacceptable, because it is based on difference. Strategically, it is unacceptable, because it would isolate women in an academic context which is already highly stratified. Politically, it is unacceptable, because it maintains a sex-differences approach and thus maintains male/female dualism. Women can benefit from a safe and supportive learning environment, but to suggest that they need special, separate environments to meet their essentially different needs does not address the need for safety as a political problem. It implies that the problem is located in naturally occurring differences between all women and all men. As Lewis (1989: 122) puts it:

> The language in which Belenky and her colleagues locate women's experiences in the academy – 'newborn', 'child', encouraged to 'think more', turning her into a 'real knower' – suggests that education for women needs to be focused at some primary level in order to bring us up to par with the already 'grown up' male thinkers who are posed as the norm to which we must aspire. It is easy to see how such an approach might enhance the already prevalent ideology that education for women is a prescription for lowering standards. The terms of the discourse on standards, which the language in *Women's Ways of Knowing* implies, only makes sense within the frames of a phallocentric system where being a man is not only considered to be different from being a woman but also considered to be better.

This categorisation of levels of knowing amounts to a hierarchy of ways of knowing on which the authors base a model of education that might draw women out of a state of silence. This silence is described as a state devoid of 'awareness of mental acts, consciousness, or introspection' (Belenky *et al*, 1986: 25). The aim is to draw women into a state of constructed knowledge, described as a condition of 'becoming and staying aware of the working of their minds' (*ibid*: 141). In this state, women can create their 'own' epistemological understandings.

On the face of it, these stages represent an exciting model and the idea of constructed knowledge appears to address the dynamics of the challenge brought to patriarchy by women's education (Lewis, 1989: 120). However, the authors propose to establish the frames of their educational model by connecting teaching with midwifery. They propose, following Ruddick (1980, 1984), to name the discourse through which women's education is to be articulated as *'maternal thinking'* (Belenky *et al*, 1986: 218, emphasis added). This proposed political strategy will draw a woman's knowledge out into the world.

As a proposed pedagogical strategy, Ruddick's concept of maternal thinking maintains the idea of immutable and natural sex differences and does not address at all the political climate (that is, patriarchal social relations and sexist discourses) in which learners' subjectivities are constructed. This is not to dispute the goodwill of the authors or their genuine concern about 'why so many women students speak so frequently of problems and gaps in their learning and so often doubt their intellectual competence' (*ibid*: 4). But, because of the lack of a clearly articulated political agenda, the authors inadvertently slip into the language of women's deficiency and thereby fail to address the deeply complex ways in which women's constraints and possibilities are constructed (Lewis, 1989: 121).

Belenky *at al* fail to analyse the structural inequalities in educational environments, most particularly the sexual harassment, abuse and incest that form a pervasive background to the lives of the women surveyed for the book. While the authors conclude that sexual abuse and harassment *may* affect women's ways of knowing and learning, they do not analyse *how* this happens. They do not address women's knowledge as socially and politically organised, but as something intrinsic to women. They describe ideology about women, but they take this as evidence of natural differences between women and men. In doing this, they promote a discourse of male/female dualism. As Brookes (1992: 58) points out, they do not address how an explicit theoretical validation of difference – an assumption implicit in mainstream curriculum and academic programming – might further disempower women in an educational system which already is failing to meet their needs, insofar as it is organised to reflect male experience and hence to entrench male power and authority. Such models also overlook the importance of politically conscious resistance experiences (Maher, 1987: 98).

Although they initially reject Perry, Belenky *et al* (1986) build on his work later when they organise women's learning perspectives into the five categories of silence, received knowledge, subjective knowledge, procedural knowledge, and constructed knowledge. While the authors clearly state that these are not universal categories, that they are abstract and hence cannot capture the complexity of individual women's thought, and that men show evidence of similar categories (*ibid*: 15), implied in their work, nonetheless, is the assumption that one stage builds upon the other in a linear and hierarchical manner. Belenky *at al* have produced knowledge about women which proposes a universal, unitary female subject, existing in a dualistic and therefore hierarchical relation to a unitary male subject. They preclude the possibility of moving out of or of deconstructing or subverting dualism, by their reliance on maternal practices as the vehicle for their pedagogy and by their use of restrictive educational categorical ways of knowing, which implicitly deny the possibility of generating new knowledge, given different social circumstances.

The theoretical divisions set up in the work of Belenky *et al* echo the work of Chodorow (1978) and Gilligan (1982). They support a dualistic approach to knowledge and the human subject which, far from challenging the status quo, functions to reinforce it. Instead of looking at supposedly naturally occurring differences, pedagogy, if it is to rise to the challenges posed by poststructuralist feminist insights, needs to investigate how different gendered experiences are *produced*, how difference can be celebrated without resorting to essentialism and how human subjects are organised to know.

Like Hollway (1991b: 31), I am constantly struck by how dominant is the idea among feminist educational practitioners and theorists that there exist natural differences between the genders and that there are naturally different women's and men's ways of knowing. In common with both Hollway (*ibid*) and Segal (1987), I am disturbed at these easy polarities and what I see as the negative effects on feminism which follow from them. Hollway's and Segal's work, along with Crawford (1997: 277–81) gives a convincing account of the extent to which polarised thinking about femininity and masculinity dominates white Western feminism. This kind of thought depends to a considerable extent on psychological concepts:

> The most accessible feminist writing today is one in which we are likely
> to read of the separate and special knowledge, emotion, sexuality,
> thought and morality of women, indeed of a type of separate 'female
> world' which exists in fundamental opposition to 'male culture', 'male
> authority', male-stream thought', in opposition to the world of men.
> (Segal, 1987: ix)

Hollway (1991b) asks why white Western feminist thought in the 1980s and 1990s has been so psychologised, unlike the socialist feminism of the 1970s. She believes significance in accounting for the psychologisation of adult education is

> the closeness of a psychological vision of the world to the dominant
> popular assumptions of Western culture, since what the two have in
> common is an outlook which understands the world in terms of the
> individual. (Hollway 1991b: 30)

Psychology plays a part in reproducing and legitimating popular assumptions about individuals and their femininity or masculinity. It places a particular model of the individual at the centre of its explanatory world, and while it does so it cannot reconceptualise gender issues in terms of the constraints and forces which shape a person and how these may be changed (*ibid*). While adult education continues to rely on unitary models of the subject, whether these are unitary and male, or unitary and female, it will not escape the limitations of popular assumptions, legitimated by psychology.

Similarly, if adult education remains within psychology's terms of reference in the use of the categories 'femininity' and masculinity', it cannot avoid reducing them to natural differences or to cultural differences, even while applying a social analysis. The solution for adult education is not necessarily to abandon psychology. One of the reasons that the socialist feminisms of the 1970s became concerned with psychological questions was that feminists operating in consciousness-raising groups realised that the personal is political and that change is not simply a matter of economic resources, equal opportunity, correct political intentions and voluntarism. Adult education has taken these lessons on board also. But as long as the reliance on femininity and masculinity remains, the personal will be reduced to the psychological and the individual, losing in the process a vision of the politicised personal and the personal nature of the political. The only difference between such use of femininity and masculinity and the old patriarchal psychology of sex differences is that adult education, relying on feminist psychology, has re-evaluated femininity as superior. This is not enough to make a political difference in a world of complex social relations characterised by 'shades of grey' rather than clear-cut essential differences (cf Cocks, 1989). As Segal (1987: 5) points out, some renowned misogynists are not averse to claiming that women are superior to men. It excuses all sorts of bad behaviour, legitimates double standards and does not disturb the expectations that women will take primary responsibility for caring, feeling and nurturing.

Experience and description in feminist research and education

In a great deal of feminist theory and research, especially in research based on the cultural feminist epistemologies I have discussed, experience has been made the most reliable guide to reality. Feminists have shown the importance of recognising and describing women's experiences and in thus giving them a valid voice in research and education. They have demonstrated the importance of recognising that the personal aspects of one's life are related to the social and political spheres. This was a major factor in feminist consciousness-raising and continues to be so. But there are all sorts of theoretical questions behind the concept of experience and they have political effects. The models of the subject implicit in many feminist approaches to research have tended to be humanist and/or essentialist. In these approaches, experience, approached through description, tends to be reified as the most valid and most stable ground for knowing and for building an epistemology. It is seeing as representing an essential reality about women's lives.

The poststructuralist objection to this use of experience is not a repudiation of grounds of knowing per se (Fuss, 1990: 27), nor of experience as one of those grounds. It is based on a belief that experience is socially constructed and that it is a sign mediated by other signs. It is also based on deconstructing a dualistic relationship between essentialism and constructionism (Potts and Price, 1995). That is, it does not want to privilege either side of the dualism, but to see them in a mutual and dynamic relationship. As Hollway argues (1989: 42), the use of women's experience as a basis for research is subject to the same kind of theoretical problems which surround models of the human subject. Humanistic psychology and Verstehen-based sociology assume that accounts given in answer to sympathetic questioning will be an expression of the 'real' person. Much feminist theory has actually had the effect of reinforcing orthodox social theory, in assuming that the meaning of accounts is unproblematic.

The social and historical conditions which gave rise to this approach by feminists are also important: they can be seen in terms of women's need for their subjugated knowledge to acquire status. These approaches take seriously people's accounts as a direct expression of themselves, rather than directly trying to measure performance or attitude. The approach is based on the assumption, which at a deeper level is shared with orthodox psychology, that an account will produce facts whose truth-value is not problematic for the research. It is believed that an account can reflect directly that individual's experience (*ibid*: 41). But these similarities are based on humanist assumptions about the individual which rely on the metaphysics of presence, that is, on the belief that one can be fully present to oneself and to other people.

Poststructuralist developments in theories of subjectivity, on the other hand, can draw on the value of experience and of accounts which were once ignored, but are able to see subjective accounts as produced within discourses, history and relations. This is my starting point for examining and interpreting experience in the accounts of feminist women in Chapter Five. To strengthen its achievements in asserting the importance of personal experience, feminist method needs to interpret experience, not just describe it, and, furthermore, needs to jettison the belief that there is no theory behind 'plain description'. We need to combine the value of experience with Foucault's idea that truth is a historical product and therefore not absolute (Walkerdine, 1989a: 40).

Descriptive research

Many earlier feminist approaches rightly saw that power was being exercised in the process of analysis and theorising about people who participated in research but who did not have a chance to participate in the analysis or, often, did not have a chance to even read the research publications. A common response to this was to democratise the relations of research and also to refrain from theorising and theory building and to view research as a means of giving voice to previously silenced views on the world (*ibid*). The method most commonly adopted in this response is one in which women are directly asked for accounts of their experience, referred to as descriptive interviewing. Hollway (1989: 40, 41) notes:

> The method of descriptive interviewing represents a consistent application of the political principle that women's experience can provide a direct route to women's consciousness or identity. That principle provides the answer for feminist method: ask women directly for an account of their experience. It is also consistent with the humanist criticism of traditional psychology that people's experience was neither sought nor valued. Again, the assumption is the idealist one that the knowledge is there, based on experience, and can be represented in an account.

Descriptive research can tell us a lot about women's lives, and how they report them, but it cannot theorise about or explain women or men, or gender. But in its unproblematic reliance on experience, it has retained a focus on the individual, rather than relations, power and difference, and the conditions that give rise to a person's account (*cf* Hollway and Jefferson, 2000). This is a theoretical lack which undermines the potential of research to be emancipatory.

The issue of experience raises theoretical questions about the concept of women's interpretive repertoires, of power, resistance and agency. In the research and pedagogy I report on in the following two chapters, I do not treat experience as revelatory of some female or feminist essence. First, I try to uncover the constructed nature of experience. Although I have no male participants, I put a special focus on the construction of feminism and feminist subjectivity in relations, including heterosexual couple and work relations. Second, because of the way I lay out my analysis, readers may make connections with their own everyday experiences. Women's experiences, I argue, need to be included in research and education, but as a starting point for developing less rigid gender hierarchies, not for showing the true nature of women. Research and education need to develop the capacity to theorise experience, in a context that does not treat the category as unproblematic, or neutral.

Collecting data for this book: feminists' interviews, conversations and discussions

The study employs grounded theory (Glaser and Strauss, 1967; Strauss and Corbin, 1990) techniques for information gathering, including theoretical sampling, the delineation of broad categories and their development through subsequent fieldwork and analysis. However, the techniques are set within a more diverse epistemological stance than the scientific epistemology of its proponents. I conducted interviews and discussions with women who self-defined as feminist, concentrating on feminist changes and how they were defined and achieved. The sequencing of the analysis in Chapter Five reflects the ways that I moved in my interviews from fairly broad discussion, to detailed accounts of private and emotional changes, drawing on only a few cases.

The theoretical sampling process began when I asked six women who had defined themselves as feminists through public speech, work or writing, to take part in research on feminist identity and how they put their feminism into practice in their everyday lives. Two of these women knew me already. All of the women were aware of the current personal/structural debates. All had significant experience of self-reflection, in relation to personal change embraced for political reasons. The initial six women all came from a similar age group, class background/present class status, educational and professional positions and cultural history, similar to my own. All six contacted responded positively to my letters and before conducting interviews, I discussed in more detail with them, over the phone or in person, the sort of research I was hoping to do.

I conducted interviews between January and August, 1996. At each interview conducted between January and May, I asked the women for the names of one or two other feminist women who might be interested in participating in the research. Such 'snowball sampling' is capable of facilitating the theoretical sampling procedures. In January 1996, I began a series of individual interviews with eight women (the original six contacted and two others whose names had been given to me by the first group), conducted over four weeks. Most women did one interview, three did two. I taped and transcribed all interviews. I did some preliminary analysis on these, drawing up categories and concept lists. I then conducted a group interview with four women. Another single interview and a pair interview followed. At this point, I felt that the categories of discourses and relations (see Chapter Five) were saturated, at least insofar as the discursive analysis went.

Many of the interviewees thus far had referred to the importance of the emotional work, connected to political change, but the interviews/discussions had not developed in such a way that produced material pertaining to the details of this work. Drawing on my theoretical sensitivity (a combination of cultural and personal experience, theoretical reading and emerging data (Glaser, 1978; Strauss and Corbin, 1990), I decided 'to concentrate on a few situations where the theoretical yield should be high' (Connell, 1995: 90). In June 1996, I drafted a letter telling potential new participants about the work so far and describing the kind of intimate discussion I was looking for, focusing particularly on overcoming crises of identity or feelings of being blocked or stuck in feminist effectiveness. Five people agreed to take part in this exercise. I supplied them with drafts of the analysis of discourses and relations, and with a short paper of my own which I had called *A Voyage Round My Feminism* (Ryan, 1995). I met them in a pair and a three, during August 1996, spending about six hours with each group.

My approach in all of the interviewing and discussion was based on exploring contradictions and keeping the focus on relations, rather than on individuals. I regarded all participants (myself and the interviewees) as equals, I voiced my own opinions and encouraged the interviewees to ask questions of me, although I was careful not to dominate the discussions or conversations. I was trying to record and document slices of information about ongoing social practices in which all the research participants were involved and to use this as a basis for theorising.

We met at locations like workplaces, or our homes, often over tea or a drink. I usually initiated the conversations by explaining some of my interest in doing a study of feminist identity and knowledge. I checked with the participants if they were willing to have the sessions recorded on tape and all were. Most of the participants had experience of group work or facilitation and were able to be active listeners as well as able to voice their own thoughts, or to develop thoughts in discussion with others. There was never a problem getting discussion started. As soon as possible after each interview, each participant was provided with a transcript of the conversation or discussion in which she had taken part and, where requested, with a copy of the tape recording.

I stopped holding recorded sessions when I had material from 20 women, amounting in all to 37 ninety-minute cassettes, most of which I had transcribed. In the course of analysis, I played back and listened to the tapes, as well as reading and re-reading transcripts. Clearly, much of the material gathered is not reported in the book. Nevertheless, every interview gave me something to think about. Transcription was an enormous amount of work, which I did as soon as possible after each interview/conversation or discussion, in order to keep on top of the work. I could probably just as well have listened to the tapes for the kinds of analysis I did. However, several women thanked me for supplying a transcript promptly and expressed appreciation at having the opportunity to read their words. As well as the formal data gathering sessions, I held many informal conversations and discussions with friends about the research. Some of these have also shaped my theorising. I think of these participants as secondary participants (*cf* Mama,

1995: 74). While I have not quoted directly from them, they have also played an important part in the research.

The ways that I developed my information gathering and my subsequent analysis of the material came directly out of my own feminist interests and reflect many of my feminist concerns. I drew constantly on my experience and use of feminist poststructuralist concepts for its analysis. I believe that we can research another's subjectivity, identity and knowledge, only if we have done similar research on ourselves. Thus, I was sensitive to other feminists' similarities to and differences from me, and wanted to give their experiences a theoretical treatment.

How the information was analysed

I used a method of analysis which is loosely called 'interpretive discourse analysis' (Gavey, 1997; Hollway, 1989; Potter and Wetherell, 1987), or 'interpretive analytics' (Cherryholmes, 1988). I focussed on accounts rather than individuals, by identifying the discourses shaping the accounts, and by examining how and why participants took up positions in different discourses (see Chapter Two).

Although I am a feminist researching feminists, I cannot assume that I can accurately 'represent' them, or that feminism will mean the same thing to them and to me. The problem is partly overcome by focusing in the analysis on issues pertaining to identity, signification and knowledge, not on individual feminists. Nor is the focus on searching for a real, true feminist identity, but on the accounts of feminist 'success' and agency provided. 'Feminist knowledge' is intended to characterise the meanings ascribed by a woman to whatever social, emotional, sexual, political or personal configuration she has learned about in the course of constructing a feminist identity. A feminist identity is a woman's subjective experience or intrasubjective account of her own feminism. The accounts are not assumed to give access to an essential identity, but must rely on what the participants are able and willing to say about it (cf Kitzinger, 1987: 90). I tried therefore to avoid treating accounts as derived solely from the psychology of individual women (ibid), and looked for evidence of the discourses with which the accounts are associated, drawing attention to the political and personal features of feminist accounts of knowledge.

Within the accounts, I looked for evidence of discourses, by following Foucault's points:

1. Seek in the discourse not its laws of construction, as do the structural methods, but its conditions of existence.
2. Refer the discourse not to the thought, to the mind or to the subject which might have given rise to it, but to the practical field in which it is deployed. (Foucault, 1973b, cited in Cherryholmes, 1988: 161)

In examining reflexive and interactive positioning within discourses, I used the Freudian and Kleinian notion of defence mechanisms. These mechanisms protect a person against the intrusion of repressed material, and they are relational: that is, they operate not simply by having an effect at an individual level, but also by projection. In accounts, therefore, I looked for examples of habitual reflexive take-up of certain discursive positions, or the interactive positioning of others. I also looked for the repression of certain discourses and emotional investments, their splitting off from the account giver, and their projection onto others. Nevertheless, even though psychoanalysis has given us valuable insights, my project is not to interpret people's unconscious. I was trying to describe feminist subjectivity at the level of consciousness, because the world of culture and politics is a consciously experienced world (Cocks, 1989: 14). This is not the same as reifying experience but more like deep analysis on a social scale (cf Cain, 1993).

I spent hours poring over the accounts and immersing myself in the data. I did not break up the data into small fragments, but analysed it at a more whole or *Gestalt* level (see Hollway and Jefferson, 2000: 68; West, 1996). My analysis is clearly laid out in Chapters Five and Six: I number each part of an account that I considered important to the development of a theme, and then made a correspondingly numbered comment, under the heading 'Points of analysis'. Rather than describe in detail here how I conducted the analysis, I lay it bare in Chapters Five and Six, so that readers have the opportunity to see exactly how I did it, and on what evidence I base my claims and my interpretations.

One of the intentions of the methodology was to encourage interpretation and exploration of feminist knowledges by the participants, as well as by me. However, I think that in the final resort, I achieved this with the participants Maureen and Sinead (see Chapter Six), but less so with the other participants. In those other cases, the conclusions are more mine than they are shared. It was I who spent hours pouring over the data and trying to connect themes, and I reserved the right to make interpretations, although I offered the participants the power of veto and the opportunity to comment on my analyses of their accounts.

Conclusion

Feminist poststructuralism challenges adult educators and researchers to create a changed conceptual framework for their practices concerning gender. Practices, discourses and orthodoxies of education and research emerge out of dynamic relationships between social and historical events and human actors, who have personal affinities and individual biographical details which must be taken into account. Knowledge production, including knowledge about the subject, is political activity. It is important, however, to move beyond critique towards discourses of agency, by suggesting ways of shifting and adjusting the meaning of the human relations, self-esteem and personal development projects within feminist educational politics. Along with accounts of contradictions and the acknowledgement of the complexity of subjectivity, we also require accounts of how transformation and movement in subjectivities can come about or can be achieved and lived. These questions are addressed in Chapters Five and Six, where I examine how feminists construct knowledge. In Chapter Seven, I discuss how I draw on the analyses of Chapters Five and Six, to inform my own practice of personal development education. I am especially interested in how theory and practice become one, how the production of knowledges and their communication as part of everyday life may be experienced as part of a whole, and how radical critiques can connect with people's lives in practical ways.

5   Discourses and relations in the present: the content and strategies of feminist knowledge

Introduction

When I began the research for this book, I wanted to investigate ongoing instances of feminist social practices, especially instances of successful feminism. In theoretical terms, I wanted to research effective resistance, rather than to map oppression. I wanted to specify the ways that the participants constructed feminist knowledge: that is, how they made sense of feminism, and the effects their interpretation of feminism had on their thoughts, emotions and actions. I had most of the ideas from the preceding chapters floating round in my head when I conducted my interviews and discussions. I knew, therefore, that I would examine participants' accounts for evidence of different discourses, and that in the course of data generation and analysis, I would also look for evidence of psychodynamic processes. The data also suggested an important third element: that of strategic responses to situations in the present. In this chapter, then, I analyse feminists' accounts in terms of discourse and relations in the present moment. In the next chapter, I go on to examine psychodynamic processes, and I illustrate how the three elements exist in dynamic relationships with each other, in the construction of subjectivity and knowledge.

Discourses of feminism

Within the framework of analysis for this chapter, discourses carry the content of subjectivity. They position individuals in relation to one another socially, politically and culturally, as similar to or different from; as 'one of us' or as 'Other' (Mama, 1995: 98). In this way, different positions and powers are made available to people. Three main feminist themes emerged from the participants' data, to qualify as discourses in the way I have defined the concept. They are:

> Discourse One: feminism as an expression of a naturally occurring femininity which is oppressed under patriarchy
> Discourse Two: feminism as a rejection of women's and men's socialisation into different roles
> Discourse Three: feminism as a move away from male/female dualism.

The three discourses reflect Kristeva's three stages of feminism (see Chapter Two), although they are not identical to them. Discourses One and Two especially have long histories in feminist theory and practice and have entered popular collective awareness as the face of feminism, although not without modification. Discourse Three is more recent and more complex and fewer people take up positions in it.

Discourse One: feminism as an expression of a naturally occurring femininity oppressed under patriarchy

At times, this discourse is expressed in accounts as the repression of a universal and essential feminine and at other times as the repression of a female culture, not necessarily based on a pre-existing femininity, but on a way of being derived from women's positions as primary care-givers in social relations. Denise is chief executive of a development organisation, and her account illustrates this discourse [1].

> **Denise**
> I have much stronger views now on feminism and women's issues than I did twenty years ago. I also think that living with men, which I did for fifteen years, was terribly anti-stuff – I don't think that men understand these issues, especially men who are radical, socialist, have a liberal agenda. Whatever about the others.

Can you dismiss them?

> Well, you can, I suppose. I just feel that even people like that just don't have a sense of what it is like for women to make it in the world. Mind you, I think that women have a different way of operating. You know, the argument can be levelled at you, 'Well, why don't you – join in?'. But I actually have problems with that, because I think that they join in, or people like me do, but in a different kind of way – different ways of communicating things, we have different ways of operating [1], which often don't fit very well with – you know, hierarchical, very male structures and political parties [2]. I think that's a problem.

> *I sometimes feel that there are two spheres that never meet. There are these non-hierarchical attempts at being egalitarian and then there are male-centred, hierarchical, party-political structures [3], even though there are women involved in that too. And I often feel they don't meet at all. How would you see that?*

> It's true. Well, I would say there are two different classes. But I think it's difficult. On the one hand, you could say, well, the only way to change things is to get in there and reorganise the structure. But I don't actually agree with that argument any more. I think that what you need to develop is a completely different sort of structure. I think it's the same argument that people use about women priests. They say, oh, the church will change if there are women priests [4]. But it won't. What will happen is you get a lot of women buying into a very male-oriented structure which doesn't allow them any equality in a real sense and where they will probably get treated

just as second-hand as people get treated in other spheres. But it won't change the thinking. Whereas if they allowed priests to marry, that might change their thinking, because they would have to think about a few other things, apart from themselves [5].

And it's almost like that with political structures as well. For example, our own experience in working with women's groups, you very quickly realise that women operate in a different way. They'll operate in a way where they network, they're concerned with what other people's needs are, and they operate I think in a more caring way. And I think that's a huge disadvantage when you come to joining in the rest of the world [6] – things like organisation of structures that are very much the old male-oriented county council, VEC [Vocational Education Committee] structures. Where they put up their hands to speak and stuff like this. And when women come on, I think actually there's an argument for learning to operate like that, because I don't think you can survive without it. But on the other hand, there is an argument for the structure changing to accommodate that. But women need a lot of time and they need a lot of support to do that, because they are not used to operating like that, especially women who are not involved in work outside the home [7]. And even women who are involved in work outside the home, for example, if you are operating at quite a different level. In which case, you will be isolated, you know.

But in a way, this is very funny, because we are all women members of staff, which is sort of weird. But that didn't happen deliberately. It happened because women work for money in an organisation like this that is sort of pathetic. But the advantage of that is that you have a very different sort of team operation or managerial operation than you would if you had a mixed population, I think [8]. I don't know, I mean, I haven't had really time to sit down and look at it in much detail [9].

– Statistically, that's not happening much outside. But yes, it's a sort of organic growth and then, actually, if that happens and if it's managed carefully [10], then people can develop skills that they wouldn't develop in other kinds of hierarchical structures. For example, here somebody starting off as a clerical assistant would now be working in some kind of other area, where they can – develop more skills, you just have to allow that to happen. And I think that in a lot of work structures, that doesn't happen. If you look for example at the Civil Service, you find a lot of good women stuck at HEO [Higher Executive Officer] level. You're not out around town with the boys, so it's not possible to make all those promotional moves [11].

Points of analysis

1. Statement that women have ways of doing things: part of Discourse One's central proposition.
2. Distinguishes women's ways from male ways of doing things and characterises these male ways as hierarchical: Establishment of dualism.

3.   I am drawn into the discourse. I know how to operate in it, even though I don't completely accept its central proposition, as readers know already. Yet, I am not 'faking', because I can read feminism through this discourse and I can act in this discourse when I need to do so, in order to make contact with another woman about issues of feminism. I also imply by my remark that power continues to reside in the 'male' space, that a power imbalance will continue to be constituted through any discourse which holds intact a male/female dualism.

4.   Denise explicitly distinguishes the discourse in which she is operating from a liberal feminist, access discourse.

5, 6. Recognition that the existence and separate nature of a women's culture won't change gender relations. The main discourse of essential differences begins to break down here, or at least to reach its explanatory limits. Thus the account is produced not just within the essentialist discourse, but also recognises that gender is relational, which contradicts the main discourse through which the account is constructed.

7.   Recognition that women's way of operation is cultural and based on the prevailing conditions of their existence. This is a recognition of the constructed nature of experience.

8.   A reassertion of the existence of a separate female culture.

9.   Describing acceptance of a female culture as a 'gut' reaction implies a recognition that looking at it in detail would reveal more of the contradictions and explanatory limits referred to in comments 5 and 6. Even while drawing on a particular discourse, the account recognises that the discourse might not be capable of explaining things completely.

10. It is a culture that can be fostered and encouraged. This is a further recognition of its constructed nature.

11. Assertion that a 'male 'culture prohibits women's development. Acceptance of the existence of separate cultures of male and female. This interpretation of her experience reinforces Denise's belief in the discourse's central proposition, that women operate in a different, specifically female, culture.

Discourse One can exist in conditions where women are downgraded, or in contexts where women are considered equal but different. On coming into contact with this discourse, which had frequently been their first contact with feminism, many participants experienced it as both liberating and enabling. They spoke of 'women's power', 'getting in touch with my femininity', 'feeling a female energy'. It enabled them to reject the negative and inferior definitions of women afforded to them by sexist and anti-women discourses. Culture needs major symbols, so if we talk about a women's culture, it is most likely that an essential femininity will become one of the major symbols, because it meshes so easily with patriarchal culture that people can understand it readily. Because of its tendency towards separatism it doesn't reach its explanatory limits as often as Discourse Two does (see next section). At the collective level, this discourse provides an explanatory framework for women's networks, women's art and women's cultural expressions (Ryan and Connolly, 2000). At a personal level, it offers women a way of seeing themselves as superior to men. Although it inverts rather than subverts gender relations, it is sometimes a necessary discourse, given the division of the world into female and male, under patriarchy, with a devaluation of traditionally female ways of doing things.

Discourse Two: feminism as a rejection of women's and men's socialisation into roles

The central proposition of Discourse Two is that gender is purely social. It relies on the concept of the conditioning or socialisation of a neutral person into differentiated sex roles. Justice and equality are ideals that can be achieved through rational action and legislation, although the complexity of this is not underestimated. It reflects the liberal feminist idea that access to areas previously denied them is important for women, in 'desocialising' or 'de-roling' them, and that the same applies to getting access for boys and men to roles traditionally associated with women. Many of the women in the study found this discourse was their mothers' attitude: gain good education, good employment, and financial independence. Some participants had experienced it at school, although schools were also recognised as prime sites for socialisation into traditional roles. Those participants with daughters were trying to pass it on to them.

Sandra

I think that my interest in the whole role definition [1] and because of my consciousness of it given my subject area [home economics], in some ways, that strengthened – I became more aware of the anomalies that existed, whereas maybe if I had stuck with hotel management [her original choice of career training], I would probably have become aware of it in terms of hotel work, maids, housekeepers and so on. But I mightn't have been challenged as much – I wouldn't have come across all the inequalities in the school system, for example [2]. That wouldn't have met me like a slap in the face, in terms of the attitude to certain subjects, and I might have been more like the women who say 'well, if you really want to do it, you should do it' [3]. I might actually have gone that way, because there are a lot of women who have made it in management. And they think, 'I've done it, why can't everybody else do it?' and it's more for them that we don't have the neck or we don't have the academic ability or whatever [4], rather than looking at the things that have happened throughout our life or what are the things that have been dished out to us to make us take different paths or that have forced us in some way into different positions [5]. And if I had done the hotel management, I wouldn't have gone to do social studies probably [6], probably wouldn't have got into union activities as much … but with other people I can understand that the contradictions are too much and they don't become active [7] … They would more say that women don't want it, where I say that women are conditioned into things [8]. They say that women are more suited to the classroom or it doesn't suit them now [to go for promotion] because they have young kids. It could suit their husband, but he might have young kids as well [9]. They wouldn't be as aware of all the inequities that exist in the wider society in terms of women's roles, because they wouldn't be touched by it [10]. I have always had a wider interest in the role of women, beyond my own career.

I think that a lot of women I have met who are into equality for themselves are not so much interested in equality for everybody – they want equality for women, but once they see it in their own set context, they don't think about it beyond – in all layers of society [11].

Even in terms of class, they wouldn't see that some upper-class women are very traditional in terms of their relationship with men. Or in terms of working-class women who might be suffering violence, they would say, 'Well, why don't they just leave?' But they don't take time to think about all the other issues that are stopping them from getting out – like their own conditioning in their families [12], or that women aren't as important in the economy [13]. So a lot of the stuff I would be conscious of wouldn't have come from picking up books on feminism [14], or socialism even [15], it would more come from trying to analyse what was happening around me [16] and listening to discussions and so on... But I have actually been pleased over the last while when I have actually done some reading to see that a lot of the research matches what I would have thought anyway [17] and that it is a matter of putting the academic language on it.

Points of analysis

1.   Statement of central proposition of the discourse: socialisation into roles.
2.   Schooling seen as a site of socialisation and a place where role differentiation can be clearly seen.
3, 4.   Rejection of individualism and meritocracy as explanation of inequalities.
5.   Almost a structural interpretation of the socialisation model is developed in the account, in contrast to a meritocratic méodel.
6.   Recognition that a social studies course has shaped her thinking. (Social studies theory, or any body of theory, represents certain discourses.)
7.   Recognises the effects of power and gender structures in everyday life, in constraining or enabling actions. Acknowledges that socialisation theory does not explain investment in gender difference for other people
8.   Again, rejects individualistic interpretation and asserts socialisation discourse.
9.   Uses role differentiation to explain or interpret different attitudes and behaviours in men and women.
10, 11. Reads other women as positioned in a discourse of individualism, which precludes them caring about equality as a social or collective aspiration.
12.   Recognition of the family as another site of socialisation.
13, 15. Recognition of the limits of a socialisation theory (economics is also important).
14.   Associates feminist awareness with knowledge of socialisation and role theory.
16.   Recognition of the effects of everyday life on the development of a discursive position and on politics.
17.   Belief in the central proposition of the socialisation discourse is confirmed.

Drawing on Discourse Two is not simple for Sandra in this account. Its explanatory limitations are frequently exposed. She expresses awareness of this when she refers to 'all the other issues'. She sees the limitations of the discourse in schools where equal opportunities initiatives are in place, but where 'de-roling' people has not worked. The discourse fails to problematise the investments that people make in taking up gendered positions, and fails to examine the content of those positions. It therefore is constantly coming up against challenges to its central proposition that roles can be changed.

Sandra's account recognises how things signify differently for different people [8] and how women can be positioned against their will in powerful gender structures [7, 10, 11]. Yet the discourse's regime of truth constantly brings her back to socialisation as her explanatory framework. This discourse has not the explanatory power of Discourse One, which draws on patriarchal and deeply ingrained notions of what men and women are really like, to assert the value of women, as women. Neither does it have the radical and productive uncertainty which is evident in Discourse Three.

As a content of subjectivity, it is not as satisfactory for a feminist as Discourse One. Yet many women in the study who accepted Discourse Two saw Discourse One as regressive, in its acceptance of a special women's way of being. Some people had drawn on Discourse Two earlier in their feminist lives and had been radicalised into Discourse Three. Others talked about women they knew who had 'given up on feminism' when a socialisation discourse could not deal with the complexities of gender change.

Discourse Three: feminism as a move away from dualism

The central proposition of this discourse is that feminism involves confronting one's own identity as it relates to 'masculinity' or 'femininity'. Maleness and femaleness are revealed as multiple and fragmented and any sense of opposition or hierarchy, or essential difference, is removed. However, it is not a move towards sameness, but towards multiple ways of being (Kristeva, 1986; Davies, 1990b). Its effects are complex and include an awareness of the other two discourses and acknowledgement of their strategic value and necessity in different contexts. It relies on an awareness of oneself and one's desires and investments (insofar as these can be made present to oneself or others). In some ways, though, this is not a discourse in the sense that Foucault described discourse as appealing to 'truth' for authority and legitimation. It is a more critical discourse than the other two.

Ursula
And it's only now I'm working out the personal side of it. And that can be very confusing then, because there were times when I would ask myself, 'am I still a feminist?'[1] I'm beginning to see things very differently [laughter].

You're talking about the story of my life, nearly – it sounds so familiar [more laughter].

Yes. Yes, and now coming to the place that: 'yes, I am feminist'. And I don't feel as black and white or as straightforwardly as I used to, you know [2].

Yeah, I used to have this thing that there was a proper, a real feminist way to be. And if you're not that way, you can't call yourself that. And like you say, I used the political to work out the personal side of things. I intellectualised and analysed and rationalised all the time, without realising that things were going at a very personal level too. Things that needed a deeper look, in a therapeutic situation – even though I was aware that the personal is political.

Yes, that's it.

And I began to realise at one stage, just how personal the political goes – just how deeply inside us, or inside me at any rate, the social is.

Yes, I think a lot of women of our generation – feminist women [3] – are beginning to come to that realisation now, to see things like that, in that way. And also things like Greenham Common, you know, where boys over a certain age wouldn't be allowed [4]. That kind of separatist stuff. And seeing now that that was growing out of pain. But also seeing now that that wouldn't be an answer either. You know, that that would be just another violent and painful answer to what we have now [5]. What we have now is a very violent painful kind of society, the way – what's done to women and what's done to men. But that wouldn't be an answer either. You know, there's healing for women and there's healing for men and there's some way for women and men to work together. I really disagree with that, as if just by going off on your own you can solve it. And even the therapeutic group I'm in is a mixed group and a few years ago, I would have said, 'No, I don't want to be in a group with men'. And I don't see things like that at all now. I believe that I can't look at my issues without men, and they can't without women either [6]. You know – so that would have really changed for me [7]. And I suppose it's about a more holistic look at society and looking at the whole thing of – that male is bad [8]. And I don't accept that at all, now, I really don't. And I think we put out all our own badness, all the things we didn't like onto men [9].

Projected it –

Yes. And I just wouldn't, I just couldn't go along with that at all now. I think it does me an injustice as well. That by virtue of being a woman, I'm a saint. And I think that that's what was done to women anyway, you know, the virgin or the whore [10]. And I think in some ways, feminism did that again [11]. You know, the Greenham Common stuff and all that, that women have no violence in them. And that's not true, we have violence in us as well [12]. But how we deal with it is the thing. I think we often do it against ourselves, rather than out there. But that's no better.

Yes, and it doesn't move us on.

Yeah, it isn't progressive or growthful, or [long silence].

Points of analysis

1.   Effects of the 'real feminist' discourse lingers in her present life.

2. Acknowledgement of multiplicity.
3. Reflects Kristeva's notion of the 'generations' of feminism, especially of having arrived at a third generation, having gone through the other two stages.
4. Recognises the effects of an essentialist and separatist discourse on practice.
5. Awareness of essentialism, its rejection as inadequate, but also acknowledging its origins and necessity in certain situations.
6. The 'issues' of gender difference are read here as relational.
7. Effects of discourse on practice.
8. Recognises the harm essentialism does to men also.
9. Projection of what is repressed in the 'feminine' onto the male is seen as an effect of essentialist discourses, in this instance.
10. Recognition of dualism in patriarchy.
11. Recognition that essentialist feminist discourses reproduce definitions of women which are the same as those produced under patriarchy.
12. Confronting personal identity as it is constructed for her/us in essentialist discourses.

The three discourses and the regimes of truth they provide about gender difference

The discourses discussed do not form a comprehensive description of feminism. Neither do they determine the types of subjects produced; rather, they 'texture subjectivity' (Mama, 1995: 111). Feminism is only one of many dimensions of subjectivity, and each discourse is responded to in ways unique to each individual (Hollway, 1989, 1995). This means that discourses are not constant, monolithic forces acting on passive victims. Instead, they are responded to collectively by the creation of new discourses and by individual movement between discourses (*ibid*).

Feminism signifies differently in all three discourses. Discourses One and Two have a certain social and explanatory power, because they are derived from dominant humanist discourses about the human person. Nevertheless, Discourse Two does not have the certainties of Discourse One, because it is not premised so heavily on the idea of an essential femininity. Nor does Discourse Two have the benefit of the radical doubt which is encouraged by using Discourse Three as an explanatory framework. In Discourse Two, multiplicity does not explicitly structure feminism. Nevertheless, the account I have chosen as representative of Discourse Two recognises multiplicity. That is, where Discourse Two reaches an explanatory limit, the account has to reach outside the discourse for an explanation. For example, Sandra refers to the 'contradictions' which prevent other people from becoming active in feminist initiatives. Her own explicit account uses Discourse Two (socialisation) to explain difference for herself, but: 'But with other people, I can understand that the contradictions are too much and they don't become active' (Sandra, above).

The account I have chosen as representative of Discourse One also has to reach outside the discourse's central proposition. It recognises gender difference as relational, that is, constructed in social relations in the present: if they allowed priests to marry, that might change their thinking, because they would have to think about a few other things, apart from themselves (Denise, above). Denise is acknowledging here that subjectivity is produced in relations between people. In the next section, I explore this relational aspect of subjectivity further by taking a closer look at Denise's account of her own feminist subjectivity in a specific relational context. Nevertheless, Discourse One's construction of difference encourages separatism as a feminist strategy and therefore does not come up against its explanatory limits as often as Discourse Two does.

None of the participants operate in just one discourse. Operating in Discourse Three necessitates as a prerequisite awareness of the other two and a willingness to draw on them. Operating in this discourse means frequently incorporating the other two as political strategies, while simultaneously asserting the absence of essential female or male natures. However, Discourse Three is used least by participants as it is more complex and difficult to operate in, since so few people recognise it. It is subaltern both in patriarchy and in the practice of feminism.

The relational production of subjectivity

People take up positions in discourse which will give them enough power to protect their vulnerable selves in difficult situations (Hollway, 1989: 60). Below are two accounts of situations where feminists have analysed their actions to the extent that they were clear that they were acting strategically and engaging with dominant discourses in order to gain agency for their feminist politics. Both analyses show positioning in feminist discourses to leave the feminist women vulnerable, and they have to position themselves in different discourses in order to gain agency.

Denise wanted to protect not only herself, but also a women's network and the principle of women's culture. We have already seen that Denise's preferred discourse is Discourse One. However, in the meetings which she describes below, if she had continued to allow that discourse to dictate her positioning, she would have been marginalised and powerless.

> Denise
>
> Actually, it was interesting, there was a huge kind of backlash thing against the local groups and we went through a very difficult period where I had to organise and chair meetings. And there were guys in there who – you know, I'm talking about politicians, local councillors – who use all this legal stuff to try and really shaft you and I thought, 'No, I am not going to allow them to do this'. But what I had to do was I had to use tactics that they employed, which didn't, which I don't care to use myself. But I thought, 'No, in this situation, you're going to *have to*.' [1].
>
> *What did you have to do?*
>
> Shaft the bastards [laughter]. ... There were a couple of guys there who decided, who tried to take out the local groups. They tried everything. Legally, they tried to talk you down in the chair, they tried everything you could

think of. And I just thought, 'I'm not going to allow this to happen, I am not going to allow it to happen'. And I didn't. I had a support group around me, but at the end of the day, it was a sort of battle of strengths, in a sense [2]. I knew that if there was any chink in the armour at all, the whole thing was gone down the tubes. I really knew that. It took an awful lot of energy, it was very stressful, but, in time, it worked. Now it's funny really, because as I say, I didn't feel comfortable using those tactics, they're sort of bullying tactics, if that's what you'd like to call them, or they're very aggressive ones. But sometimes that's the way you have to operate, you know, to survive [3]. So that, actually, I decided to do that, to be very pragmatic about it. I haven't had to do it again, but I would do it again if I had to. I would have no difficulty doing it again if I had to. I think that wouldn't happen to a guy in the chair, you know.

You think they saw you as a soft target?

Initially, yes. But they very quickly realised that that wasn't the case, yes. It took about two meetings, that's all. And in fact, that challenge came at almost the first meeting I conducted. It's interesting now that I think back on it. I think they thought it would be easy [4].

It wasn't just a challenge to you, it was a challenge to the way the local groups were organised. In other words, it was a whole culture they were fighting.

Oh, absolutely, that's right. And I think when you're working in a group like that, you personify it in some way, or you're seen to be leading it [5]. So I think those were the sorts of things that, in the educational sphere, the reason I wanted to hang on in there and still would, is that I have a basic belief in adult education anyway, I believe in the development of the women's sector. I really do. I think it's just a lot of untapped potential. But I think it's very difficult to organise and when we encourage women to come up from the ground, it takes a long time to get into positions where you can really use your power [6]. It really does, it's very difficult.

Points of analysis

1. Recognition that the discourse of feminism as an expression of women's culture is subaltern in comparison with dominant discourses in mainstream culture. It has outsider status in this situation and cannot influence the 'ball game' in insider culture. Continuing to operate within it in these circumstances will marginalise it even further. There is also recognition of the importance of circumstances in the present moment, in deciding how to act.
2. Enactment of personal authority in her conduct of the meetings, by drawing on a different discourse and positioning herself in it, in order to be agentic and affect the 'ball game'.
3. Recognition of the power relations involved. Recognition of the necessity of taking up a position which will give her enough power to protect the women's networks, even if this is at odds with the culture of the networks themselves.

4. Recognition that her opponents at the meetings also make a similar reading of the power differentials between the two discourses. They thought it would be easy to defeat her, because they assumed that Denise would continue to operate within the subaltern discourse.
5. Drawing on the dominant discourse gives a more powerful status to the women's networks, and possibly to the subaltern discourse of feminism (in relation to the mainstream), on which they draw for explanations.
6. Recognition of the power differentials between the discourses again, along with recognition of the slowness and difficulties of change.

By positioning herself in a dominant discourse, outside feminist discourse altogether, Denise is able to play her opponents at their own game and win. She is capable of taking up positions in many discourses in their various manifestations. Depending on present circumstances at the meetings described, she chooses from moment to moment which discourse to position herself in. Within these situations in the present, specific instances of agency are negotiated. Therefore, she takes up a position in a dominant discourse for the strategic purpose of gaining power. Nevertheless, that dominant discourse is modified by her dominant mode of explanation, which is feminist Discourse One. Once she has got what she wants, she does not continue to position herself in the dominant discourse.

A collective strategy

Patricia and Moira, both teachers, worked together to achieve agency in their second-level school.

Patricia
We were involved in this project [a specially funded project for children at risk of early school leaving] in school and because of the special funding that this project had, we were able to have regular meetings of the staff involved, with an outside facilitator, and one of the issues that began to come up was the gender balance in the class involved in the project and then, later, in all the classes in the school. There was a lot of sexually abusive language going on between the two girls and the twelve boys in the group concerned. In the beginning, they were seen as just horrible people [1]. Moira and I talked a lot about it to each other and we thought very similarly on it, that it was a gender issue [2] and that something needed to be done about the gender balance in groups in the future. Eventually, the other staff on the project began to see it from that point of view and as a group we made a recommendation to the management that there should be something about gender balance. Moira, do you want to talk about it?

Moira
Um, yeah. It seemed to me that we had to be really careful about it [3]. We knew from experience that going in with all guns blazing on a gender issue didn't work [4]. But we didn't want to go along – but if we started talking about it in those technical terms, and about the need to examine school structures, if we started that straight away, we would have alienated the rest of them from the start [5].

Patricia
I mean, some of the time, I thought I would go crazy, bringing it up at every meeting and being restrained about my own opinions, just stating the problem over and over and saying, 'This is a problem for everyone in the class, what can we do?', or words to that effect [6]. How many meetings did we have before it got taken seriously? Eight, ten?

Moira
About that, yeah. We were able to let off steam to each other though. That was important. I'm not sure if I could have done it on my own [7].

Patricia
Me neither. Through talking to you about it, I began to see how some of the men were threatened by us, by our ideas– and by our anger, I suppose, when we let them see it [8]. There was one time near the start of the project that I had a huge row with one of them, over the same kind of thing, though not specifically about gender, but about working out of a deficit model of the kids. Of course, that wasn't the language I used. I really lost my cool over it and so did he, in front of the group. After that, well, the two of us talked a lot about it and we really decided to keep it cool and play a game to get what we wanted. And it wasn't just to get what we wanted, but what we believed in [9].

What happened in the long run?

Moira
We began to develop a good relationship with one of the older men, an A post holder [member of senior staff of school], very influential, but involved in the project just as an ordinary subject teacher. We sort of cultivated his good will towards us and towards our ideas [10]. I mean, after meetings, we used to say to each other '[name]'s beginning to move, he's coming over to our side'.

Patricia
Oh yeah, that's exactly how we used to talk about it. When he began to see it in terms of gender, he carried the others with him. They were all men, some of them teaching here thirty years, really set in their opinions, probably couldn't care less what happened to the girls. [The A post holder] suggested making some kind of recommendation about gender balance in classes to the management, from the group as a whole. That was a great day [11]. They listened to him. We were so pleased. It wasn't just a recommendation coming from us, the well-known feminists on the staff, who were dismissed as extreme [12] most of the time, but it was coming from all these men who normally didn't get involved in issues like that. And it was supported strongly by this influential person in the group.

Yes –

Moira

We managed to make a mainstream challenge out of something that was earlier just a marginal challenge [13] from two women teachers who were seen as a bit awkward, feminist, and, like Patricia says, extreme. And that was a feminist success for me [14] – we got a group of men teachers who had been there thirty years and were mostly very complacent about issues like that to actually go to the management and ask for a change [15].

Patricia

I think it also shows you how we felt as feminists within the school, that we felt it would be better – have a better chance of succeeding coming from them than from just the two of us [16]. But we did manage to make them think about it. I look on that as an educational success, the fact that they thought about the issue and moved on it, not just passively followed whatever was happening. Them thinking about it was just as important for me as any direct consequences for the girls in the group [17]. I think they learned something. I look on that as more of a success than a lot of other things I've done in my time. But we almost had to do it by stealth.

Moira

We knew from experience that we couldn't be open about it and get anywhere [18]. We had to be devious about it.

You weren't really being devious about it, you could call it being strategic, along with being assertive in not letting it drop.

Patricia

Yes, strategic, I suppose, but that meant we had to really hold back. We couldn't show our emotions about it. We did have to work at it strategically, you're right, we had to say, 'When is the right time to bring this up, when is the right time to push, when is the right time to lay off?' It was really difficult [19].

Moira

It relates back to what we were talking about earlier, about how, when you push, a person becomes defensive. So it's like a long-term strategy – that you hold off at the time. And I don't think we were – that they didn't consent to it all [20].

Patricia

By the end, I suppose, they kind of owned it. And in fact, I would never have been able to do that, in that situation at school, if I hadn't worked out how to make changes at home [21]. I really would never have been able to make those connections. I suppose it's very much like learning how to take people where they are at, you know [22].

Points of analysis

1.   The dominant model of the girls in the school is a deficit one: they are deficient in relation to the school norms.

2.   A gender perspective constitutes an explicit challenge to the dominant model.

3, 5.   Playing down the political viewpoint is necessary for strategic reasons.

4.   Recognition of the vulnerability of a feminist perspective.

6.   Drawing on a child-centred discourse, which does not pose such a threat to the dominant model as would a feminist or gender analysis.

7, 9.   Emphasis on the importance of a collective approach from the feminists in the group.

8.   The two women recognise other people's emotional investments in the positions they occupy. This includes their own investment in a feminist position.

10.   They try to find common ground, as a strategic measure.

11.   It is important that they do more than analyse the situation from a feminist perspective, they want to be able to effect change also, that is, to be agentic.

12.   Feminism is mostly seen as extreme, but now a feminist initiative is coming from within the mainstream, even if it is not explicitly named as feminist.

13, 14.   Again, it is important for the women to be agentic.

15, 17.   The effects on non-feminists, that is, the girls and the other staff, are important and are part of the process of being agentic. There is also a pedagogical dimension to the way they want to relate to the other staff.

16, 18.   Recognition of feminism's vulnerability and susceptibility to marginalisation.

19, 20, 22. Explicit recognition of the use of strategy to achieve feminist agency and to produce certain ways of thinking (knowledge) in their colleagues.

21.   As part of an earlier interview with Moira, we had discussed the relational nature of feminism in the heterosexual dynamic. I do not go into it in this section, but it arises in the next section, in the account of another participant, where we discuss emotional investments in femininity, as part of heterosexual couple relations.

There is a pedagogical focus in this case, in that the women wanted their colleagues to learn something and to own that learning. Again, this case illustrates that subjectivity in its relational aspects is connected to power. In this case, the power relation is twofold. The women want to protect themselves from being vulnerable and being 'defeated' in their efforts to get gender balance seriously considered at the meeting. They also want to see other staff members move towards a feminist position, even if they do not name it as such. Hence, they take up a position in a child-centred, humanist discourse *vis-à-vis* the other staff members, recognising their colleagues' emotional involvement in the anti-feminist discourses and the threat to them if they shift positions. They also take up a tactical position of not pressurising them. In a strategic move, they avoid acting recognisably in a feminist discourse, which would allow their colleagues to position them as extremists and dismiss them. Importantly, in this case, the two women mount their challenge in a collectively worked strategy. They convince each other that what they are doing is worthwhile, and they support each other in their frustration and anger, because the end result will have feminist effects for the girl students and their colleagues.

The difficulties of acting strategically, in order to produce feminist agency

I have conceptualised both pedagogy and subjectivity in terms of recursive relationships between discourse and situation in the present moment. This conceptualisation has meant analysing the effects and limitations of various feminist discourses in the everyday world. Where feminist discourse of whatever hue has minimal capacity to challenge the mainstream dominant discourses, feminists can resort to strategically drawing on the dominant discourses in order to gain power for the feminist discourses. As Harre (1979: 405) puts it: 'The task of the reconstruction of society can be taken up by anyone at any time in any face-to-face encounter'. But the trick is to have others recognise and accept the discourse through which the reconstruction is taking place (Davies, 1990b: 137).

One of the unifying features of feminism is that it aims to have practical effects. To this end, all women and men, feminist and non-feminist, are an important component in the achievement of feminist goals. The nature of the 'target group' is thus so diverse that the meaning of the term radical varies greatly, and important changes which people make may not always be easily visible to observers. For Patricia and Moira, being recognised as feminist in the situation they describe is less important than achieving change within the social world of their school. The men in the staff group are as important in the achievement of their goals as the young women who were the subject of their concern initially.

In identifying the intersection of discourses and situation as important, these accounts illustrate how meaning and knowledge are created. A person's words and practices are only half the person's. They are brought to completion by the group (cf McDermott and Tylbor, 1987: 160). It can be seen as necessary to collude with these practices, in order to modify them and cause them to signify differently from the dominant significations. Collusion literally means a playing together (from the Latin col-ludere). Less literally, it refers to how members of any social order must constantly interact with each other to posit a particular state of affairs (ibid: 154). The situational or relational analysis gives us a picture of the institutional constraints on feminist discourses. The feminists in question have to align themselves to a certain extent with the dominant discourses, in order to make links with feminist discourses and to achieve change. The boundaries between discourses are seen to be fluid. This kind of analysis not only gives us an account of social structure, but an account of the tools that people use to build social structure (ibid: 164) or change existing structures.

Finely balanced strategies influenced by situations in the present moment

Being proactive about feminism in certain situations can paradoxically mean the strategic playing down of feminist discourses in ways that could be described as contradictory. However, within the theoretical framework I have adopted, acting thus is evidence of the relational, dynamic and multi-layered nature of subjectivity, knowledge, politics and communication. Nevertheless, the strategies are finely balanced. In playing down feminist discourses for strategic reasons, it is easy to become completely taken in by the dominant sexist discourses (cf Thompson, 1996: 12): We need to be vigilant, imaginative and courageous in order to make sure this does not happen (ibid).

> Patricia
>
> You have to be so careful. You want them to think you're a decent human being, so that they will listen to you and your ideas and maybe change the ways they act. But if you're too willing to listen, they assume you're agreeing with them, and next thing, you're being treated like one of them and it's too late to pull back.

Being multiple in this way would be characterised in traditional left political discourse as deserting principles. It would be pathologised in psychological discourse as not being authentic. But it can be re-theorised as politically acceptable and agentic once we view subjectivity as multiple and dynamic. The women cited in this chapter are describing their own movement between various subjectivities, displaying a skill that is developed and refined as they interact with all kinds of people, groups and situations. This kind of multiplicity is a feature of the complexity of contemporary political life. It is evidence that the dominant power structures are not monolithic and that feminist interactions with them can modify them and advance feminist discourses.

Conclusion

As I have discussed in Chapter Four, many of my early interviewees referred to the importance of the emotional work of feminism. Yet the early accounts did not get beyond references to such work, and illuminated only the fields of discourse and strategy, or relations in the present moment. Therefore, I decided to ask potential new participants if they would be willing to give accounts of some of the emotional work they had done in connection with their feminism. Five people agreed, and I sent them a paper I had written on my own feminism and emotional work (Ryan, 1995), as well as descriptions of the discourses and relational processes I had identified thus far in the study. For the next chapter, I have selected the accounts given by two participants of their own self-analysis, in relation to emotional investments in certain discursive positions.

6 Emotional and psychodynamic dimensions of feminism, learning and change

Introduction

This chapter examines two feminists' accounts of private and emotional change and the ways that such change is affected by the discursive and relational contexts in which it takes place. The chapter thus continues to develop the concepts of discourse and relations in the present, as analysed in Chapter Five, but concentrates on the intimate and immediate operations of power, although without divorcing it from its social context. The women cited engage in self-reflection which further develops the explanatory power of a discourse of a multiple subject and undermines male/female dualism. The analysis also shows how psychic life is relational and social, as opposed to being a purely intrapsychic and individual phenomenon. Material repressed in the psyche is seen to be reproduced in discourse, and the analysis draws on the psychodynamic concepts of repression, splitting and projection, and uses them as tools for examining why a person habitually takes up certain positions and not others (see Mama, 1995: 130).

Feminist emotional work within the heterosexual dynamic

Sinèad's account takes up in more detail the dynamic within heterosexual couple relations, which was previously mentioned by other participants, but not developed. As part of her account, she discusses what she sees as her earlier failure to create the degree of egalitarianism she would have liked within her relationship with her husband, even though they were both committed to feminism and were economic equals. Her account is concerned with the process by which she learned to make what she considers feminist changes in the relationship.

Sinèad
I was just so depressed; I thought that I was the cause of all my own problems. In spite of all my feminist knowledge about the messages given to women and girls, and so on, I failed to see that I was buying into all of that [1]. I was accepting my failure as a feminist as a personal failure, a personality deficiency, if you like, that the relationship could not be made more equal.

That deep socialisation was there and I didn't recognise it for ages. Actually, on the surface, when I spoke to him, I was blaming him for all the problems in the relationship, but now when I look at it, I think that deep down I was really angry with myself, that I really blamed myself for not being able to cope with it [2]. Here was this feminist [3], supposedly knowing about equality and all that, who still couldn't make her own relationship work. I mean, he would say to me: 'what do you want me to do? You're the one who wants changes, tell me what I should do?' And I did take on all the old shit about being responsible for the relationship, managing, caring, all that, I took it on deeply [4]. Any good feminist would have left, I thought, but I didn't want to [5].

So what happened?

Well, things were so bad in the end that we did separate. I wanted him to come to counselling with me, but he wouldn't, so I went by myself. I felt like a complete mess.

What were the outcomes?

I can't go into the whole thing, but one of the things I learned was about my own manipulation of [her husband]. I always felt that he manipulated me, that he pushed my buttons, to use that phrase. I felt that he had all the power emotionally in our relationship, because he was able to walk away, while I ranted and raved and got all upset over his lack of participation in the housework and the emotional and caring work [5]. Slowly it dawned [6] on me that – well, that I was manipulating him as well. I was getting what I wanted out of those situations too, because after every row, we eventually made up, and he apologised for walking out, and told me he loved me. The counselling helped me see [7] all the patterns that I was trapped in. For a good while, I blamed myself totally, which was wrong too, but then I learned to tell the difference between taking responsibility for my part in the destructive patterns and blaming myself [8]. The next step I suppose was to see how to change the patterns. I realised that I was getting a lot of power out of those patterns, that it is very hard to disagree, for an educated man like him to disagree with the idea that he should share the housework [9]. So that gave me power, I mean, he agreed with feminism, that was one of the reasons he got to know me in the first place, was because I was – we were politically very much in tune about a lot of things [10] ... Of course, I knew that women tended to do the emotional work in relationships and that I tended to do it in our relationship, but I didn't see for ages that I was getting something out of it, a payoff, if you like, from continuing to do this – this emotional work. I could claim to be a victim [11], I could say to him, 'I have to do it, because emotional work needs to be done, it's really important, and you won't do it'. I was able to make him feel both inadequate and a lazy sod at the same time, because we both knew that it was – you know – *good* to be able to do emotional work, to be able to express feelings and that sort of thing [12]. So – so that meant he was inadequate and – well – by his laziness in not even trying, he was dumping more work onto me, so he was also being oppressive. Because of his own politics, he knew that I had a point, so he felt guilty [13]. But he didn't make any changes, I mean, that's what really annoyed me and made me angry. Talking to him about this, at the times when we tried to talk rationally and calmly about it, he said that he felt I had all the power [14]. And I felt that he had all the power. It was a complete mess, as far as I could see. Of course, talking about it didn't solve it, I needed to *do* [15] something. In fact, it wasn't really that I needed to do something, as much as that – well – what I needed to do was to *stop* [16] doing something, doing certain things. I would agree with your analysis of yourself that you had double power in a way, in your relationship, because you were both the feminist and the caring, feminine one. In a relationship with a man interested in equality – that seemed very familiar to me [17].

How did you make the changes you talked about, when you said you had to stop doing things?

The counsellor asked me to look at *how* [18] we had reached this division of labour, not what the division of labour was, because I knew that already, God, did I know it, I knew exactly how much I did and he didn't do. But what she got me to do was to look at the *ways* that this had happened – been allowed to become the pattern [19]. It was very painful, very, very difficult for me, because I realised just how much a part I played in it [20]. She helped me to see what I had been getting out of the situation, the payoffs [21], as we learned to call them. I blamed myself totally for a while, saw myself as a complete failure as a feminist [22].

I found it much easier to give out to him for not doing his share, but to continue doing his share myself, than I found – well, it was much easier and familiar for me to do that [23], than to actually stop doing his share, or doing things for him [24]. I kept complaining to the counsellor about how he wouldn't do things in the house. She would say to me things like, 'why are you doing them for him?' [25] and I would reply that somebody had to do it. But of course, then I could take the moral high ground. I mean, I knew that he, as somebody who professed a commitment to equality, would feel guilty at not doing his share. So I was always in the right [26]. In the end, I realised that this was giving me power, but it wasn't the sort of power that was helping me get the changes I wanted [27]. I had a very strong sense of myself as a political person, in the outside world, but in my home life, I felt a fraud – completely confused [28]. I couldn't get any of the things I wanted, like – like the sort of equality I wanted in this relationship, but I knew that a lot of people – that the relationship looked good from the outside [29]. ... I didn't know how to recognise, let alone manage, all the raging emotions I was feeling [30]. Sometimes, he accused me of being completely over the top, impossible to reason with [31]. But on the other hand, my emotionality and my feeling side were things he said he liked in me: I mean, this was when we talked rationally about things, the ways that I cared for people and had so many friends – all that [32].

Points of analysis

1.   'Buying into' the 'messages' can be analysed as accepting the positions made available through a discourse of femininity, which is the classic story for women.

2.   Acceptance at the time of giving her account that she once positioned herself in a discourse of femininity, but repressed this for a time.

3.   Reflexive and interactive positioning in a feminist discourse by herself and others. In such positioning, feminists know the answers, they know what is wrong, so they should know how to 'fix' the situation. A discourse of the rational unitary subject facilitates this perception.

4.   Simultaneously (that is, at the same time as the positioning in discourses of feminism), she is positioned in a discourse of femininity. In such a discourse, the woman is supposed to take care of relationships and emotions and to be good at it 'naturally'. This is supposed to be a trait of the unitary female subject. Nevertheless, Sinèad's experience is contradictory.

5.   Evidence of her reflexive positioning in a discourse of 'real feminism'. It is also evidence of her refusal of the unitary subject of this discourse. In spite of the contradictions she is experiencing, she wants to continue in the relationship, rather than withdraw. By continuing in the relationship, she is going against a certain feminist orthodoxy, but is increasing her chances of constructing something outside this orthodoxy.

6.   Projection of the undesirable act of manipulation onto the other (in this case, the male) and simultaneous repression of manipulation in oneself.

7.   Recognition of own previous projections and repressions. Reading her own situation retrospectively, giving it meaning in time: a meaning different from what it had at the time it was happening.

8.   Failure to recognise repressed material resulted in blame being placed on her from two discursive sources: feminist and feminine.

9, 10.   He positions himself and is positioned by her in feminist discourse, which says that men should do housework. This gives her a feminist power to make him feel guilty, because he accepts the feminist arguments, but does not act on them.

11.   Separatist feminist discourse can be interpreted as positioning women as victims, which could facilitate this view of the woman in a heterosexual couple relationship. The notion of woman as victim is based on a unitary view of the subject.

12.   They are both positioned also in a human relations discourse that emphasises the importance of emotional literacy. He is guilty of failing to become literate, within the terms of this influential discourse.

13.   He is also guilty in the terms of the feminist discourse that, at least partly, constructs their relationship.

14.   Both made completely different readings of the situation, according to this account. He recognised the power conferred on her by her positioning in and taking up of positions in a socially dominant discourse of femininity. He did not say this outright, at least according to this account, possibly because he knew that in the feminist discourse that they shared, this is not

acceptable. Yet he recognised her power. A phenomenon such as power has effects on a situation, even if it is not acknowledged. At the point that Sinèad is describing here, she had not recognised this positioning in femininity and the power it can confer on her in heterosexual relations. At this point, none of the discourses that either of them was positioned in was capable of moving forward the situation.

15. Recognition of the situational and relational nature of the situation and the need to act.

16. Recognition that she is maintaining the situation unchanged.

17. Recognition that I have helped to construct this account, through the relationship I had developed with the research participant, and through my self-disclosure.

18,19. Points to the need to deconstruct the situation, to examine the processes that brought her here.

20. Evidence of her investment in the outcomes of the processes. They are very much part of her subjectivity, even though she has repressed them, because of her desire to be feminist.

21. Recognition of her power through her positioning in feminine discourse.

22. Effects of positioning in real feminist discourse again.

23. Positioning as feminine is socially approved, it is easy, it is like 'second nature' for many women.

24. Feminist positioning exists simultaneously with feminine positioning.

25. Counsellor encouraging her to examine her emotional investments.

26. Feminist discourse positioning her powerfully.

27. Explicit recognition of the power she achieved through taking up feminine positions. But also a recognition that for a feminist, there is little movement available through take-up of such positions.

28. Constant and rapid shifting of discursive positions, without recognising what was going on, at the time. While still denying or repressing the existence of one of the discourses and her take-up of positions in it, such shifting caused her to feel confused and inauthentic. Because of the dominance of the unitary rational model of the subject, this is how people most often interpret experiences of simultaneous positioning in contradictory discourses.

29. Recognition that power is more than economic and material issues.

30. Pointing to the necessity of dealing with the emotions as social phenomena.

31. Effect of positioning in a dominant liberal-humanist discourse, which includes liberal feminism. Such positioning can facilitate a reading of excess emotionality as irrational and therefore as weak.

32. Simultaneously with her positioning as weak [31 above], she is positioned as strong. This is an effect of both discourses of femininity and of difference feminism, which read emotionality as women's special domain and strength.

Emotionally charged relations and cathectic structures

Heterosexual relations provide a fertile site for the production of new feminist discourses concerning gender identity. In addition, heterosexual couple relations provide the sites where feminism is hardest pressed. I contend that this is due to the social construction of cathexis, underpinned as it is by emotional investments (see Chapter One), and its implications in power relations. Even within an egalitarian relationship, femininity can confer power on women. Anxiety and discomfort with traditional feminine roles in domestic and personal heterosexual relations can lead women to take up positions in feminist discourses, but because of the multi-layered nature of subjectivity, traditional feminine identity is not discarded, but continues to be present and to produce significations for each individual. In examining the emotional dimension of subjectivity, then, I am examining in detail the emotional consequences of positioning oneself in feminist discourses, especially in the discourse that embraces multiplicity (Discourse Three), with accompanying anxieties and contradictions. These anxieties and contradictions are pronounced in heterosexual couple relationships. Particularly in egalitarian couple relationships, power is seen to be more than an effect of material or economic issues. At the same time, I take into account the emotional consequences of being positioned in sexist discourses, which is an experience common to all women, including feminist women.

Analysing heterosexual couple relationships carries with it the danger of a focus on individuals which ignores power relations. This is the major critique of therapy and counselling interventions which exist within liberal-humanist metadiscourses (see Kitzinger, 1987: 197, 8; Goodrich, 1991a). In this chapter, I have examined Sinèad's relationship and the emotions involved in it, but within a specific power analysis.

In the next analysis, I use material gathered from Maureen in the same discussion, about her relationships with and attitudes to other women, particularly non-feminist women. I use the account to further demonstrate the existence of repressed material about femininity and investments in feminine positions and the way that acknowledgement of these phenomena may result in transformatory experiences. The analysis develops the two points which I have begun to explore: first, that every situation has psychodynamic aspects which are related to the discursive and relational aspects. Second, that no discourse, including feminist discourses, is without power relations, but that the self-conscious divestment of the power which can be an (albeit unconscious) outcome of the take-up of feminine positionings, can result in an increased 'power to', or agency.

Maureen's account: femininity and feminism

Maureen

You asked us in your letter to think about where we had been stuck and where things had been – become unbound. I suppose I thought – used to think – that what should happen was that I should challenge other women, challenge their internalised oppression, the awful things they believed about themselves, get them to be more assertive, get away from that awful passive, door-mat stuff that women did. I thought they should just say no, as it were. I suppose, really, I thought I could get them to be more like me. I pitied them for being blind to their own oppression. I thought – if they would only look at themselves in a politicised way. I thought that would be very radical and that was how my activism should take shape. But that's where I got stuck, that wasn't happening, and I was getting more and more frustrated. But you know something? What I needed to do – and this was the most radical thing I could have done in the circumstances [1] – was to, I needed to look at my own internalised oppressions and work out how they were leading me to be stuck … The most important thing I learned was that I am not so different from them, you know, I'm not so different [2] from those poor, weak women that I pitied and despised at the same time. Exploring the ways that I was like them was exceptionally liberating [3]. I realised that I was very like a lot of so-called traditional women [4] – I hadn't managed to get rid of all that stuff that I saw other women doing – the caring, the working too hard, taking on too much responsibility, always being available to help out, or to get someone out of trouble [5]. I saw other women doing it in relation to their families. I saw girls and young women doing it – trying to please. But I didn't see it in myself for a long time [6], because, well, I had, you know, a different lifestyle. I wasn't in a relationship with a man, I was single, financially independent, all that. But I was doing those things in my own circle of friends and colleagues anyway. I always had to be giving, caring, sorting things out, available for people, lending them money. I wasn't much of a listener, though, I can see that now, looking back. I actually realised that my self-esteem was very low. In some ways, I cringe when I say it, because I know how some people slag all that as trendy liberal jargon [7] – but it was – that's how it was for me. I read the Gloria Steinem book [Steinem, 1993] and, I suppose I just recognised a lot of myself in it. I was really all caught up in meeting my 'obligations' – you know, what I felt were obligations [8].

How did it change?

At my lowest, when I was really depressed and fed up, I was invited to lunch with some friends and I met a woman I liked a lot. She talked very openly about herself. She was clearly feminist and very politicised and of course that made me pay attention to her from the start. She also talked a lot about her emotions in relation to a project she was involved in, but it was very different from the kind of talk about emotions I was used to. It wasn't the sort of analysis I was used to, but it wasn't counselling jargon or pop psychology individualist shit either [9]. She just talked about what she had experienced in a work situation and how she had dealt with it. I was really struck by her capacity to – to understand why she acted in certain ways and, also, not just to understand, but to *do* something about it, something that made her change the situation, or, you know, to get things moving. Later, I said to her that I'd love to be able to understand myself so well. She recommended *The Dance of Anger* [Lerner, 1985].

Maureen goes on here to talk in some detail about how she did a great deal of 'personal work', including seeing a counsellor for a period.

Maureen

developed a self-awareness that has made me feel much more whole as a feminist. I used to get angry about being taken for granted. I did the 'poor me' thing a lot. I blamed other people for asking too much of me. And at the same time, you know, like I said, I was really pitying traditional women for doing the same things in their family and with their partners [10.] I really couldn't let go of the idea that I had to be the great – the great – I don't know – the fixer, the earth mother, the all knowing, all – [11]. You know, I'd have done anything for people, I'd take classes for colleagues, help them out, give people money. I never said no. And I was doing all this in the name of feminism. I mean, that's not something I shouted about, but to myself, that's what I thought. I suppose I was a bit smug, really. I saw myself as superior [12]. I simply couldn't say no to people who asked me to do things or get involved in something. And not only that, but, you know, I volunteered to do things, I constantly took on too many responsibilities, and then I would end up exhausted and resentful And eventually, I began to feel that this was an oppressive situation [13]. Eventually, I had to look at my own impulses towards this way of being – this way of being all things to everybody and at the same time being, well, feeling so superior and so elite, but at the same time so put-upon. You know, I considered myself to be more aware than other people, I thought that non-feminist women suffered from false consciousness, and I didn't like the Mary Daly stuff and I didn't like the Carol Gilligan stuff either – that was just too much like the stuff I was trying to leave behind [14]. And in spite of all that, here I was, doing all the really feminine things, just like they were [15].

But I suppose what was the hardest thing for me to come to terms with was that I had created the situation for myself [16] – no, actually, I think the worst thing was that I began to understand that I hadn't really always liked other women, especially so-called traditional women. They were too weak [17], they needed me to sort them out, to tell them how oppressed they were, but even when I did, they couldn't see what I was talking about [18]. And I made a point of not needing anyone. I was able to fix my own car, do my own household repairs, I was fit and strong, it was very important to me to be different from other women in that way, to be able to do anything that other women relied on a man to do [19] ... I thought I was really good at talking about feelings, but I was just good at analysing them, not at *doing* anything about them. I'd never really worked on my emotions, I had never been in a situation where I opened up about anything apart from my anger. I didn't really trust other women, or anyone, enough to do that. I didn't want to identify with other women, because – why? I'm not sure, well, I have a good idea – really, I know this sounds a bit confused, but I didn't want to identify with feminine things, with femininity [20]. Yet, I was doing feminine things, in the ways I was acting. And I suppose those ways were giving me a power [21] because I was always the caring, good one. I didn't accept the label feminine about myself, but I did things traditionally associated with femininity, all the same [22]. And when I realised a lot of this stuff, I went through a time when I really hated myself even more, I was very low, I blamed myself for being so stupid. I questioned whether feminism was possible at all [23] ... I had to learn to be nice to myself, stop driving myself so hard. I had to stop blaming myself. When I read your paper, I felt that I could talk meaningfully to you about all of this [24]. I learned to accept parts of myself. In a way, that seems like the exact opposite of what I – what a feminist needs to do. But it wasn't a matter of accepting them and things staying the same. Through some kind of acceptance of myself, of the feminine parts of my being, through me no longer fighting them, things began to change. I accepted that, yes, I was like many other women, in a lot of respects. I feel sometimes like I became a nicer person and that by becoming nicer, that created some sort of space for change to happen [25].

How do you mean – what sort of change?

I felt – well – blocked, I felt that my feminist aspirations were getting nowhere [26]. I just got angry all the time about injustice and about the lack of progress on feminist issues. And my anger was futile, it got me no results. I was very depressed at that time, because I could see no way out. I felt completely and totally hopeless. Just – focusing on myself, becoming nicer to myself and becoming a nicer person, accepting myself more, I became more accepting of other people. Warmer, I suppose – better able to relate. I think I understood more about my own emotions, so I could understand other people's emotions too – not understand them, exactly, but understand the strength of them, how they can hold you back, or keep you in a certain place [27]. I seemed to mellow – and I don't want this to be taken as becoming more tolerant – but I just – in mellowing, I got a much better view of other people, and that included – that there didn't have to be just one right way for feminist change to happen [28]. I didn't feel the need to be in control of situations all the time. I learned to relax and to listen to other people and being much more sure of my own feelings and emotions, I became much more assertive, instead of being aggressive. I mean, I – there was a real feeling of before and after. I'm just sorry sometimes that I didn't learn all this sooner, but, anyway, I didn't. So – I suppose, though, if I had got into the personal stuff earlier, I mightn't without have had the political resources to help me have this kind of outcome, I might have got much more into myself and left politics behind [29].

I did get very into myself for a while. I suppose I was making up for lost time. I learned to relax and to feel more creative. I knew I didn't want to be side-tracked into navel gazing or all that personal growth stuff, a feminist and political perspective [30]. But I really needed this, I devoured it, and what was really exciting was that I could do that stuff, the personal stuff, without having to leave my politics behind ... and I didn't lose my anger – you have to hang onto anger, but now I had a different way of hanging onto it and dealing with it. Because I couldn't cope with my anger before, I often used to feel I was like a child, not fully mature, or it was easy to dismiss me because I was immature or over the top, an irrational female [31]. I'd try to control it, keep it in [32], but then it would get too much for me and I'd explode or get depressed [33] ... But – yes, that was it, really – starting with *The Dance of Anger*, I learned how to use my anger, how to state my case and *then* how to do something constructive [34], I can deal with it now in – in ways that aren't just aggressive, or passive, losing the head or getting withdrawn and depressed and blaming other people. As I said, I've done some work in family therapy with a woman therapist that I like. But I'm sure that if I hadn't been a feminist to start off with, my personal work would not have been like this, I mean, it wouldn't have had these results [35]. I've come such a long way – my feminism is more productive now [36]. I can connect with other people, instead of doing things for them all the time. I'm not saying it's perfect, but I don't expect that any more [37].

Points of analysis

1. Equation of being radical with being agentic and able to make changes.
2. Recognition of the source of the aspiration towards feminism as arising from solidarity with other women.
3. Deconstruction of the feminism/femininity dualism experienced as liberating.
4. Possibility of a new reading of herself through doing emotional work.
5. Recognition of the take-up of positions in discourses of femininity by others, but not by herself (projection).
6. Projection of femininity onto other women.
7. Awareness of the ideology of liberal humanism and also the general disdain of politicised people for individualistic interpretations of social conditions.
8. Realisation that she has investments in the pattern she thought was imposed.
9. Juxtaposition of political analysis of emotional issues with liberal individual analysis and indication that there is a different, more politically productive way than either of them.
10. Positioning of other women through discourses of femininity or sexist discourses. Using those discourses to read other women.
11. Recognition of the power attached to these positions and drawing on them, while rationally denying their power, or denying that she might be taking up positions in sexist discourses herself.
12. Opposition of feminism (herself) to femininity (other women), but also a demonstration that she has reached awareness of how such dualism is implicated in power relations and hierarchy.
13. She both positions herself (reflexive positioning) and is positioned by other people (interactive positioning) as responsible. Because of the lack of variety in her positioning, becomes oppressive.
14. Explicit rejection of essentialist feminism at an intellectual level.
15. Recognition of contradictions again. In spite of rejecting the unitary female model of women posed by essentialist feminism, she is still positioned in a unitary discourse of the human subject.
16. Further recognition that the pattern she thought was imposed is one in which she had emotional investments.

17. Projection of the aspects of herself which she repressed psychodynamically and also the aspects of women which she rejected intellectually, onto other women
18. Recognition that her route into feminism owed more to feelings of alienation from other women, rather than solidarity with them.
19. Feminism taking the shape of 'being like men', or being as good as men.
20. Feminism equated with being different from women. It is opposed to the sort of feminism she has explicitly rejected, which extols an essential femininity. Yet, her feminism based on identification with men is at the same time reaching its explanatory limits and her own unique combination of politics and experience is on the verge of pointing her into a third, deconstructive way of approaching feminism.
21. A power associated with women, even if suppressed in sexist discourses.
22. Contradictions again.
23. Experience of lack of agency or ability to influence events.
24. Recognition that we (she and I) share a particular feminist discourse.
25. Production of knowledge about herself: that which is repressed is reproduced unchanged, what is acknowledged can be produced in different ways (cf Hollway, 1982).
26. Experience of a lack of agency again.
27. Stress on her experience that a lack of attention to emotional processes has an impact on agency.
28. Leaving behind the filtering of experience through a discourse of prediction and control and moving into a more poststructuralist discursive mode of understanding human action.
29. Recognition of the constructed nature of experience and the self and an implicit recognition and simultaneous rejection of the liberal-humanist belief that the politicised individual represents the penultimate step on the way to maturity (cf Kitzinger, 1987).
30. Implicit recognition of the self as a production, not as a discovery.
31. Within liberal humanism, anger represents immaturity, a 'phase' which has to be gone through on the way to the well-adjusted mature personality (see comment 29 above).
32. Perception of a 'choice' between rationality or emotionality.
33. Contradictions between the expression of anger and the 'manly' feminist she tried to be.
34. Capacity to act has grown out of a deconstructive approach to the choices between rationality and emotionality.
35. Recognition of the constructed nature of experience and the self. The self is a production, not a discovery (cf comment 30 above).
36. Experience of agency.
37. Awareness of the need to keep a political perspective alive, even if a feminist 'end point' is not reached.

Earlier in her feminism, Maureen read femininity as negative resulting in her wanting to be like men. Her unease with femininity and her negative evaluation of other women were produced through sexist discourses. This characterises early second-wave feminism, where not just men, but some feminist women also, read women through sexist discourses. Maureen managed that contradiction by distancing herself and marking the difference between herself and other women. At the same time, she was positioned by others as a woman. Nevertheless, in this way, she was able to draw on the 'double power' of being like men, but of also having the power of the feminine, caring, maternal woman. This was unsustainable, because if people are always positioned as responsible, strong, having obligations, the lack of variety in the positioning becomes oppressive. The unitary rational subject to which many aspire is itself oppressive.

This is where a person positioned in dominant discourses of the human person may succumb to the idea of a core femininity and conclude that feminism can never work. But Maureen had already strongly rejected essentialism at an intellectual level. She had an identity investment in being feminist, but outside essentialist discourses, and the particular discourses which made up the content of her feminism had an effect on how she interpreted her emotional self.

Doing politicised self-reflection

Practices of therapy and self-reflection are frequently and accurately seen by people on the left as reclaiming people for liberalism and individualism. Maureen and Sinèad constructed radical accounts of themselves when they filtered their reflection on their psychodynamic processes through the feminist discourses in which they had positioned themselves. Because of their theoretical and political convictions and refutation of essentialism and an essential feminine nature, neither woman interpreted her identification of reflexive positioning in a discourse of femininity as evidence of getting in touch with a 'real' feminine self. They recognised it as the taking up of positions in socially approved discourses which almost every woman experiences. Each woman discovered a sense of herself beyond her own previous image of herself, but did not interpret the repressed part as in any way less social. Sinèad's description of herself in her time of confusion is reminiscent of what Gramsci calls a disjointed and episodic conception of the world (cited in Grimshaw, 1986: 137). The more coherent (but not unitary) and critical conception (*ibid*) which she reached allows her to acknowledge her multisubjectivity, and incorporate contradiction and confusion in politically productive ways. The knowledge that Maureen and Sinèad constructed of their psychodynamic processes helped them to become more critically aware of things which had deposited in them the 'traces' of which Gramsci wrote. The construction of this knowledge was facilitated by their anti-essentialism, and of discourses that challenged liberal-humanist discourses.

Feminist women, even though they may reject traditional discourses of femininity, are still positioned interactively in discourses of femininity, which gives them a certain power that they may be reluctant to recognise. But even if not recognised, the positioning continues to have effects on relations and on subjectivity. Repressing the knowledge that one is taking up feminine positions has the effect of reproducing the discourse unchanged. Recognising it, on the other hand, can have major effects in terms of movement, a sense of agency and discursive interventions. The discourse of femininity is not abandoned, but can be reproduced in different ways, mediated or filtered through a feminist awareness of the multiplicity of the subject. Identifying a repressed attachment to or investment in femininity can lead to the pushing forward of psychic development and the parallel construction of a discourse of multiplicity, in which one's construction as both feminine and feminist can be productively used.

Sinèad's account shows her identifying repressed elements of a situation that arose as a result of her politics. So the emotional work and the identification of emotional investments carried out as a result of her counselling is not just therapeutic at an individual level. It is therapeutic at a political level and is a politicised practice of therapy and emotional work. She also identifies the process as pedagogical. The comments highlight an earlier confused switching of positioning and take-up of positions between several discourses of feminism and a discourse of femininity and, before the counselling work, a denial or repression of positioning in feminine discourses, with feelings of contradiction and confusion. Her recognition of the tensions between the different positionings has allowed movement to take place. Her refusal to adhere to one single explanation based on one discourse has had the effect of disrupting the model of the unitary subject.

Sinèad has read her situation retrospectively, giving it a different meaning from the time of the event. A radical and politicised reflection on the situation, facilitated by the counselling process, has allowed her to construct a different meaning, and to construct herself as an agent capable of making a discursive intervention. This discursive intervention moves both her and her husband beyond all the discourses in which they can be seen to be positioned, throughout the account. These are not jettisoned, they remain part of their identities, but, through the identification of the repressed, the reproduction of femininity and emotionality in the same old traditional ways is stopped. In the space that is thus cleared, new discourses can emerge. These may exist at a practice level at first, as Hollway (1995) suggests. Practice is not the same as full discourse, in that it does not provide recognisable discursive positions which people can take up. But it is a forerunner of discourse in that it is produced in language. Practice which does not reflect either dominant culture or dominant feminist discourses will be hard to maintain. The new is always constrained by pre-existing discourses, structures and practices.

Multiplicity in the psyche can be acknowledged, although not without difficulty, due to the dominance of the unitary rational subject as a discursive position. Such acknowledgement in turn helps to push forward the subversion of male/female dualism and the production of a discourse of a multiple human subject. Davies (1990b: 136) asks:

> How are we to move beyond male-female dualism? The simple answer is that all we have to do is to *stop* doing the work that maintains the difference. That, of course, is more easily said than done.   (my emphasis)

One type of work that maintains the differences is the use of power conferred on women by sexist discourses. This is often not acknowledged by feminist women who have attained power in the social spheres of paid work or egalitarian relationships. Yet even powerful women can find themselves hesitating in their assertion of power, turning it into domestic, 'female' or feminine ways of action. Even where feminists rationally and intellectually resist typically feminine positionings, they nonetheless have also learned the patterns of power and feelings through which male-female social relations are organised (Braidotti, 1989: 86). All women are positioned in discourses of femininity, which read women as powerful mothers and carers (even if this power is repressed). Thus, recursive positioning (interactive and reflexive) in any discourse through which a woman can be read as powerful will produce an identity investment which can co-exist with the politicised identity investments (as feminists, in this case) adopted in adulthood.

However, feminist women who have access to resources such as income and education, as the participants in this research have, are likely to suppress the power of their femininity altogether. Acknowledging their construction in discourses of femininity and the ways they take up feminine positions was transformational for Maureen and Sinèad, in terms of producing feminist agency. Their experience of this and our shared analysis of the phenomenon goes some way towards developing a discourse of feminist multiplicity, where femininity is not jettisoned, but is acknowledged and construed in ways that have potential for a poststructuralist feminist praxis. There is a need to express, in feminist poststructuralist terms, the power of femininity, not to suppress it, as happens in sexist discourses and in the earlier feminist positions that these two women took up. This is not, however, the same as lauding an essential feminine as better than an essential masculine, as 'difference' feminisms do. It is a deconstructive move which promotes a discourse of multiplicity, in which women do not have to be 'either/or', but can experiment with different ways to be both feminist and feminine.

Accepting oneself as partially constructed in femininity can help feminists to accept the diversity of other women's experiences and resistance and to understand other women's actions. It also helps feminist women to find more points of intersection with women who do not accept the label feminist. Instead of differences between feminism and femininity being seen as uncrossable boundaries or as battle lines, they can be seen as meeting points. Understanding the ways that one's own subjectivity is gendered and the social nature of one's own and others' feelings can allow feminist activists to connect more empathetically with other women and to interact or 'collude' with them in ways that may alter gendered practice. An exploration of one's own psychodynamic processes, outside dominant liberal-humanist models of the human subject, seems crucial to such projects. Neither a discourse of the rational unitary subject nor of a unitary female feeling subject provides the conditions for these moves.

A liberal-humanist analysis might have led Maureen and Sinèad to conclude that they were after all determined by an essential and pre-given femininity and that they might as well give up their feminist aspirations (*cf* Coward, 1993). Instead, because both of them were aware of discourses other than essentialist ones, they interpreted their emotional experiences in ways which facilitated feminist agency and a recognition of their own multiplicity. That is, they were able to recognise femininity as part of their subjectivities, but not as an essence.

It is clear that their rational intellectual take-up of positions in Discourse Three is implicated in the very construction of their psychodynamic processes and in the radical outcomes of their reflection on those processes. Thus, the personal is seen to be not only political, but also theoretical (*cf* Braidotti, 1989: 95), insofar as an exposure to the broad range of feminist theories provided anti-essentialist discursive positions through which the women could filter their experiences.

Conclusion

In traditional terms, power is the exclusive property of dominant groups. The analysis made here demonstrates that the person who would be traditionally characterised as victim has power to move or to change positioning, or to take up new positions. The emphasis is on the relationality of power, that it is a two-way production. This is not the same as equating men's and women's power in social relations. Men's power (and the power of members of any privileged group) is backed by material resources and reproduced through dominant discursive power, which is the kind of power that produces oppression.

The analysis in this chapter provides a means to explore the possibilities for action towards change, by examination of contradictions, such as women's positioning in sexist discourses and what is suppressed (women's power) in these discourses. This was sketched in the section on relations in Chapter Five, but has been further developed in this chapter's analysis of emotional investments in certain discursive positions which may confer power, but whose acknowledgement may remain repressed or misread. Thus, the chapter has also provided some answers to Braidotti's (1989: 95) questions: 'how does the "woman-in-me" relate to the "feminist-in-me"? What are the links and the possible tensions between my "being-a-feminist" and "being-a-woman?"'.

The essence of a liberal-humanist approach to contemporary femininity is to make inequalities appear as equalities (Hare-Mustin, 1991: 82). In drawing attention to the ways that positioning in discourses of femininity can provide positions of power for women, as I have done, there is a danger that such power may be regarded as equal to men's power. This kind of analysis is something I would have attempted to do only with feminist women who have thought in fairly radical feminist terms about themselves. Expecting women in personal development courses, for whom the courses are often a first step outside their immediate circles and into adult education, to engage in this kind of analysis would have the effect of reinforcing the status quo. Such an analysis of women's investments in femininity is radical only insofar as it is mediated through discourses which challenge liberal humanism. This is an appeal to readers not to misread the analysis in this chapter. In some ways, it is only relevant to women who have been engaging with feminism for some time. 'When I read your paper, I felt that I could talk meaningfully to you about all of this' (Maureen). What I think *is* useful for the practice of personal development education is the way that attention to contradictions can be a starting point for altering practice. The radical self-analysis of Maureen and Sinèad hinges on contradictions. The pedagogical challenge is to share feminist poststructuralist insights about contradictions in ways that can articulate or collude with the positioning of each woman who comes to a course.

7 Radical personal development education

Introduction

In this chapter I discuss the ways that my epistemological stance and my theorising of politicised feminist subjectivities and ways of knowing undertaken in Chapters Five and Six influence my pedagogical practice. I expose my practice as a personal development facilitator who is trying to work from a feminist poststructuralist perspective in a field dominated by liberal-humanist discourses. I am not trying to present a formula for this kind of work, since each course and each situation is different, but I discuss issues I have found to be important in Stage One personal development education (see Chapter One, for an outline of the content).

This chapter represents research on myself and on my practice of adult education, which draws on my experience of facilitating several personal development courses over a period of five years (permission has been given for any material quoted). I do not come to these courses as a neutral facilitator. Since hundreds of Irish women take the first step into community-based adult education via personal development courses, I believe that this educational arena is far too important to be left to supposedly neutral liberal-humanist facilitators. I want to make feminist poststructuralist ideas available in a way that is meaningful to the women I work with. But I also have to find a balance between my desire to predict and control the outcomes and the women's rights to take my theory and engage with it in their own ways, and to modify it.

Locating resistance and constructing agency

All women, to a greater or lesser extent, are positioned in patriarchal relations and interactional processes (which include discourses of femininity). Feminist responses to them are multiple, collective and sometimes internally contradictory. We have to choose, as educators, where to intervene. For women coming to Stage One personal development classes, the family, power in the family, and heterosexual relations, are often the place to do that, when we are responding to their need to make changes. These sites are bearers of the gender status quo and a site of the production of gender differences. They are where patriarchal relations are at their most naturalised and normalised. Issues of domesticity and maternity surface time and again in the personal development courses I facilitate. Dealing with these issues is a major challenge to contemporary feminism.

A 'radical' or separatist feminist approach would be to dismiss the family and heterosexual relations completely. But the problem with this perspective is that it fails to deal with the large numbers of people who live in families and in heterosexual relationships of one kind or another. Another way of approaching the issue of family and heterosexuality is to ask how we can reshape families and heterosexual relations for feminist ends, that is, to disrupt the gender status quo. These structures, as we know them now, are generally self-contradictory in any feminist terms. But family and heterosexual relationships, which are arenas for a radical democratisation of the emotions (*cf* Giddens, 1994), may be very important images for the future of feminism. What is more, they allow the women I have met in personal development courses to have the things they say they want, namely intimate relationships with men and children, as well as the changes they desire. Such a vision of radically changed families is inclusive of women who choose to live without men. It is also recognition of the fact that masculinities are constructed and can change (see, for example, Connell, 1995; Segal, 1990).

Women coming to Stage One personal development courses are invariably nervous, often losing sleep the night before the first class. It may be their first experience of an educational setting since leaving school, which may itself have been a painful experience for them (see, for example, Kiely *et al*, 1999; Gilligan, 1999; Quinn, 1999; Rath, 1999). The need for a facilitator to be gentle, while at the same time challenging women, cannot be overemphasised. Some may have difficulties with reading and writing, while others are highly literate and enjoy reading. For many, speaking in a group is terrifying at first. At the same time, it would be wrong to assume that they are not politicised. All have experience of power and resistance, as well as of conformity, although they may not use these terms to describe their experiences. Some have highly politicised consciousnesses and vocabularies. In their resistances, they have devised strategies, some of which may have been successful, some not. I am concerned with facilitating them to examine the ways their resistance can be agentic. The challenge for me as a personal development facilitator is to find a pedagogical method adequate to my analysis of feminist subjectivities. I believe that the content of a standard personal development course can be used to position women in a feminist discourse of multiplicity, just as much as it can position them in essentialist discourses. I use the course structure and content outlined in Chapter One, but I approach courses as educational and learning events, not as therapy. To encourage women to read themselves as multiple feminist subjects, I filter the content through the following pedagogical tools:

- The productive and positive nature of the experiences of contradictions, and how they create possibilities for movement.
- Kristeva's (1986) three tiers and other feminist analyses of women's situations, which I regard as discursive content.
- Lerner's (1985) idea that relationships are like a dance. People need to *stop* doing certain work, to unlearn patterns that maintain dynamics of power and of male/female dualism. I see this as a pedagogical tool suitable for exploring the relational elements of subjectivity and resistance (see Chapter Five).

- A focus on one's own needs, 'treats' and bodily relaxation, as a means to producing self-awareness. By mediating this self-awareness through discourses of multiplicity and discussions of power, I aim to facilitate acknowledgement of unconscious investments in certain 'feminine' positions and recognition of repression and projection in intimate relationships.

Facilitating skills for politicised personal development

Any exploration of agency in personal development must begin with recognition of the power dynamics embedded in the personal development process itself. Feminist practice of personal development is not a neutral endeavour. There is a hierarchical relationship between a facilitator who is paid for her expert knowledge and skills, and the group members who are seeking the benefit of that expertise. The facilitator is in a more powerful position than the group members by virtue of her expertise, qualifications, status, position, and the fact that the women are probably paying for the course, even if it is a nominal sum. Consequently, the group assesses the facilitator's words, directions, questions, beliefs and interpretations as more powerful than their own. Only by recognising my power and privilege in teaching/facilitating relationships can I use this power in ways that facilitate agency. I try to produce conditions in the personal development classroom that will facilitate self-understandings of the participants which are not confined to liberal-humanist discursive interpretations. I do this particularly by naming power and by emphasising the social nature of feelings, emotions, desires and contradictions. If I do not name power in the personal development classroom, then I mask it and its relations and I individualise women's experiences of contradictions and desires for change. At the same time, I want to promote feminist poststructuralist ideas about power and multiplicity, not essentialist ones. Yet I must let go of my own desires to predict and control the ways that the women will engage with these ideas.

I wish to be an empathic listener and encourage the women to be the same for each other, but I also want to take a critical role in examining the stories that they tell, such as life-maps, check-in stories at the start of each class, and the stories they tell about relationships and feeling. As Stephenson, Kippax and Crawford (1996) point out, such stories are recounted because they are formative. I believe that they can be loci for change, if I can engage with the women in ways that facilitate more social and multiple readings of them. Some of the stories may be expressed in terms of regulatory discourses and how I respond to them can have the effect of disrupting these discourses, or not.

The power of the facilitator is considerable. By virtue of my position, I have credibility and clout and my comments and information carry weight. My way of being can produce ways of being in other people. That is, I can attempt, by my method of relating to them and by the content and information (discourses) that I introduce to the course, to interactively position them in ways that assist them to recognise and negotiate their own multiplicity, rather than bury it.

I know also that there are limits to personal development. So one of the things I need to do is to be active outside the class and to share that with the women and encourage them to become active also, in their own ways. In changing beliefs, it is important to work on an action level as well as a conceptual level. But if action tasks are encouraged too early (either outside the family arena or within it), results may be superficial. Agency needs to be collective as well as individual, in order to have maximum social impact. But I must not replicate the agency/structure or individual/society dualism, by implying to the women that public action is superior to private actions.

In my practice of personal development facilitation, I find that such exercise of power involves walking a fine line of deliberately reducing hierarchy by using self-disclosure and by putting as much information and control as possible into the group's hands, while at the same time not denying or undermining my own authority and competence. I try to be as aware as possible of the values I express, either directly or indirectly, and to be open about what I believe. Following Avis (1991), I clarify for the group what I believe: for example, 'I believe we need to examine power in our lives', or 'I believe that relationships work best when people have equal power'. I also make it clear that each person should reveal about herself only what she wants to reveal and feels comfortable about revealing, and that it is fine to decide not to continue with the course. I also tell the group that the course is not counselling or therapy. I explain that it is an adult learning programme, but one that is not like the schooling they may have experienced.

Women's experiences of schooling have generally demanded that they embrace socially acceptable forms of femininity (Lewis, 1993: 155, 185, 6; Ryan, 1997; Spender and Sarah, 1980). Many of the stories I have heard illustrate women's bad experiences as children at school, a great deal of them related to their social class positioning and poverty. Many of the women learned to cope with this as children by trying to please the teacher and to develop a special relationship with her and this may continue to happen in the adult learning situation of the personal development course. I need to remember that my relationship is with a group and that the members can provide support for each other when I am gone, and in between class meetings, since I don't usually live in the areas where I teach.

Because of positioning in discourses of femininity, frequent patterns for some women are to 'rescue' others in the group and to avoid looking at themselves. When caught in this pattern, we (both myself and the other women) may make the error of giving advice, telling a woman what she should do, or encouraging her to take a particular direction such as leaving an abusive relationship. Women also often attempt to be the all-powerful, nurturing, and wise mother in relation to others in the group. This is disempowering for the woman who is the focus of it (Avis, 1991). I find that by talking about these things on the first day, when we are setting ground rules for the group, we can avoid it, although I need to continually watch out for it. Bringing up the issue in this way on the first week also has the effect of sometimes making women reflect on it in relation to their behaviour as mothers in their own families, so the seeds are sown for discussing such patterns when we come to examine relationships.

On the other hand, it is not necessarily indicative of a lack of politicisation if a woman focuses on the situations of other women in the group. This may be part of her process of consciousness-raising. Although I believe that each person needs to look at how the personal and political are implicated in each other, not everybody does this in the same sequence. It is important, however, that women do not get into the role of advice-givers for other women in the group. I usually deal with the possibility of this by reminding the group about the ground rule of not giving advice, but of sharing what may have worked for oneself.

As facilitator I need to continually work on myself in these issues also, in some kind of supervisory relationship. As Chapter Six has shown, it is an issue of both politics and power to avoid focusing on one's own internalised oppressions and focus only on other people's. A facilitator's politicisation needs to be sustained and developed by a continual radical self-reflection on the ways in which she interacts with the group members.

The facilitator needs a thorough understanding of the economic, political, social, cultural and biological constraints that shape women's lives and behaviour. This includes a knowledge of the variety of feminist discourses and analyses, as well as understanding issues of poverty, violence, sexual abuse, gender construction, guilt and ambivalence about change. Even if we consider ourselves feminist, we must examine ourselves for any anti-women biases we may have absorbed from dominant discourses (*ibid*).

A facilitator must evaluate women positively, which includes recognising and acknowledging the strengths of the women before they come to personal development, while simultaneously acknowledging their desires for changes. When I feel irritated because women don't seem to be making changes, I need to understand their behaviour in the larger context of the oppression of women, and not to draw on liberal-humanist discourses which psychologise them as inadequate or not wanting to change. Emotional investments in power and in femininity, and embeddedness in patriarchal social relations mean that the process of becoming agentic is simultaneously threat and desire (Lewis, 1993: 154, 5). The dynamics of agency *do* involve contestation of the status quo, however small or slow these changes may be. These dynamics are born of knowledge that, once acquired, changes the way a person views the world. Challenging the status quo can result in women getting 'change back' (Lerner, 1985) messages from men and children, who also have emotional investments in power and their identities. These identities are threatened when women change their relationships to power (*cf* Hollway, 1994: 268).

Naming power and facilitating women to take action in their lives

I use the word 'power' in the courses as early as I can. This can be difficult, because it can put women off and it is important to keep them attending from week to week. It is rare that people coming to courses articulate power differentials as a reason for their desire for changes or for some of the difficulties they experience in making changes in their lives. The maintenance of men's power in the family is arguably the most diverse in its forms. In marriages, there is often not outright oppression, but the unacknowledged pre-eminence of men's desires and the subordination of women's desires (Avis, 1991). The patterns of desire, desirability and object choice moulded within the family extend beyond that institution to permeate the wider world of labour and authority (Segal 1990: 99, 100). The challenge for me is to get the women to see relational patterns as political patterns, or patterns of political institutions, with all the power implications of that view, as well as simply relationships, which is how they would be portrayed in a liberal-humanist personal development framework.

I describe power initially as an ability to have control over one's life and to be able to influence other people and the decisions that affect one's life. I explain that women often have difficulty using the word power. A gentle way to introduce it is to use some elements from Jeffers' (1987) 'pain to power' chart:

PAIN	POWER
I can't	I won't
I should	I could
If only	Next time
I have to be perfect	I'm a fine person, just as I am
I have to please others	I want to look after myself
I have to always be strong	It's alright to have needs
I should try harder	I'm doing the best that I can
Hurry up	I can take my time

I tell women that it is often difficult for women to think of themselves as powerful. We are taught that powerlessness is appealing, submission is erotic and helplessness is feminine. Yet they all know how much they do in their own families, how they are far from helpless in many different ways. I ask them to think of a story where they were not helpless, and to talk to another person in the group about it. I do not ask to hear the stories, but afterwards I ask how they felt. Feeling powerful is not the same as having power, or being agentic, but it is a necessary step. Understanding different ways that power can work and how a change in positioning can change those workings is part of a production of agency

Bernadette

My mother-in-law visits every Sunday and stays for tea. I always used to cook a full fry, set the table, all that. And this was one thing I wanted to change. It was putting too much onto me every Sunday. I thought of changing 'I should cook a fry' to 'I could cook a fry, but I don't want to and I don't have to'. The Sunday after that, I just had sausage rolls and apple tart, and we ate off our knees, by the fire. Nobody said anything, but I felt much better. It really made me think about the way to change things, small things, and how they make you feel much more in control.

In talking about communication and assertiveness, I also focus attention on situations where the other party has the power to refuse a woman's request for change. It is not always the case that if a woman communicates clearly what she wants, a reasonable other will facilitate her. It is necessary to know what one wants and needs, but getting it may be much more a matter of strategy and power than simply asking for it. Nevertheless, it is important to know what one wants. Discussion based on these issues can be a good lead-in to the social nature of feelings, especially feelings of anger and depression at powerlessness. In naming power, I am articulating a collective feminism that provides terms outside of individualist discourses in which the women can interpret their experiences.

Challenge and empowerment

In personal development education, challenge and empowerment are each part of the other. I cannot facilitate women's empowerment or the construction of agency if I do not challenge their beliefs, their expectations of themselves and others and their learned behaviours, thus making them conscious of how their lives are structured. To do this, I again draw on Avis (1991: 189) and strive to:

1.   provide a context in which the processes of politicisation and becoming agentic can occur;
2.   communicate my own politicised views, along with my beliefs in the value of women and every woman's potential to be agentic;
3.   provide social analysis which gently challenges internalised belief systems which may keep women from moving in the direction of agency. This includes overtly challenging sexist or demeaning or essentialist views of women which may be discussed in the group and which often arise from discussions of current news stories and media representations of women;
4.   help women to take actions in their own lives, however small, according to what they identify as necessary and as best for themselves.

Avis' (*ibid*) work on women and power in family therapy has provided these four headings. The rest of this section examines their use and potential for personal development education and continues to draw extensively on her work. Importantly, however, I situate the work in the arena of feminist pedagogy, as distinct from a one-to-one therapeutic relationship. The collective nature of an educational setting is important for the process of politicisation in the context of critical adult education. The list is not exhaustive, but represents my beliefs in the potential of personal development education for feminist ends. The beliefs are not distinct from each other. They overlap and complement each other in relation to the course content.

Personal development education as part of a critical adult education project

Personal development education can provide a context within which the process of becoming politicised and agentic can begin and develop. The women who attend are taking time for themselves and beginning a process of individuation. Individuation is a political act and statement for women who are often constructed in an ideology of women's relatedness and connectedness. Traditional femininity is not geared towards the individuation of women. In the very act of individuation, 'the subject becomes an active agent, a point of intelligibility, a self that constitutes itself in relation to history' (Poster, 1989: 61, cited in Faith, 1994: 42). Emphasising individuation is not to deny the connectedness which so many of the women value, nor the importance of relationships to them, but it is often the first time in a long time that they have had a space in which to think of themselves as distinct. It is a process distinct from individualism and it is often immensely liberating for women. This space allows women to reflect on and discuss their needs, without worrying about protecting family members, partners and friends. It also allows new relationships and/or friendships to develop within the group, fostering collectivity as well as individuation. Working on one's individuation in a group context can counteract the individualisation of women's problems. It also breaks down the isolation and shame that women often feel.

The presence of other women allows women to build up personal authority through the telling of and listening to their stories and they may re-view them through the use of key questions from the facilitator. These key questions often concentrate on *how* and *why* certain situations have come about, rather than on the telling of *what* the facts are. For instance, by using 'how' and 'why' questions, Margaret, a woman in her sixties who had been 'churched' after the births of her four children, was able to connect this to the oppression of women within the church and to connect her feelings of hurt with anger at social injustice.

With regard to relationships, I emphasise to women that the reason for paying attention to them in the course is so that women will stop assuming the burdens for them, not because they are responsible for the relationships. Such an emphasis allows me to communicate a view of women as separate individuals from their relationship systems and allows the women to develop this view of themselves. I point out that motherhood, for example, is on the one hand a relationship, but also a political institution, as are all relationships (Avis, 1991). I talk about culture and beliefs about motherhood, as a way to make such theory accessible. Forming friendships with other women is an important resource for women in discussing and taking on board such theory.

Life-stories and narratives

Women can 'share the stories of their lives and their hopes and their unacceptable fantasies' (Heilbrun, 1989: 44).

> One studies stories not because they are true or even because they are false, but for the same reason that people tell and listen to them, in order to learn about the terms on which others make sense of their lives; what they take into account and what they do not; what they consider worth contemplating and what they do not; what they are and are not willing to raise and discuss as problematic and unresolved in life. (Brodkey, 1987: 47, cited in Brookes, 1992: 33)

I have to listen very carefully to people's stories, in order to discern the women's current understandings of power and control in their lives. Maybe I can create a shift, by the way I ask a question, and thereby emphasise a different aspect of the story or of her character from what she has emphasised. This is part of the creation of belief, a very complicated task and more complicated than the sharing of facts and details (Avis, 1991). I may be able to lead to the creation of multiple interpretations of the same event, which may contradict each other. The same set of events can inspire a story in which great personal authority is demonstrated, as well as stories emphasising passivity, weakness, or deprivation. In this way, I emphasise the multiplicity of each person. Just as the problem of experience – its production and interpretation according to available discourses – is at the core of my approach to research methodologies (see Chapter Four), it is also central to my practice of personal development education.

Through attention to their stories, the women can reclaim aspects of the past and present not readily apparent to me. Much of this reclamation, as Brookes (1992) suggests and as I have suggested already, is dependent upon the quality of the questions asked. This situation is distinct from the process of collaborative memory-work within groups (Haug, 1987, 1990; Stephenson *et al*, 1996), because here, I am a teacher, set apart from the group by virtue of my status. But I do not have to set myself apart completely, in that I share my story with them, and encourage them to ask questions of me. The way that I share my story is also important, in giving information about me and about feminism. In this way, I can try to keep a check on power imbalances that might occur between me and them.

A lot of the storytelling process is not so much telling new stories, or new things, but saying the same basic things again and again, and examining them from different angles. Brookes (1992: 156) cites Williamson (1981), suggesting that it makes little difference what we teach, as long as it leads to questioning of the assumptions informing our social practices. Consciousness-raising through autobiography and storytelling are practices that can be taken up immediately, in any classroom, with both women and men, without devising a separate curriculum (Brookes, 1992: 156). Groups can discover their collectivity, as well as affirming each member's personal authority to 'tell' their lives. This is in contrast to Belenky *et al*'s (1986) suggestion that we need to devise a whole new curriculum for women, and it is one way of integrating a feminist perspective into women's interpretation of their everyday experiences.

Communicating a belief that women can be agentic

I try to communicate to the women that they are all competent and capable of agency and that they know what is best for themselves, each one in her own situation. This is in line with my belief that every moment of power and resistance devises its own strategy. Women who come to personal development education are often out of touch with their own needs and are accustomed to meeting and responding to others' needs. One of my first goals as a facilitator is to help them develop relationships with themselves and to listen to, validate, articulate and meet their own needs (*cf* Avis, 1991). Ways of tuning in to the self and one's needs are listening to the body's symptoms and what they can tell us about our situations. Headaches, fatigue, overeating and depression can all be listened to as messages from the self denoting fear, anger, lack of agency, and inequality. I emphasise listening to themselves, as well as listening to other people in the group. I advise daily relaxation and/or visualisation to help them make contact with their own needs. I devote nearly half an hour of each class period to meditation, relaxation or guided visualisation.

Writing, drawing and collage-making can also be tools for women to develop relationships with themselves. In the process of these activities, they often discover new and powerful self-awareness and self-appreciation, making conclusions and generating knowledge they were not aware of before and which they may not even articulate during the course. Resistances can be produced which I am not necessarily aware of. That is, they may not be shared with the group, or articulated verbally, but this does not mean that they are not happening.

I try to affirm each woman's reality and feelings, ideas and experiences, accepting them as unique to each person, yet emphasising that they are social in origin and are often shared by other women in the group. It is usually a relief for women to find that other women share their feelings of anger, guilt at feeling anger, resentment, being burdened and powerless (*ibid*). 'The discourse of silence is one salient feature of our engagement of the social world' (Lewis, 1993: 105). Yet in overcoming silence and learning to talk to each other, women need to be presented with discourses that position them with agency, rather than with discourses that simply map their oppressions. Women often bond around the experience and the telling of abuse and oppression (Bart, 1993: 248), but they need to develop the resources to go beyond simply describing them, to identifying where they already resist and where they can resist further and make changes. I try to assist this development by pointing to the strength and resilience that they have shown in the past, when dealing with oppressive situations (*cf* Avis, 1991). However, I need to be careful not to situate women's strength within a discourse of essential feminine qualities, rather to show it as constructed out of social relations.

Because of my own positioning in discourses of femininity and caring, I have to work hard at avoiding over-helping (*ibid*). I have to communicate my belief in their competence, by not giving too much help. I can give information and encourage people to meet and support each other outside the group. As a facilitator, I must not be over-protective towards the women, if I feel that they are depressed about their situations. This can increase women's feelings of inadequacy and prevent them from becoming agents of their own lives. I can lead the women by making suggestions or giving advice, and encouraging them to meet each other for mutual support outside the classroom. This active stance on my part will provide a model for the women of being assertive, as well as caring (*ibid*). I must offer gender-sensitive and feminist perspectives, which may differ from some of the values held by some of the women. I have to do this in ways that challenge the women without alienating them from me and from the course.

Often, halfway through a course, women say that they feel strangely depressed, in contrast to the first few weeks of a course, when they often feel excited at the newness and the prospect of the changes they envisage. I emphasise the importance of going slowly and of paying attention to the parts of themselves that are being cautious. I affirm the importance of waiting until they are ready to make changes and of making small changes to start off with. At the same time, I can affirm that change will take place, using terms such as 'when', rather than 'if' (*ibid*). One can also reassess as strengths what might otherwise be regarded as deficits or illness. Thus, depression can be seen as a healthy normal reaction to difficult circumstances and can be examined for what it tells women. Normality can be redefined to highlight women's strengths, rather than their deficiencies.

Providing information which may be contrary to the discourses through which women interpret their experiences

Providing information, in the shape of feminist discourses and social analyses, is indispensable to both the politicisation and the becoming agentic of women. It is partly rational, intellectual and theoretical, and it is where I, as an intellectual, try to make feminist poststructuralist theories available to women, and can facilitate connections between the personal and the political.

Many women who come to Stage One personal development education believe that their problems are of their own making and that they are inadequate, stupid, ignorant or inept. When they tell their various stories, to each other in pairs, or to the group, I draw again on Avis (*ibid*) and ask questions, or provide them with questions to ask each other, such as:

- where did you learn that you are responsible for making other people happy?
- who told you that you shouldn't ask directly for what you want?
- where does this belief come from?
- does this still make sense to you?
- how were you taught to look after children?
- how were you taught to look after men?
- what would happen if you said no?
- what would happen if you stopped doing something?
- what do you need?
- how did things get to be the way they are?

Since information is one form of power, it is important to find as many ways as possible to put this power in women's hands (*ibid*). When people first tell their stories, and I have had a chance to identify some of their beliefs from these stories, I provide information which challenges these beliefs and supports alternative constructions of reality. I do so in several ways:

1. I discuss and elaborate the process of gender socialisation, which helps women to understand that their beliefs have been taught to them, that they are not absolutes. I keep it simple, but not reductionist, with sentences like 'women are taught from birth that other people's needs are more important than theirs'; 'women are taught that it's not respectable to want sex'; 'I'm not surprised that you feel guilty about not making the beds for the whole family – most women feel guilty when they make changes, because they are taught to put everybody else first before themselves'. These are simple statements, but I have learned that, when a course is going well and women are enjoying it, they hang onto every word that the facilitator says. I have met some women months or even years after a course ended who are able to repeat things I said during the course.
2. New information can also be provided in the form of statements which challenge women's beliefs about themselves and other women, such as 'women need to take care of themselves in order to be able to really care for others'; 'by caring for yourself and meeting your own needs, you are teaching your

children how to respect and care for themselves'. It can be also useful to report on research findings about issues like sexual abuse, housework, or depression (*ibid*). This research adds weight to my message, while at the same time giving the women more information.

3. I try to introduce the idea of multiplicity in this way also, making statements like 'we can be different people at different times, depending on the situation'. I use games, especially remembered childhood games, to illustrate that we do not jettison parts of ourselves that we may have thought were in the past. The use of games and laughter also gives a pleasurable dimension to the course which is crucial in forming feminist subjectivities (*cf* Kenway *et al*, 1994).

4. I give information through reading material, in the form of handouts which I produce myself and in the form of recommending books. I can use cartoons, poems, newspaper and magazine articles, as well as books. It is important, however, to be aware of literacy difficulties that may exist within the group and not to disempower women by giving them material to read that is too difficult, too academic or too long. For women who do enjoy reading, I lend books and articles and recommend that they buy some of their own.

I have found that making 'We' statements is a simple and powerful way to connect the personal and the political, to decrease hierarchy between me and the group and to encourage a collectivity with other women and in particular with the other group members. Again, Avis (1991) provides suggestions:

- As women we have been taught that ... (we should not get angry)
- Many women feel ... (depressed, angry, guilty)
- Most of us have learned ... (to blame ourselves when things go wrong)
- A lot of the groups I work with ... (have had similar experiences about this issue)
- As women, many of us have experienced ... (harassment, intimidation, violence)
- As women, we are often ... (badly paid)

'We' statements are also ways to examine Kristeva's three tiers. I explain about different 'stages' of feminism, showing that they can exist together. If we talk about women's need for access to jobs, education and economic independence, then we are articulating a liberal feminist perspective. If we talk about women as a group and their ways of doing things, or if we laugh about how hopeless men are at certain tasks, then we are articulating radical feminism which values female ways of doing things, but without necessarily being essentialist (Davies, 1990c). This can be one way to discuss projection and how we may project the parts of ourselves that we do not like onto other groups or individuals. This can again lead into discussion of multiplicity and the idea of Kristeva's third tier, where gender identity is not fixed. The challenge is to be able to 'know' where a group is 'at' and to give them the next piece of information that will lead them to a different way of looking at themselves, at other women and at men.

I use Dolphin's (1994) spiral model of social analysis to help women examine and analyse the workings and the power relationships operating in their lives. I use a big poster of the spiral, designed to show how each level – personal, social, cultural, political and economic – interacts, interlocks and influences the others. Becoming aware of these levels enables an understanding of the roots of oppression and inequalities. I generally introduce the spiral in the same session where I introduce human rights. I ask women to reflect on the following questions:

- Personal: how do I experience things?
- Social: how do people relate to each other?
- Cultural: what are the dominant beliefs and values and how are they passed on?
- Political: how are decisions, policies and laws made and who makes them, at all levels of society – homes, workplaces, parishes, communities, the state?
- Economic: who controls and owns resources of money, raw materials, land, equipment and technology.

Fran worked as a cleaner in a hospital. On the first day of the course, she talked about how she felt invisible and 'nothing' when medical staff walked by her without a greeting or acknowledgement, 'as if I wasn't there'. In an interview after the course, she commented:

Fran
I came to the course because I felt very down in myself. I thought that it would help me feel better. The most important thing for me was the day you showed us the spiral. I took it home and stuck it on the fridge. I talked about it to my husband. I brought it to work and showed it to my friend. I was raging, really raging I was. I decided to do something about it. You remember I asked you to photocopy the human rights for me? Well, I gave them to her and we decided to stick them up in the kitchen at work. I often saw people reading them. That was really important.

Taking action

Many women come to Stage One feeling and believing that they are responsible for every aspect of their family life and intimate relationships. I find it helpful to clarify the things for which women are and are not responsible (*cf* Avis, 1991). I use the concept of human rights to do this, emphasising that other people have rights and responsibilities also. This is often a first step in helping women to understand that there are power differentials at work when they experience difficulties in making changes. The second step is to help the women to see what they *are* able to change and where emotional investments may be blocking change. Women may not always be able to make changes in their relationships with their husbands or partners as fast as they would like, but they often are able to make changes in their relationships with their children and with friends.

I find that a trigger for these changes is often the 'treat' for themselves that they have to do for 'homework'. Taking time for themselves apart from course time often triggers a release of the excessive responsibility that some of them feel for their children. Success or agency in changing relationships with children can lead to a consideration of patterns of power and control. I find that women reflect a great deal between the weekly classes. Reflection on successful changes, that is, where they have been agentic, is important in learning to make further changes in heterosexual relations. Often, at check-in at the beginning of a class, they talk about their engagements with the previous week's material and how they acted, or not, in relation to it.

Josephine

My friend wanted me to go guarantor for her at the Credit Union. It was for a big sum of money. And anyway, I didn't want to go guarantor, even if it was a small sum. She just took it for granted I'd do it, gave my name without asking me and told me on her way home. I thought about what we had learned about saying 'no'. I didn't want to do this for her, I went round to her house and said it straight out. It took an awful lot out of me. I said I didn't want to break up our friendship, but that I didn't want to be her guarantor. I asked her to go back to the Credit Union and tell them. She did. She's not speaking to me yet, but I'm just glad I did it.

I often use the metaphor of martial arts to examine power, emphasising that *not* doing things can be as important as doing things. This is useful in helping women think from a power perspective about situations they want to change and understand that head-on resistance is not always the best strategy for agency . This requires self-awareness. It has also led some women to take up martial arts, or self-defence classes based on martial arts.

Helping women to acknowledge and to express their anger and to use it to make changes is potentially one of the most politicising, resistance-focused and agency-producing actions that personal development education can do. It is also potentially the most depoliticising action, depending on the discursive framework of the course. Politicisation is often represented by liberal humanism as a passing, even if necessary, stage in identity formation: anger represents this phase (Kitzinger, 1987: 56). Radical political identity is seen as a penultimate step in achieving maturity: the liberal-humanist well-adjusted and non-politicised identity is the final one (*ibid*). But maturity is a concept that is socially constructed and therefore reflects the values and interests of the hegemonic culture (Clark and Wilson, 1991). Writing about the construction of lesbianism, Kitzinger (1987: 56) asserts: 'In directing the lesbian's attention away from the outer world of oppression and offering a satisfying inner world as a substitute, psychology offers salvation through individual change rather than system change'. If the facilitator does not recognise the necessity of politicisation, as well as attention to individual needs, personal development education will have the same effects that Kitzinger discusses: it will encourage women to 'deal with' their anger within the gender status quo, rather than use anger to disrupt it.

When we discuss feelings and relationships in courses, anger is always brought up. I tell the women that anger is a vital part of becoming more conscious and of making changes and I deliberately try to mobilise anger by predicting it and affirming it as a highly positive emotion for women, as recommended by Avis (1991). I use social analysis to point out how women have been robbed of anger and taught to be docile and therefore out of touch with power and strength.

Women's relationships with others are affected by the necessity to deny and disguise the anger that arises from a lack of power. The only acceptable voice for women in a male world is a voice that does not directly express anger. Caring, represented as a fundamental female quality, can be better understood as a way of negotiating from a position of low power. Patriarchy is represented, not by outright oppression, but by the unacknowledged pre-eminence of men's desires and the subordination of their own. If a woman wants to exercise authority it must be indirect or manipulative, or else in the service of others. The same is true if she wants to show anger (*ibid*).

I explain how, because of these social conditions, we may project anger onto others and not acknowledge it in ourselves. This facilitates a view of the person as multiple and is able to accommodate both anger and caring in the one person, thus undermining male/female dualism. I share some of my own experiences of anger with groups. This always catches their attention, because they are surprised that somebody whose manner is as mild as mine appears could feel anger as strongly as I describe. I talk about the cost of anger to women, whether it is directed at ourselves in the form of depression or illness, or directed at other people, where it affects relationships with bitterness and resentment. All the time, I emphasise the social nature of anger.

I often use the metaphor of a cleansing white light to describe the benefits of anger, pointing out that it is a clear and strong emotion with the potential to energise and focus attention onto the areas where change is needed (*ibid*). I make it clear that the experience of anger in situations of oppression is to be expected. I explain how anger can affect the body and I encourage physical release by pounding pillows or screaming into them. I encourage women to see where their anger is coming from and to make plans in the group for dealing with certain anger-causing situations where they *can* make changes. Again, I find Lerner's (1985) book about anger an invaluable tool to share with women.

I ask the group where in their lives they want to say 'no', but have difficulty. I ask them to role-play situations where they practise saying no directly. I encourage them to examine how they could stop doing an activity that they no longer want to do. We discuss the guilt that women can feel when they say 'no' to demands or expectations from partners, children, friends or colleagues. I emphasise again that each situation demands its own strategy and its own ways of resisting. The more agentic women become in their families and in other close relationships, the more changed will be the emotional patterns that have shaped experiences and dynamics in those relationships. We discuss how it can be difficult for us to learn to tolerate not being seen as healing and helpful.

We discuss how relationships can be reorganised to support women's new interests and activities. By being different, they are creating different situations, and have to learn to deal with them. They may get strong 'change back' messages from family and friends (*ibid*) and it is essential that I warn women about them. The family can be threatened, because of the ways that traditional families revolve so completely around women, so that even small changes in the woman's role may mean that work and emotional patterns are disrupted. I explain that everybody is capable of the emotional work that the mother or wife traditionally did, but that women sometimes find it difficult to let other people do their own emotional work, because it is one of women's few traditional sources of power. In the meantime, it may be enough for women to learn to say 'no', in small things, perhaps not even to say no directly, but to take time for themselves. I explain that this is not just to feel good, although that is one of the effects of taking time for treats, but also to get rid of some of the burdens they are under, including housework and emotional labour.

The beginnings of a pedagogy of the body

We are embodied subjects. Feminist resistances of the 1960s began with the body and a woman's right to choose how it is or is not used. For both women and men, the body is one medium through which the world is experienced. On the other hand, women are objectified bodies. 'Under constant critical surveillance by others, women begin to experience their own bodies at a distance. They view themselves as the objects of the intentions and manipulations of others' (Davis, 1996: 115). At Stage One, the body approached via the relaxation and visualisation exercises already mentioned. It is also dealt with when we discuss feelings and relationships. I give people a blank drawing of a body and ask them where they experience various feelings. Relaxation helps to restore 'sensual authority', without which we can become muscularly rigid and perceptually dulled (Taylor, 1991: 62). The body is a meeting point between private and public. For women, particularly, patriarchal power can dictate how the body is constructed and social (Davies, 1990c). I ask women to talk to each other about what they learned about their bodies as children and as adolescents. They often focus on commands such as 'keep your legs together while sitting' which held the secret to becoming respectable (cf Haug, 1987; Stephenson et al, 1996).

Attending to the body can contribute to a growing awareness of the structuring of subjectivity through the embodiment of dominant ideologies (Taylor, 1991: 72). Yet, to move beyond unconscious challenges or emotional defiance, there has to be a critical connection able to thread together the fragments of the contradictions, accommodations and resistances. Resistance that is not grounded in political critique is limited in its effects on everyday practices and existences (ibid). In the sharing of stories and narratives, a common experience of resistance and oppression is recognised, in relation to the body as well as other aspects of women's lives. Paying attention to the body in this collective setting is capable of beginning a process of a critical pedagogy of the body, although such a pedagogy is one that is ongoing. Stage One personal development education is just a first step.

Personal development education: part of a feminist project

My analysis of feminist subjectivities in Chapters Five and Six has shown that a person is never totally powerful, or totally powerless. I posit, then, that if, in my courses, I can get women to focus on contradictions, that is, the reasons why they want changes in their lives and came to the course in the first place, and where these desires show up the cracks in the social façade, then there is the possibility of politicisation. If I can facilitate women to see where they *are* powerful and resisting, as well as seeing how constraining power relations work in their lives, this can help them make changes and be agentic. We can look at intimate and immediate manifestations and operations of power in this way. Nevertheless, the discursive analysis does not deal with questions of authority and the powerful social status of experts to produce 'truth' (see, for example, Fraser, 1989: 173,4; Kiely, 2000). This is an aspect of power that I try to make explicit through the use of the spiral analysis.

The personal extending which personal development education can bring about is necessary, then, but not everything. It is necessary to acknowledge the limits of personal development, both to myself and to the groups I work with. Sometimes, recognising limits can be comforting, by allowing us to say, 'I've done all I can do here' (Avis, 1991). Part of my feminist project is to encourage the women to move into other groups that will continue to develop their politicisation.

The possibility of reorganising families as a result of personal development education is limited by the gender relations sanctioned by the larger society. The options open to the facilitator are limited too, by the dominant discourses in the larger social system of which women and their relationships are part. Nevertheless, by opening up the possibility of alternatives to the dominant discourses in personal development education, we can begin to transform practice in the existing social order. Foucault identifies liberation with resistance rather than revolution, the acting out of refusal at multiple points of power relations (Faith, 1994: 53). The task is to change the regimes that produce truths about people. In changing family and relationship dynamics, women can begin to change one of those regimes of truth.

> Feminisms produce a mosaic of resistances which address the family, language, courts, churches, media, welfare, educational and health institutions, violence against women, political economy, heterosexism, colonisation, racism, imperialism and all other impositions of patriarchal truths. The targets of feminist wrath and appeal are vast, deep, intricate and constantly shifting. Whereas individual feminist voices may convey a dogmatic certitude of analysis, as a broad and internally diverse social movement feminism moves beyond the model that would simply replace one regime of truth with another. Feminisms are local in their expressions and global in their collective, potential force. (*ibid*)

Resistances can occur beyond that which is articulated, observable or conventionally politicised. As a facilitator, I need to be aware of this. It is not always possible to measure learning outcomes, and I must not make assumptions about what course participants have or have not learned. Too many women make personal development education their first or only contact with adult education for us to leave it untheorised and to neglect its politicised practice.

There is a problem for the feminist poststructuralist facilitator, regarding the content of such courses. She is constantly in competition with dominant discourses (feminist and non-feminist, and all drawing on liberal humanism) of what it means to be a woman, while simultaneously using human relations processes, such as empathy, participative techniques and drawing on personal experience. She also needs to be aware that it is not enough to ground her practice in simplistic notions of false consciousness and to see feminist personal development teaching as mediation or, worse, as a charitable act (Lewis, 1993: 177). Experiences in the feminist personal development classroom can be deeply emotional for many women, offering the opportunity to claim relevance for the lives they live as the source of legitimate knowledge (cf ibid). Women don't need to be taught what we already know: that we are marginalised in a mainstream culture for which our productive and reproductive labour is essential. We need opportunities to reflect on our situations outside dominant discourses of the personal. From that viewpoint, a personal development course can construct for women an island, or a 'holding environment' (Avis, 1991), in which they recognise, understand and change their role in inequitable power relationships and cathectic relationships. This may include deciding to leave those relationships.

I want courses to end with 'woman' signifying differently for the women than it did at the beginning, that is, with interpretations available to them that are not mediated by the dominant discourses of woman. In this way, the signifier 'man' can also begin to be changed. Any changes that women make also interrupts men's positionings.

> Concern for this basic struggle should motivate feminist thinkers to talk and write more about how we relate to men and how we change and transform relationships with men characterized by domination. (hooks, 1989: 130)

This is feminist work that focuses on strategies women can use to speak to men about domination, oppression and change. It is the sort of work that is not readily available (ibid). Yet, many women have a deep longing to share their desires for change and their feminist consciousness with people to whom they are close and to reach into their lives and relationships, in order to transform them. How we understand 'femininity' and 'masculinity' affects how we see our options for doing such transformative work and our choices for the future. It is crucial that personal development facilitation practices do not actually produce women in liberal-humanist terms and then claim to 'discover' what they have produced. It is essential that the facilitator have a keen political awareness of the conditions of her own production.

Naming power and the multiplicity of power and the social nature of feelings and contradictions are concepts central to my assertion that personal development practice can be politicised and can produce feminist agency. Personal development education deals primarily with intimate relationships (structures of cathexis), underpinned by emotional investments. Being involved in intimate relationships, including marriage, can be a source of agency and power, as well as constraint (Hollway, 1995). Through personal development, women can learn not to do the emotional work for others in their relationships and thereby affect structures of labour and power as well.

In discontinuing both emotional and practical work for others (including projection of certain qualities or feelings onto men as individuals and as a group), they often need to learn to deal with guilt and ambivalence which arise because they are leaving behind traditional positions of power for women, with their associated emotional investments in those positions. Chapters Five and Six have shown that women who can deal with uncertainty, contradiction and feelings of ambivalence are likely to be agentic in pursuit of feminist goals in a multiple and complex social world. Learning to deal with these feelings of ambivalence requires a strong sense of what one's own needs are (Coward, 1993), which many women are lacking, when they first come to personal development education. The examination of psychodynamic processes in Chapter Six has shown that what is unacknowledged is often reproduced unchanged. Constructing self-awareness in feminist poststructuralist discourses can lead to the abandonment of such reproduction and the take-up of new positions for women and men. Feminist personal development done outside liberal-humanist discourses of the self can thus play an important part in the construction of new selves.

Conclusion

This chapter has put forward a way of facilitating politicised personal development education, based on my own practical experience and on my theorising earlier in this work. While my practice may be flawed, if I have no practice, then there is only empty theorising. Yet, if we do not theorise in order to inform our practice, then our work is open for colonisation by the dominant discourses of the self. These liberal-humanist discourses depoliticise our feelings, desires for change and experiences of contradictions, and reduce them to effects of our individual psychologies and/or pathologies. Where Chapters Five and Six address the first of my research questions about the nature of feminist subjectivity, this present chapter has tried to examine the second question: under what conditions can we do politicised personal development education?

A politicised practice of personal development education has the potential to be a successor to earlier feminist practices of consciousness-raising, incorporating its strengths, while avoiding its downside, that is, a lack of a nurturing dimension and support for women in working on feelings of guilt, ambiguity, and ambivalence. In this, personal development education is capable of living up to consciousness-raising's theoretical goal of examining lives with all senses, including an equal emphasis on feelings. Drawing on feminist poststructuralist theory, it is capable of challenging the gender status quo by demonstrating that gender differences are produced and thus available for modification.

8 Politics, subjectivity and adult education

Introduction

In this chapter, I draw together the threads of the book, and attempt to 'cast off', in two senses. The first sense in which I use the term is taken from knitting, where casting off implies working with the stitches to create a neat, finished edge, which will not unravel. To some extent, I want to do this with my work, by summarising the implications of my attempts to theorise feminist ways of knowing. Yet I do not want to cast off so tightly that the stitches cannot be picked up by others, and the work continued. So I also want to cast off in the nautical sense of freeing a boat from its moorings and beginning a passage. Stimulated by an intense personal engagement with feminism and issues of agency, I have researched and theorised feminist subjectivities, and the ways that feminist women produce knowledge about themselves and about feminism. Along the way I have attempted to indicate the resources made available to adult education by radical approaches to subjectivity.

Subjectivity has been treated in this book as a process by which a person discursively, relationally and psychodynamically constructs a sense of self, or constructs knowledge and identity. I have also shown that feminism 'comes together' very differently for each person, depending on individual histories and psychodynamic process, and in engagement with discourses which carry the social and historical content of subjectivity. These discourses are in turn inserted into a cultural web of understandings available to each individual. In addition, each situation, or moment of the process, is an important site for the production, circulation and consumption of feminist knowledge. I have attempted to take this further and see how these feminist ways of knowing can provide sources and themes for another meeting point between adult education theory and practice: that constituted by feminist personal development education. I have shown that reflection on the self does not have to be purely individually focused, or individualistic in its effects. In doing so, I have indicated a framework whereby adult education can theorise the person without falling into dualism.

Theoretical conclusions

The knowledge produced for this book has implications for both feminism and adult education, because it has developed a way of theorising the person that can cope with adult politicisation. The multi-layered nature of knowledge and subjectivity must be taken into account in efforts to develop critical thinking, and to support progressive social movements. Because of the focus of my research and my pedagogical interests in the personal, there is a danger that this work could be dismissed as a study of change at the level of the individual. However, in my treatment of subjectivity as constructed in a dynamic three-way relationship between discourse, relations in the present and psychodynamics, I believe it is possible to avoid the reductionism about the human subject which plagues many approaches to adult education and social movements.

Building on the work of Hollway (1984a, 1989), I have taken signification as a starting point for examining the self, the person, or subjectivity, because the concept does not privilege either side of the individual/society dualism. Situations and events signify differently and uniquely for each person but this must not be taken to mean that the process of signification is not social: the only way to express emotions is via discourse. Signification is thus produced in relation to discourses which pre-exist a person. By refusing certain discursive practices or elements of those practices, and by searching for new ways to position themselves, individuals can construct new and different forms of practice, and thus work towards new discourses and new ways of understanding emotions. By examining investment, power and discourse in each case, an analysis based on signification privileges neither individual nor structure.

Signification, by allowing for psychodynamic processes, gets us beyond discourse determinism, into 'the capillaries of the structures' (Beckwith, 1999). The concept allows for the uniqueness of individual histories, and each person's unique relation to different discourses. But at the same time, it acknowledges that individuals are constrained by existing discourses, structures and practices. These are not simply external constraints, but are also responsible for the psychic patterns through which individuals position themselves and through which they privately and emotionally experience themselves in relation to the social world (Davies, 1990b: 13). The idea of emotions as discursively constructed connects discourse, the unconscious and subjectivity, and allows for different individual reactions and responses to discourses. It also challenges the notion that desires, emotions or feelings are an expression of the real or true essence of an individual. People can be controlled by perceptions of what is true or real about them. Perceptions of women's true nature, illustrated by the expression of their 'real' desires, have been shown to be open to challenge.

> The profound complexity of the third tier is knowing oneself as a woman
> and in that knowing breaking the bonds of words and images and
> metaphors that have held oneself inside the male/female dualism, that
> have made one a woman in phallogocentric terms. (Davies, 1990c: 514)

Signification also attends to the ways that discourses circulate between people, in addition to the ways that they operate intrapersonally (Mama, 1995). Meanings can be changed through inter-discursive work, that is, through the articulation of concepts in new and different ways. People participate actively – even if sometimes unwittingly – in the production and reproduction of discourses, and therefore of change. Numerous small everyday significations, which occur from moment to moment in relations with other people, must be taken into account in the search for a useful theory of change, and the construction of new knowledge. From a feminist poststructuralist point of view, 'it does not make sense to think of political change simply in terms of emancipation from oppression, as feminists conventionally have done. It does make sense to think of transforming political relations through the production of new discourses and so new forms of power and new forms of the self' (Ramazanoglu, 1993: 24). Some of the meanings that emerge, when feminist poststructuralist discourses engage with other discourses, may stand in stark contrast to other feminist theoretical traditions, but they nevertheless have concerns about women's oppression, which have much in common with these other traditions (cf Kenway et al, 1994: 190).

This study has illustrated the 'extreme proximity of the thinking process to existential reality and lived experience' (Braidotti, 1989: 94). Power was analysed as a relational phenomenon, through the use of the concepts of discourse and discursive positioning. In addition to being a way to protect vulnerable selves through the take-up of powerful positions within any one discourse, power emerges as the energy which motivates investments in certain positions, whereby one can meet one's own (possibly unacknowledged) needs. Because different positions in different discourses are being taken up from moment to moment, it is no longer adequate to theorise people as always victims or as always oppressors. In traditional terms, power is the exclusive property of dominant groups. The analysis made here demonstrates that the person who would be traditionally characterised as victim has power to move or to change positioning, or to take up new positions. The emphasis is on the relationality and multiplicity of power.

Implications for feminism

When people come to read themselves through new discourses, the structures of labour, power and cathexis and the system of gender difference production which they facilitate are challenged. Many women and men do not recognise that other discourses, practices and possibilities exist, apart from those based on an essentialist perception of what it is to be women or men. Their incorporation into femininity and masculinity comes about not only through divisions of labour and imbalances in material and economic power, but also through complex and less acknowledged emotional, psychic and sexual workings of desire and cathexis. Dominant sexist discourses encourage them to interpret these workings as evidence of their true 'feminine' or 'masculine' selves. In dominant feminist discourses, these are interpreted for them as evidence that attention to the personal will never achieve emancipation, or, alternatively, for women, that they need to leave the heterosexual relationships within which they experience these feelings (Hollway, 1995).

Challenging perceptions of what women are really like from a radical feminist or liberal feminist perspective alone is not enough (although it may sometimes be necessary), because these feminisms rely on a model of the human subject which allows that there is such a thing as a true femininity. They thus lend themselves to universalisms regarding women, which feminist poststructuralism considers inimical to emancipatory moves. The bases of the other feminisms in essentialist models of the subject make their approach to change reliant on rationality and voluntarism. These may be useful tools, depending on the situation, but they are not sufficient to deal with people's investments in certain discursive positions and their resistance to transformation.

Feminism has been preoccupied with power throughout its history. In this book, I have concentrated on discursive forms of power. I have examined emotional investments in certain discourses, discursive positions and cathectic relations. This analysis has shown that women are not without power, as women, or as feminists, when it comes to getting people to engage with feminist discourses and thereby having feminist effects. But I have emphasised also that this does not mean that women's and men's powers are equal, nor that the power of feminist discourses is equal to the power of dominant sexist discourses. The power conferred through positioning oneself as feminist or as feminine operates at the same time as many other powers, such as socially sanctioned authority and material resources. Such alternative sources of power and power relations also operate in heterosexual couples and between adults and children, resulting in social sources of power within intimate relations, and implying that we need to include materialist and economic analyses. When women do not have material or economic power, they are less likely to critically examine the power conferred on them by virtue of their take-up of feminine positions. My analysis also makes it clear that power and agency are not always the same thing. Having certain types of power is not the same as being agentic, or influencing the 'ball-game'. Nevertheless, to achieve agency, it is vital to understand politically the different ways that power works and how one is implicated and positioned in those workings. The analysis of power as multiple indicates additional moves that women can make to achieve feminist agency.

The concept of positioning was again useful for feminism, in analysing patterns of power relationships and the construction of agency. It allows women to approach change when they are feeling 'stuck', through an examination of their own reflexive positionings and the ways they position other people. 'Conscious choices, even when they are less than ideal, help us to transcend our sense of entrapment' (Lipman Blumen, 1994: 128). Personal development education can help people to make some choices, from a positional perspective. But collective agency is necessary also: the limits of personal development education are recognised.

Another benefit of the concept of positioning is that it allows women to recognise that they simultaneously occupy a range of social and cultural positions and to incorporate the social into their reflection on experience. This was illustrated in this study as occupying simultaneously feminist and feminine positions, but does not have to be confined to such positionings (see, for example, Kenway et al, 1994: 199). By focusing on positioning, it is possible to come to see power as multiple. The implications for a theory of change and hence for a meaningful feminist politics are significant. It takes us beyond a view of women as either stuck in a system where they have no meaningful access to power, or, alternatively, as powerful in the maternal, domestic and sexual arenas only.

Gender is a system of difference production which depends on labour, power and cathexis for its effects. This means that feminists must focus on gender *relations*, as well as on women. Men and men's subjectivities, especially as they engage with emancipatory discourses, including feminism, cannot simply be left out of the equation. Moves that women make to change their positions have effects on men's positioning: theoretically speaking, if signifiers of 'woman' change, due to the effort of feminists, then signifiers of 'man' will change also. The difficulty with this is that change involves feminist women trying to change both themselves and men at the same time. It is nevertheless encouraging that any changes women make have the effect of changing men's positioning in discourses as well as women's. Men can also participate actively in this kind of signification work and they have been encouraged and sometimes precipitated into it by women's feminisim (cf Connell, 1995; Griffin, 1997).

Implications for adult education pedagogy

The concept of pedagogy draws attention to the process through which knowledge is produced: the relational nature of teaching, learning and the production of knowledge. 'How one teaches is therefore of central interest but, through the prism of pedagogy, it becomes inseparable from what is being taught and, crucially, from what one learns' (Lusted, 1986: 3). Generating new theoretical perspectives from which the dominant can be criticised and new possibilities envisaged is especially important. As an instrument of social change, a truly transformative pedagogy requires the embodiment of a subjectivity conscious of her own subordination (Lewis, 1993: 54). But if our understanding takes us only as far as pinpointing the construction of femininity and oppression, then it is inadequate for a transformative pedagogical practice. We also need a means to examine and theorise successful resistances, including the social transformation of gender identities.

Including a psychology of women in adult education has historically been seen as radical in the face of a mainstream psychology which tended to take the male as the norm against which women were to be measured and most often seen as deficient. This explains the enormous popularity of the work of Gilligan (1982), Brown and Gilligan (1992) and Belenky et al (1986). These ideas need to be seen in the historical context in which they first became popular, but the insights produced by feminist poststructuralism mean that these approaches are no longer satisfactory. Adult education needs a theory of how gender differences are produced, reproduced and subverted. The theoretical focus needs to be on new forms of femininity and masculinity, on politicised subjectivities formed in the struggle to challenge the gender status quo. It is not enough to focus on women and men as they are, because gender is produced through difference, in relations. Focusing on sex differences in adult education leads to comparison, but does not fundamentally challenge the categories male and female.

One challenge for both feminism in Ireland and critical adult education pedagogy (especially where they come together in women's personal development education) is to find a praxis adequate to the accounts of feminist knowledges presented in this book. The requirement of the pedagogy is that it can provide a framework where people can go beyond rational accounts and can do this without slipping into mere feeling accounts (cf Hollway, 1989). In other words, it has to avoid dualism. I have asserted more than once that any curriculum that places personal growth at its centre must negotiate some tricky ideological ground

(Kenway and Willis, 1990). It has to prevent gender studies from falling into 'psychobabble' on the one hand, or a structural-based movement incapable of politicising the personal, on the other hand (cf Burman, 1995: 132).

Much feminist exhortation and adult education practice in Ireland comes down on one side or other of the dualism. Reactions to rationalism tend to concentrate on the spiritual and emotional. Reactions to the personal call for more emphasis on the structural. Humanist practice is seen as a radical alternative to religious practice in personal development education, but when humanist practice is then found to be inadequate for forming politicised subjectivities, the call is made to leave the personal, or to move beyond it, and to concentrate on the structural. The call to 'move beyond' personal development (cf Mulvey, 1995) assumes a hierarchy of development from personal to political, from individual to structural.

When women and men studying gender issues arrive at radical feminist and social constructionist ways of seeing things for the first time, it can be enormously exciting. This produces the 'aha!' factor. But, even though these ways of interpreting the world provide very important insights, they are not the sole explanations for women's condition. Unfortunately, because we are so attuned to the idea that fundamental truths exist, most people stop there. They look for reductionist explanations in all walks of life. So, pedagogically speaking, we need to go beyond the reductionism of 'aha!', while acknowledging its importance. This is reminiscent of Kristeva's project of operating in three stages of feminism – radical, liberal and deconstructed – all at once. If women consider that an essential femininity is the whole truth about them, this can operate to perpetuate the current power status quo. If they consider that the only way to emancipation is to tackle social structures, it can have the same effect, because the personal is left untheorised in a politicised manner and the assumptions of a liberal-humanist perspective are taken for granted.

Pedagogies that support progressive social movements therefore need to produce ever more useful understandings of power, capable of dealing with the complexity and multiplicity of its late twentieth-century expressions. Old dichotomies led to clear explanations and impetus for action; the new complexities of power may have the opposite effect (Jones, 1993: 165), if we do not develop ways of using them in classrooms to spark militant oppositional efforts (cf Cocks, 1989: 6). The concept of multiple and contradictory discourses, powers and subjectivities can act as a resource for women, and for men, who want to make changes. Radical self-reflection can create awareness of how all of these positions and discourses overlap in the same person, that is, how the person is multiply constructed.

But how does radical self-reflection differ from a human relations discourse, when people want to know 'Who am I?' It can be frustrating not to be able to settle on an idea of who one is, even while at the same time accepting the constructedness and multiplicity of human experience. Wetherell (1995: 135, 6) draws on Hall (1988: 44) to address this issue. Hall argues that we do, indeed, answer the question and come to conclusions and settle on positions in various relationships and often maintain these versions of ourselves for a considerable length of time (or find that others maintain them for us). The construction of knowledge is thus about closure, as well as fluidity and multiplicity. It is about refusing all the possible versions and choosing one, for a time. So knowledge, to borrow a phrase, is often formed 'at these points where we place a full stop' (Wetherell, 1995: 136). Critical pedagogies, then, have to work with the constructed nature of knowledge, but also facilitate choices for action, even if those choices are flawed.

Such an assertion has consequences for the practical shapes that pedagogies take. It means that not all of the forms of pedagogy can be student centred, in the sense that they provide a response to the immediate needs and experiences of students (cf Grimshaw, 1993: 61). Adult education has a responsibility to provide new forms of knowledge, such as feminist poststructuralist discourses, and to facilitate students' engagement with them in productive ways. Otherwise, dominant assumptions about women and men will be reproduced unchanged. For many intellectuals and deeply committed radical feminists, this entails a possibly difficult 'reconciliation of radical political commitment with an appreciation of the shades of grey in the social world' (Cocks, 1989: publisher's introduction). It also involves taking a close look at our own powers.

A self-consciously feminist poststructuralist adult education praxis could provide one model for such a practice. This would involve laying bare the power dynamics of different discourses of femininity and feminism, openly questioning the formulation of dominant discourses about women and men, and pushing forward subordinated and barely formulated alternatives. The knowing subject of such a model of pedagogy will take on board the poststructuralist lesson *par excellence*, which is to be suspicious of authority and authoritative versions of who we are. It is important that feminist teachers can somehow make accessible to learners the various theoretical tools that are available for doing this, but it is equally important that such teaching does not take the form of an initiation into feminist theory as a disembodied form of knowledge. Feminist teaching projects must devise means of teaching students about the various feminist perspectives in ways that focus them on students' everyday personal, intellectual and political dilemmas (Middleton, 1993: 31) and provide positions from which to act effectively for political change.

> Much of the unfamiliarity and strangeness of poststructuralism recedes when applied to everyday life. Work, relationships, beliefs, skills, and we ourselves are not identical from one day, or even one moment, to the next or from one place to another. There are always differences ... What we do in everyday life is negotiated, compromised, contingent, subject to miscalculation, and flawed. (Cherryholmes, 1988: 142)

While authoritative and foundational theories may promise redemption, they cannot help us deal with confusion and imperfection, mingled in with success, as well as poststructuralism can. Poststructuralism has room for both constructors and deconstructors. Construction is based on the realisation that what is built is temporal, fallible, limited, compromised, negotiated and incomplete or contradictory. Each construction will eventually be replaced. And deconstructive argument must be shaped so that construction will be encouraged and follow (*ibid*: 143).

Adult educators need to work in a way that is both intellectual and facilitative, in order to clear the 'roadblocks' (Cain, 1993: 83), from the standpoint or site of the group of people with whom one wants to produce knowledge. If we fail to incorporate theories of discursive power and emotional investments certain discursive positions into our educational work, then we leave open space for others to construct – either implicitly or explicitly – theories of the person and of experience which we may well find politically unacceptable. This process also involves educators taking a close look at their own powers and investments, in other words, interrogating their own subjectivities.

Suggestions for further research and pedagogical work

This work has highlighted the role that knowledge creation can play in the formation and evolution of the social movement that is feminism and the role that feminism, in turn, plays in the construction of knowledge and subjectivity. Social movements generate knowledge and typically form an identity in opposition to a constructed Other (Holford, 1995: 103). Feminism has done this, and in large measure has constructed itself as Other to a male culture. But the knowledge generated must be viewed critically, even by those who identify with the aims of the social movement and consider themselves part of it (*ibid*).

This study has taken gender and feminism as the main lenses of the analyses, but one could equally take masculinity, class, ability, religion, nationality, ethnicity, or any other dimensions of human experience, and investigate the discourses, social relations and psychodynamics that apply to them. The study of feminist subjectivities in this book has shown that so much of feminist life is the daily project of establishing a social identity. Work on subjectivity can be applied to other social movements, and the identities and knowledges developed as part of those movements. What subjectivities are emerging among the thousands of refugees from Africa and other parts of Europe, currently living in Ireland? What discourses, relations and psychodynamics shape the identities of today's Roman Catholics? What sort of knowledge has been constructed in contemporary Northern Irish communities? The methodologies developed in this book could be used for investigating knowledge and identity developed as part of any social phenomenon, in any part of the world, provided that local specifics are taken into account. The women who took part in this study were very specific – they were formally well educated, accustomed to self-reflection, and had access to economic and material powers, and this must be taken into account when viewing the knowledge they constructed. The methodology does not purport to be universal, then, but it does put forward a framework within which specific subjectivities can be studied, and knowledges constructed.

Equally, the methodologies could be employed in treating any topic in the classroom. In whatever subject area we teach, theories of discourse, relations and psychodynamics can facilitate questioning of the assumptions that inform our social practices. Work on subjectivity provides a discourse whereby we can integrate politicised perspectives into students' reflection on everyday experiences and dilemmas. In this way, it is possible to create a dynamic educational practice where different subject positions become available to people, backed by a theory which puts forward for consideration debates about emotional investments in certain positions, the social construction of selves, and the reproduction and transformation of society (cf Stephenson et al, 1996: 184).

If we accept that people are not rigidly fixed in a single identity, then we can study the ways in which they are able to change, to resist and oppose dominant discourses, either by taking up positions outside these discourses, or by developing alternative ones, or both. When we look at the processes by which women living in a sexist and anti-feminist environment constitute themselves as feminists and take up positions in feminist discourses, we are examining how politicised subjectivities are constituted in oppressive environments and in environments of resistance. The concept of positioning in discourse is applicable in multiple situations: it allows us to see that people can be positioned simultaneously in different discourses, prompting contradictions to manifest themselves. This concept is more dynamic than a static definition of roles and is able to focus on how self-signification is achieved in encounters between people in social situations. People are positioned in discourses in ways such that they are motivated to reproduce certain positions in discourse and therefore certain significations. Because people are never positioned in only a single discourse, contradictions occur and knowledge is not determined. Change is possible through the contradictions between discourses and how people experience themselves as positioned through more than one discourse.

It is also vital that researchers investigating learning, meaning, knowledge construction, human experience and social change take on board theories of subjectivity. There is a myriad of questions about human experience which are not adequately answered, because so much qualitative research has failed to problematise issues of subjectivity and experience. The framework I have proposed could facilitate the production of richer, more complex, more detailed and more nuanced pictures of human experience.

> Layers of meaning and experience to which research (and hence policy-
> makers) have rarely had access would become visible. The human
> subjects of research might be represented with the complexity we
> currently associate with literature and works of art more generally.
> (Hollway and Jefferson, 2000: 156)

Conclusion

Adult education, in its support for progressive social movements, has a responsibility to draw attention to cultural politics, and to promote understandings of power as discursive, dispersed and subtle in its operations. But it must be careful not to allow discourse theory to overshadow the importance of parallel psychodynamic processes. Researchers and teachers must not underestimate people's emotional attachments to certain discursive practices and positions. It should also be understood that investments can seem like freely made choices, or can be portrayed as choices. We also need to be aware of discourses which challenge liberal humanism's dominant views of the human subject. We need to develop them in the collectives to which we belong, and to find ways of communicating and developing different discourses in any learning situation.

Astute educators display a judgement capable of capturing the distinctive character of both an era and a specific situation. This implies the need to understand the self, or subjectivity, in transformative, or radical, ways, both in research and in pedagogy. There is a way of understanding the complexities of how people in a particular time and place think and act, which also tells us what can be changed politically and what cannot. This is a feature of pedagogy, which distinguishes it from sociology and psychology. Knowledge, subjectivity and meaning are constructed by feminism, along with other social movements. Adult education has a role to play in this process, in that adult educators can act as movement intellectuals, not to initiate people into academic knowledge, but to take academic knowledge into the frontline of educational practice and to facilitate its development in an engagement with students. Through our research, our theorising and our classroom practices, we can produce with them new positions in emancipatory discourses, which are available for take-up by all of us. In this way, we have a central role to play in the emergence of new knowledges and thus in social change itself.

Notes

Chapter Three

1. Although recent anti-humanism is mostly associated with Althusser, it had its beginnings in the work of Merleau Ponty (1969), Sartre (1960), Gramsci (1971) and writers of the Frankfurt school, including Habermas (1971a, b). Nietzsche's 'death of man' and Levi-Strauss' 'death of the subject' had given earlier indications of this departure, as well as Marx' critique of Feuerbach's foundation of the purpose of history in 'man', and Freud's decentring of the rational *cogito* and his emphasis on the importance of the unconscious (for a discussion, see Henriques *et al*, 1984, 95ff).
2. The anti-essentialism of feminist poststructuralism also finds a forerunner in the anti-essentialism of existentialist Marxism, particularly that of Beauvoir (Schor, 1989). However, Althusserian Marxism defined itself in opposition to both existentialist and humanist Marxisms and Beauvoir's importance tends to be overlooked, particularly in Britain, because of the widespread adoption of Althusser's theories there in the 1970s (Lovell, 1990: 187, 188). While Morrow (1994: 130) asserts that Althusser's structuralism has been decisively rejected by critical social theorists, he neglects productive feminist engagements with it.
3. Few feminist poststructuralist writers refer to Gramsci's (1971) references to subjectivity. In his *Prison Notebooks* (1971), he 'discusses the way in which individuals are a mixture of "subjectivities" locked in common-sense understandings and played out in social practices' (Henriques *et al*, 1984: 94). Exceptions are Fraser (1992) and Kenway *et al* (1994), who consider it productive, 'despite their differences, to use Gramsci alongside Foucault, for it was Gramsci (1971) who developed a most persuasive account of the ways in which social groups and collective identities and socio-cultural hegemonies are formed and reformed through discourse' (Kenway *et al*, 1994: 190).
4. Both Urwin (1984: 279) and Moi (1985: 98) note the influence of existentialism on Lacan, and its emphasis on a fundamental lack of being in the subject.

Chapter Six

In this account and all following accounts, I use the following devices:

– indicates hesitation in speech
italic text indicates my speech
... indicates that a section of text has been left out of a particular account by me
[ ] is used for explanatory notes within an account, or to avoid using names as part of an account
[ ] also contains numbers which refer to the points of analysis made after each account.
All names are pseudonyms.

References

Abrahams, N. (1992) 'Towards reconceptualising political action' *Sociological Inquiry* 62 (3): 327–47.

Acker, S. (1988) 'Teachers, gender and resistance', *British Journal of Sociology of Education* 9 (3): 307–22.

Alcoff, L. (1988) 'Cultural feminism versus poststructuralism: the identity crisis in feminist theory', *Signs* 13: 405–36.

Althusser, L. (1971a) *Lenin and Philosophy and Other Essays*, London: New Left Books.

Althusser, L. (1971b) *For Marx*, London: Allen Lane/New Left Books.

An Roinn Oideachais (1971) Curaclam Na Bunscoile/Primary School Curriculum, Dublin: Brown and Nolan.

Aontas Women's Education Group (1991) *From the Personal to the Political: A Women's Education Workbook*, Dublin: Attic Press.

Avis, J. M. (1991) 'Power politics in therapy with women', in Goodrich, T. J. (ed.) *Women and Power: Perspectives for Family Therapy*, New York and London: W. W. Norton and Co.

Bailey, M. E. (1993) 'Foucauldian feminism: contesting bodies, sexuality and identity', in Ramazanoglu, C. (ed.) *Up against Foucault: explorations of some tensions between Foucault and feminism*, London: Routledge.

Balbus, I. D. (1982) *Marxism and Domination: A Neo-Hegelian, Feminist Psychoanalytic Theory of Sexual, Political and Technological Domination*, Princeton: Princeton University Press.

Barrett, M. (1980) *Women's Oppression To-day: Problems in Marxist Feminist Analysis*, London: Verso Books.

Barry, K. (1995) *The Prostitution of Sexuality: the global exploitation of women*, New York: New York University Press.

Bart, P. (1993) 'The liquidity of female sexuality and the tenaciousness of lesbian identity', in Wilkinson, S. and Kitzinger, C. (eds) *Heterosexuality; A Feminism and Psychology Reader*, London: Sage.

Beckwith, J. B. (1999) 'Editor's introduction: power between women: discourses within structures', *Feminism and Psychology* 9(4): 389–97 (Special Feature: Power Between Women).

Belenky, M. F., Clinchy, B. M., Goldberger, N. R. and Tarule, J. M. (1986) *Women's Ways of Knowing: the Development of Self, Voice and Mind*, New York: Basic Books.

Bell, D. and Klein, R. (1996) (eds) *Radically Speaking: Feminism Reclaimed*, London: Zed Books.

Belsey, C. (1980) *Critical Practice*, London: Methuen.

Benhabib, S. and Cornell, D. (1987) (eds) *Feminism as Critique*, Cambridge: Polity Press.

Bhaskar, R. (1979) *On the Possibility of Naturalism: A philosophical critique of the contemporary human sciences*, Brighton: Harvester Press.

Blackman, L. M. (1996) 'The dangerous classes', *Feminism and Psychology* 6(3): 361–80.

Bordo, S. (1987) 'The Cartesian masculinization of thought', in Harding, S. and O'Barr, J. F. (eds) *Sex and Scientific Enquiry*, Chicago: University of Chicago Press.

Bourdieu, P. (1986) 'The forms of capital', in Richardson, J. (ed.) *Handbook of Theory and Research for the Sociology of Education*, New York: Greenwood.

Bowlby, J. (1971) *Attachment and Loss* Vol 1, Harmondsworth: Penguin.

Braidotti, R. (1989) 'The politics of ontological difference', in Brennan, T. (ed.) *Between Feminism and Psychoanalysis*, London: Routledge.

Braidotti, R. (1991) *Patterns of Dissonance: A study of women in contemporary philosophy*, Cambridge: Polity Press.

Brodkey, L. (1987) 'Writing ethnographic narratives', *Writing Communication* 4 (1): 25–50.

Brookes, A. L. (1992) *Feminist Pedagogy: an autobiographical approach*, Halifax, N.J.: Fernwood.

Broughton, J. M. (1987a) (ed.) *Critical theories of psychological development*, New York: Plenum Press.

Broughton, J. M. (1987b) 'An introduction to critical developmental psychology', in Broughton, J. M. (ed.) *Critical theories of psychological development*, New York: Plenum Press.

Brown, L. M. and Gilligan, C. (1992) *Meeting at the Crossroads: Women's Psychology and Girls' Development*, Cambridge, MA and London: Harvard University Press.

Brown, L. M. and Gilligan, C. (1993) 'Meeting at the Crossroads: Women's Psychology and Girls' Development', *Feminism and Psychology* 3 (1): 11–35.

Brownmiller, S. (1976) *Against Our Will: Men, Women and Rape*, Harmondsworth: Penguin.

Burman, E. (1994) *Deconstructing Developmental Psychology*, London and New York: Routledge.

Burman, E. (1995) '"What is it?" Masculinity and femininity in cultural representations of childhood', in Wilkinson, S. and Kitzinger, C. (eds) *Feminism and Discourse: Psychological Perspectives*, London: Sage.

Busfield, J. (1989) 'Sexism in psychiatry', *Sociology* 23 (3): 343–64.

Byrne, A. (1995) 'Issues for Irish feminist pedagogy: what it is and how you do it', in Lentin, R. (ed.) *In from the Shadows: The UL Women's Studies Collection*, Limerick: University of Limerick Department of Government and Society.

Cain, M. (1993) 'Foucault, feminism and feeling: what Foucault can and cannot contribute to feminist epistemology', in Ramazanoglu, C. (ed.) *Up against Foucault: explorations of some tensions between Foucault and feminism*, London: Routledge.

Cherryholmes, C. H. (1988) *Power and Criticism: Poststructural Investigations in Education*, New York: Teachers' College Press.

Chodorow, N. (1978) *The Reproduction of Mothering*, California: University of California Press.

Chodorow, N. (1980) 'Gender, relation and difference in psychoanalytic perspective', in Eisenstein, H. and Jardine, A. (eds) *The Future of Difference*, Boston: G.K. Hall and Co.

Chodorow, N. (1994) *Femininities, Masculinities, Sexualities: Freud and Beyond*, London: Free Association Books.

Cixous, H. and Clement, C. (1975) *La Jeune Née*, Paris: Union Générale d'Editions.

Clancy, N. (1995) *Personal Development as a Tool for Empowering Women*, Unpublished M. A. thesis, Department of Economics, University College, Galway.

Clark, J. and Prendiville, P. (1992) *Report on Personal Development Training Course*, Dublin: Combat Poverty Agency.

Clark, M. (1989) 'Anastasia is a normal developer because she is unique', *Oxford Review of Education* 15 (3): 243–56.

Clark, M. C. and Wilson, A. L. (1991) 'Context and rationality in Mezirow's theory of transformational learning', *Adult Education Quarterly* 41 (2): 75–91.

Clavelin, M. (1974) *The Natural Philosophy of Galileo*, London: MIT Press.

Cocks, J. (1989) *The Oppositional Imagination: feminism, critique and political theory*, London: Routledge.

Collins, T. (1992) *Power, Participation and Exclusion*, Dublin: Conference of Major Religious Superiors.

Connell, R.W. (1985) 'Theorizing gender', *Sociology* 19 (2): 260–77.

Connell, R.W. (1987) *Gender and Power: Society, the Person and Sexual Politics*, Cambridge: Polity Press.

Connell, R.W. (1990) 'The state, gender and sexual politics: theory and appraisal', *Theory and Society* 19: 507–44.

Connell, R.W. (1995) *Masculinities*, London: Polity.

Connolly, L. (1996) 'The Women's Movement in Ireland 1970–1995', *Irish Journal of Feminist Studies* 1 (1): 43–77.

Connolly, L. (1999) '"Don't blame women": an exploration of current challenges facing feminist academics', in Connolly, B. and Ryan, A. B. *Women and Education in Ireland* Vol Two, Maynooth: MACE.

Connolly, L. (2001) *The Irish Women's Movement: From Revolution to Devolution*, London: MacMillan/Palgrave.

Coolahan, J. (1981) *Irish Education: history and structure*, Dublin: Institute of Public Administration.

Cornell, S. and Thurschwell, A. (1987) 'Feminism, negativity, intersubjectivity', in Benhabib, S. and Cornell, D. (eds) *Feminism as Critique,* Cambridge: Polity Press.

Courtney, S. (1992) *Why Adults Learn: Towards a theory of participation in adult learning*, London: Routledge.

Coward, R. (1984) *Female Desire: Women's Sexuality Today*, London: Paladin.

Coward, R. (1993) *Our Treacherous Hearts: Why Women Let Men Get Their Way*, London: Faber.

Craib, I. (1992) *Anthony Giddens*, London: Routledge.

Cranton, P. (1992) *Understanding and Promoting Transformative Learning: a guide for educators of adults*, San Francisco: Jossey Bass.

Crawford, M. (1997) 'Agreeing to differ: feminist epistemologies and women's ways of knowing', in Gergen, M. M. and Davis, S. N. (eds) *Towards a New Psychology of Gender*, London and New York: Routledge.

Culler, J. (1976) *Saussure*, Glasgow: Fontana.

Daly, M. (1973) *Beyond God the Father: Towards a Philosophy of Women's Liberation*, Boston: Beacon Press.

Daly, M. (1978) *Gyn/Ecology: the metaethics of radical feminism*, London: The Women's Press.

Daly, M. (1984) *Pure Lust: elemental feminist philosophy*, London: the Women's Press.

Daly, M. (1989) 'Women and power in Ireland, what progress have we made?', *Co-Options: Journal of the Community Workers' Co-Operative.*

Davies, B. (1990a) 'Agency as a form of classroom practice: a classroom scene observed', *British Journal of the Sociology of Education* 11 (30): 341–61.

Davies, B. (1990b) *Frogs and Snails and Feminist Tales*, Sydney: Allen and Unwin.

Davies, B. (1990c) 'The problem of desire', *Social Problems* 37 (4): 501–16.

Davies, B. and Harre, R. (1990) 'Positioning: the discursive production of selves', *Journal for the Theory of Social Behaviour* 20 (1): 43–63.

Davis, K. (1996) 'From objectified body to embodied subject: a biographical approach to cosmetic surgery', in Wilkinson, S. (ed.) *Feminist Social Psychologies: International Perspectives*, Buckingham: Open University Press.

Delphy, C. (1984) *Close to Home: A materialist analysis of women's oppression*, London: Hutchinson.

Derrida, J. (1973) *Speech and Phenomena*, Tr. D. Allison, Evanston, IL: Northwestern University Press.

Descartes, R. (1637) *Discourse*.

Descartes, R. (1641) *Meditation*.

Dinnerstein, D. (1976) *The Mermaid and the Minotaur: Sexual Arrangements and the Human Malaise*, New York: Harper.

Dolphin, E. (1994) 'Using the spiral', in Caherty, T. (ed.) *Making connections: Women Developing Links for Change*, Dublin: Banulacht.

Donzelot, J. (1980) *The Policing of Families*, London: Hutchinson.

Dreyfus, H. L. and Rabinow, P. (1982) *Michel Foucault: Beyond Structuralism and Hermeneutics*, Chicago: University of Chicago Press.

Drudy, S. and Lynch, K. (1993) *Schools and Society in Ireland*, Dublin: Gill and Macmillan.

Eagleton, T. (1983) *Literary Theory: An Introduction*, Oxford: Blackwell.

Easlea, B. (1980) *Witch-hunting, Magic and the New Philosophy*, Brighton: Harvester Press.

Echols, A. (1983) 'The new feminism of yin and yang', in Snitow, A., Stansell, C. and Thompson, S. (eds) *Powers of Desire: The Politics of Sexuality*, New York: Monthly Review Press.

Eichenbaum, L. and Orbach, S. (1982) *Outside In, Inside Out*, Harmondsworth: Penguin.

Eichenbaum, L. and Orbach, S. (1984) *What do Women Want?*, Glasgow: Fontana.

Eisenstein, H. (1984) *Contemporary Feminist Thought*, London: Unwin.

Eisenstein, H. and Jardine, A. (1985) (eds) *The Future of Difference*, New Brunswick, N.J.: Rutgers University Press.

Eisenstein, Z. (1979) (ed.) *Capitalist Patriarchy*, New York: Monthly Review Press.

Elias, N. (1978) *The History of Manners: The Civilising Process* Vol 1, Oxford: Basil Blackwell.

Fagan, G. H. (1991) 'Local struggles: women in the home and critical feminist pedagogy in Ireland', *Journal of Education* 173 (1): 65–75.

Faith, K. (1994) 'Resistance: lessons from Foucault and feminism' in Radtke, H. L. and Stam, H. J. (eds) *Power/Gender: Social Relations in Theory and Practice* (Inquiries in Social Construction Series), London: Sage.

Ferguson, A., Xita, J. and Addleson, K. (1981) 'On "compulsory heterosexuality and lesbian existence": defining the issues', *Signs* 7 (1): 158–99.

Firestone, S. (1974) *The dialectic of sex: the case for feminist revolution*, London: Cape.

Fisher, S. and Todd, A. D. (1988) (eds) *Gender and Discourse*, New Jersey: Ablex.

Flax, J. (1978) 'The conflict between nurturance and autonomy in mother-daughter relationships and within feminism', *Feminist Studies* 4 (2).

Foster, M. (1984) *Foucault, Marxism and History: Mode of Production versus Mode of Information*, Cambridge: Polity Press.

Foucault, M. (1966) *Les Mots et les Choses*, Paris: Gallimard.

Foucault, M. (1972a) *The Archaeology of Knowledge*, New York: Pantheon.

Foucault, M. (1972b) *Histoire de la folie*, Paris: Gallimard.

Foucault, M. (1973a) *Birth of the Clinic*, London: Tavistock.

Foucault, M. (1973b) 'History, discourse and continuity', *Salmagundi* 20: 225–48.

Foucault, M. (1979) *The History of Sexuality* Vol. 1, London: Allen Lane.

Foucault, M. (1980) *Power/Knowledge: Selected Interviews and Other Writings 197–1977*, New York: Pantheon.

Fox, D. and Prilleltensky, I. (1997) (eds) *Critical Psychology: An Introduction*, London: Sage.

Fraser, N. (1989) *Unruly practices: Power, discourse and gender in contemporary social theory*, London: Routledge and Kegan Paul.

Fraser, N. (1992) 'The uses and abuses of French discourse theories/or feminist politics', in N. Fraser and S.L. Bartkey (eds) *Revealing French Feminisms: critical essays on difference, agency and culture*, Bloomington, Indianapolis: Indiana University Press.

Freire, P (1970, sixth edition, 1993) *Pedagogy of the Oppressed*, Harmondsworth: Penguin.

Freud, S. (1900) *The Interpretation of Dreams*, London: Hogarth Press.

Freud, S. (1914) *On Narcissism: An Introduction* Standard Edition, Vol XIV, London: Hogarth Press.

Freud, S. (1973, first published 1933) *New Introductory Lectures*, Harmondsworth: Penguin.

Friedan, B. (1965) *The Feminine Mystique*, Harmondsworth: Penguin.

Frith, H. and Kitzinger, C. (1998) '"Emotion work" as a participant resource: a feminist analysis of young women's talk-in-interaction', *Sociology* 32 (2): 299–320.

Frosh, S. (1987) *The Politics of Psychoanalysis*, London: Macmillan.

Fuss, D. (1990, first published 1989) *Essentially Speaking: Feminism, Nature and Difference*, London: Routledge.

Galligan, Y. (1993) 'Women in Irish politics', in Coakley, J. and Gallagher, M. (eds) *Politics in the Republic of Ireland*, Dublin: PSAI/Folens.

Gallop, J. (1982) *The Daughter's Seduction: Feminism and Psychoanalysis*, Ithaca, New York: Cornell University Press.

Gallop, J. (1988) *Thinking Through the Body*, New York: Colombia University Press.

Gardiner, F. (1997) 'Gender gaps and dual cultures: are these the missing links in Irish politics?', *Irish Journal of Feminist Studies* 1 (2): 36–57.

Gardner, H. (1983) *Frames of Mind: The Theory of Multiple Intelligences*, New York: Paladin.

Gavey, N. (1997, first published 1989) 'Feminist poststructuralism and discourse analysis: contributions to feminist psychology', in Gergen, M. M. and Davis, S. N. (eds) *Towards a New Psychology of Gender*, London and New York: Routledge.

Gee, J. P. (1988) 'The legacies of literacy: from Plato to Freire through Harvey Graff', *Harvard Educational Review* 58 (2): 195–212.

Giddens, A. (1979) *Central Problems in Social Theory*, Cambridge: Polity Press.

Giddens, A. (1991) *Modernity and Self-identity: Self and Society in the Late Modern Age*, Cambridge: Polity Press.

Giddens, A. (1994) *Beyond Left and Right: the Future of Radical Politics*, Cambridge: Polity Press.

Giddens, A. (1999) *Runaway World*, London: Profile Books.

Gilbert, P. (1989) 'Personally (and passively) yours: girls, literacy and education', *Oxford Review of Education* 15 (3): 257–66.

Gilbert, P. (1990) 'Self-esteem in the English curriculum', in Kenway, J. and Willis, S. (eds) *Hearts and Minds: Self-Esteem and the Schooling of Girls*, Barcombe: The Falmer Press.

Gill, J. (1987) 'The effect of gender on schooling', *Expanding Options* 3 (1): 1–11.

Gill, R. (1996) 'Relativism, reflexivity and politics: interrogating discourse analysis from a feminist perspective', in Wilkinson, S. and Kitzinger, C. (eds) *Feminism and Discourse: Psychological Perspectives*, London: Sage.

Gilligan, C. (1982) *In a Different Voice: Psychological Theory and Women's Development*, Cambridge, MA: Harvard University Press.

Gilligan, A.L. (1999) 'Education towards a feminist imagination', in Connolly, B. and Ryan, A. B. (eds) *Women and Education in Ireland* Vol Two, Maynooth: MACE.

Glaser, B. E. (1978) *Theoretical Sensitivity*, Mill Valley, CA: Sociology Press.

Glaser, B. E. and Strauss, A. L. (1967) *The Discovery of Grounded Theory*, Chicago: Aldine.

Goldberg, H. (1976) *The Hazards of Being Male: Surviving the Myths of Masculine Privilege*, New York: Nash.

Goodrich, T. J. (1991a) (ed.) *Women and Power: Perspectives for Family Therapy*, New York and London: W. W. Norton and Co.

Goodrich, T. J. (1991b) 'Women, power and family therapy: what's wrong with this picture?', in Goodrich, T. J. (ed.) *Women and Power: Perspectives for Family Therapy*, New York and London: W. W. Norton and Co.

Goodsin, I. (1990) 'Studying curriculum: towards a social constructionist perspective', *Journal of Curriculum Studies* 22 (4): 299–312.

Graff, H. (1987a) *The legacies of literacy: Continuities and contradictions in Western culture and society*, Bloomington: University of Indiana Press.

Graff, H. (1987b) *The labyrinths of literacy: Reflections on literacy past and present*, New York: The Falmer Press.

Gramsci, A. (1971) *Prison Notebooks*, London: Lawrence and Wishart.

Greene, M. (1993) 'Introduction', in Middleton, S. *Educating Feminists: Life Histories and Pedagogies*, New York: Teachers' College Press.

Griffin, G. (1997) 'Review of Sage series: "Research on Men on Masculinities"', in *Feminism and Psychology* (3): 412–416.

Grimshaw, J. (1986) *Feminist Philosophers: Women's perspectives on philosophical traditions*, Brighton: Wheatsheaf.

Grimshaw, J. (1993) 'Practices of freedom', in Ramazanoglu, C. (ed.) *Up against Foucault: explorations of some tensions between Foucault and feminism*, London: Routledge.

Grosz, E. (1989) *Sexual Subversions: Three French Feminists*, Allen and Unwin: Sydney.

Habermas, J. (1971a) *Knowledge and Human Interests*, Boston: Beacon Press.

Habermas, J. (1971b) *Towards a Rational Society*, London: Heineman.

Habermas, J. (1983a) *The Theory of Communicative Action* Vol 1, Boston: Beacon Press.

Habermas, J. (1983b, first published in English, 1991) *Moral Consciousness and Communicative Action*, Cambridge, MA: MIT Press.

Hacking, I. (1981) 'How should we do the history of statistics?', *Ideology and Consciousness* 8: 15–26.

Hall, S. (1988) 'Minimal selves', in *Identity: the Real Me* (ICA Document NO. 6), London: Institute of the Contemporary Arts.

Hare-Mustin, R. T. (1991) 'Sex, lies and headaches: the problem is power', in Goodrich, T. J. (ed.) *Women and Power: Perspectives for Family Therapy*, New York and London: W. W. Norton and Co.

Harre, R. (1979) *Social Being*, Oxford: Blackwell.

Harris, V. F. (1989) 'Scribe, inscription, inscribed: sexuality in the poetry of Robert Bly and Adrienne Rich', in Barr, M. S. and Feldstein, R. (eds) *Discontented Discourses: feminism/textual intervention/psychoanalysis*, Urbana and Chicago: University of Illinois Press.

Harrison, J. F. C. (1969) *Quest for the New Moral World: Robert Owen and the Owenites in Britain and America*, New York: Charles Scribner's Sons.

Hartmann, H. (1979) 'Capitalism, patriarchy and job segregation by sex', in Eisenstein, Z. (ed.) *Capitalist Patriarchy*, New York: Monthly Review Press.

Hartmann, H. (1981) 'The unhappy marriage of marxism and feminism: towards a more progressive union', in Sargent, L. (ed. 1989) *The Second Shift*, London; Piatkus.

Hassan, I. (1987) *The Postmodern Turn: Essays in Postmodern Theory and Culture*, Columbia: Ohio State University Press.

Haug, F. (1987) *Female Sexualization*, London: Verso.

Haug, F. (1990) *Erinnerungsarbeit*, Berlin: Argument

Hayes, L. (1990) *Working for Change: A Study of Three Women's Projects, 1988–1990*, Dublin: Combat Poverty Agency.

Heilbrun, C. G. (1989) *Writing a Woman's Life*, New York: W. W. Norton.

Henriques, J., Hollway, W., Urwin, C., Venn, C. and Walkerdine, V. (1984) *Changing the Subject: Psychology, social regulation and subjectivity*, London: Methuen.

Hindness, B. (1986) 'Actors and social relations', in Wardell, M. C. and Turner, S. P. (eds) *Social Theory in Transition*, London: Allen and Unwin.

Hirst, P. H. (1979) *On Law and Ideology*, London: Macmillan.

Hochschild, A. R. (1990, first published 1989) *The Second Shift*, London: Piatkus.

Holford, J. (1995) 'Why social movements matter', *Adult Education Quarterly* 45 (2): 93–109.

Holland, D. and Eisenhart, M. (1990) *Educated in Romance: Women, Achievement and College Culture*, Chicago: University of Chicago Press.

Holland, S. (1979) *Rutland Street: the story of an educational experiment for disadvantaged children in Dublin*. Written for the Bernard van Leer Foundation. Oxford: Pergamon.

Hollway, W. (1982) *Identity and Gender Difference in Adult Social Relations*, Unpublished PhD thesis, University of London.

Hollway, W. (1984a) 'Gender difference and the production of subjectivity', in Henriques, J. *et al Changing the Subject: Psychology, social regulation and subjectivity*, London: Methuen.

Hollway, W. (1984b) 'Women's power in heterosexual sex', *Women's Studies International Forum* 7 (1): 63–8.

Hollway, W. (1989) *Subjectivity and Method in Psychology: Gender, Meaning and Science*, London: Sage.

Hollway, W. (1991a) *Work Psychology and Organizational Behaviour: Managing the Individual at Work*, London: Sage.

Hollway, W. (1991b) 'The psychologisation of feminism or the feminisation of psychology?', *Feminism and Psychology* 1: 2–37.

Hollway, W. (1994) 'Separations, integration and difference: contradictions in a gender regime', in Radtke, H. L. and Stam, H. J. (eds) *Power/Gender: Social Relations in Theory and Practice* (Inquiries in Social Construction Series), London: Sage.

Hollway, W. (1995) 'Feminist discourses and women's heterosexual desires', in Wilkinson, S. and Kitzinger, C. (eds) *Feminism and Discourse: Psychological Perspectives*, London: Sage.

Hollway, W. and Jefferson, T. (2000) *Doing qualitative research differently*, London: Sage.

Hooks, B. (1989) *Talking Back: Thinking Feminist, Thinking Black*, Boston: South End Press.

Inglis, T. (1994) 'Women and the struggle for daytime education in Ireland', *Studies in the Education of Adults* 26: 50–66.

Irigaray, L. (1985) *This Sex Which Is Not One*, Tr. C. Porter, with C. Burke, Ithaca, New York; Cornell University Press.

Jagger, A. (1983) *Feminist Politics and Human Nature*, Totowa, New Jersey: Rowman and Allenfeld.

Jardine, A. (1985) *Gynesis: Configurations of Women and Modernity*, Ithaca, New York; Cornell University Press.

Jeffers, S. (1987) *Feel the Fear and Do It Anyway*, London: Arrow.

Johnston, R. (1993) 'Becoming more reflexive as a researcher', in Miller, N. and Jones, D. J. (eds) *Research Reflecting Practice*, Boston, Lincolnshire: SCUTREA.

Jones, A. (1993) 'Becoming a "girl": post-structuralist suggestions for educational research', *Gender and Education* 5 (2): 157–66.

Jones, K. and Williamson, J. (1979) 'Birth of the schoolroom', *Ideology and Consciousness* 6: 59–110.

Kanter, R. M. (1977) *Men and Women of the Corporation*, New York: Basic Books.

Keller, E. F. (1985) *Reflections on Gender and Science*, London: Yale University Press.

Kenway, J. and Willis, S. (1990) (eds) *Hearts and Minds: Self-esteem and the Schooling of Girls*, Barcombe: The Falmer Press.

Kenway, J., Willis, S., Blackmore, J. and Rennie, L. (1994) 'Making "hope practical" rather than "despair convincing": feminist post-structuralism, gender reform and educational change', *British Journal of Sociology of Education* 15 (2): 187–210.

Kenway, J., Willis, S. and Nevard, J. (1990) 'The subtle politics of self-esteem programs for girls', in Kenway, J. and Willis, S. (eds) *Hearts and Minds: Self-esteem and the Schooling of Girls*, Barcombe: The Falmer Press.

Kerfoot, D. and Knights, D, (1994) 'Into the realm of the fearful: power, identity and the gender problematic', in Radtke, H. L. and Stam, H. J. (eds) *Power/Gender: Social Relations in Theory and Practice* (Inquiries in Social Construction Series), London: Sage.

Kiely, L. (2000) 'A feminist critique of the concept of empowerment', paper presented at Women's Studies Seminar, University College Cork, February 18.

Kiely, E. Leane, M. and Meade, R. (1999) '"It's all changed from here": Women's experiences of community education', in Ryan, A. B. and Connolly, B. (eds) *Women and Education in Ireland* Vol. One, Maynooth: MACE.

Kitzinger, C. (1987) *The Social Construction of Lesbianism*, Newbury Park, CA: Sage.

Kitzinger, C. (1990) 'Resisting the discipline', in Burman, E. (ed.) *Feminists and Psychological Practice*, London: Sage.

Kitzinger, C. (1994) 'Problematizing pleasure: radical feminist deconstructions of sexuality and power', in Radtke, H. L. and Stam, H. J. (eds) *Power/Gender: Social Relations in Theory and Practice* (Inquiries in Social Construction Series), London: Sage.

Kitzinger, C. and Gilligan, C. (1994) 'Listening to a different voice', *Feminism and Psychology* 4 (3): 408–19.

Kitzinger, C. and Wilkinson, S. (1993) (eds) *Heterosexuality: A Feminism and Psychology Reader*, London: Sage.

Kitzinger, C. and Wilkinson, S. (1994) 'Dire straights? Contemporary rehabilitations of heterosexuality', in Griffin, G., Hester, M., Rai, S. and Roseneil, S. (eds) *Stirring It: Challenges for Feminism*, London and New York: Taylor and Francis.

Kitzinger, J. (1993) 'Sexual violence and compulsory heterosexuality', in Kitzinger, C. and Wilkinson, S. (eds) *Heterosexuality: A Feminism and Psychology Reader*, London: Sage.

Klein, M. (1986) *The Selected Melanie Klein*, ed. J. Mitchell, Harmondsworth: Penguin.

Koyre, A (1933) *The Reformation in Medieval Perspective*, Chicago: Quadrangle Books.

Kristeva, J. (1986) *The Kristeva Reader*, ed. T. Moi, Oxford: Blackwell.

Kurzweil, E. (1989) 'Psychoanalytic feminism: implications for sociological theory', in Wallace, R. A. (ed.) *Feminism and Sociological Theory*, London: Sage.

Lacan, J. (1949) 'The mirror stage as formative of the function of the I as revealed in psychoanalytic experience', reprinted in J. Lacan (1977) *Ecrits: A Selection*, Tr. A. Sheridan, London: Tavistock.

Lacan, J. (1977) *Ecrits: A Selection*, Tr. A. Sheridan, London: Tavistock.

Lacan, J. (1981) *The Talking Cure: Essays in Psychoanalysis and Language*, ed. C. McCabe, London: Macmillan.

Lather, P. (1986) 'Research as praxis', *Harvard Educational Review* 56 (3): 257–77.

Lather, P. (1991) *Feminist Research in education: within/against*, Geelong: Deakin University Press.

Lauretis, T. de (1984) *Alice Doesn't*, Bloomington: Indiana University Press.

Lauretis, T. de (1988) (ed.) *Feminist Studies/Critical Studies*, Basingstoke: Macmillan.

Layder, D. (1994) *Understanding Social Theory*, London: Sage.

Leeds Revolutionary Feminist Group (1981) 'Political lesbianism: the case against heterosexuality', in *Love your enemy? The debate between heterosexual feminism and political lesbianism*, London: Onlywomen Press.

Lerner, M. G. (1985) *The Dance of Anger: A woman's guide to changing the patterns of intimate relationships*, New York: Harper and Row.

Lewis, M. (1989) 'The challenge of feminist pedagogy', *Queen's Quarterly* 96 (1): 117–30.

Lewis, M. (1993) *Without a Word: teaching beyond women's silence*, London and New York: Routledge.

Lipman Blumen, J. (1994) 'The existential bases of power relationships: the gender role case', in Radtke, H. L. and Stam, H. J. (eds) *Power/Gender: Social Relations in Theory and Practice* (Inquiries in Social Construction Series), London: Sage.

Lomax, P. (1994) *The Narrative of an Educational Journey or Crossing the Track*, Kingston upon Thames: Kingston University School of Education.

Lovell, T. (1990) (ed.) *British Feminist Thought: A Reader*, Oxford: Blackwell.

Luker, K. (1984) *Abortion and the Politics of Motherhood*, Berkeley: University of California Press.

Lusted, D. (1986) 'Why pedagogy?', Introduction to a special issue on pedagogy, *Screen* 27: 2–14.

McDermott, R. P. and Tylbor, H. (1987) 'On the necessity of collusion in conversation', in Kedar, L. (ed.) *Power through Discourse*, New Jersey: Ablex.

McDonald, G. (1989) 'Feminist teaching techniques for the committed but exhausted', *Atlantis* 15 (1): 145–51.

McNeil, M. (1993) 'Dancing with Foucault: feminism and power-knowledge', in Ramazanoglu, C. (ed.) *Up against Foucault: explorations of some tensions between Foucault and feminism*, London: Routledge.

Maher, F. A. (1987) 'Towards a richer theory of feminist pedagogy: a comparison of "liberation" and "gender" models for teaching and learning', *Journal of Education* 169 (3): 91–100.

Mainardi, P. (1970) 'The politics of housework', in Morgan, R. (ed.) *Sisterhood is powerful: an anthology of writings from the women's liberation movement*, New York: Vintage Books.

Mama, A. (1995) *Beyond the Masks: Race, Gender and Subjectivity*, London and New York: Routledge.

Mantel, H. (1994) *A Change of Climate*, Harmondsworth: Penguin.

Martin, B. and Mohanty, C. T. (1988) 'Feminist politics: What's home got to do with it?', in Lauretis, T. de (ed.) *Feminist Studies/Critical Studies*, Basingstoke: Macmillan.

Maslow, A. (1939) '*Dominance, personality and social behaviour in women*', *Journal of Social Psychology* 10.

Maslow, A. (1942) 'Self-esteem (dominance feeling) and sexuality in women', *Journal of Social Psychology* 16.

Maslow, A. (1968) *Towards a Psychology of Being*, Second edition, Princeton: Van Nostrand.

Maslow, A. (1970) *Motivation and Personality*, Second edition, New York: Harper and Row.

Mednick, M. (1989) 'On the politics of psychological constructs: Stop the bandwagon, I want to get off', *American Psychologist* 44: 1118–123.

Merleau Ponty, M. (1969) *Humanism and Terror*, Tr. J. O'Neill, Paris: Gallimard.

Mezirow, J. (1978) 'Perspective transformation', *Adult Education* 28 (2): 100–10.

Mezirow, J. (1981) 'A critical theory of adult learning and education', *Adult Education* 32 (1): 3–24.

Mezirow, J. (1991) *Transformative Dimensions of Adult Learning*, San Francisco: Jossey Bass.

Mezirow, J. (1996) 'Adult education and empowerment for individual and community development', in Connolly, B., Fleming, T., McCormack, D. and Ryan, A. (eds) *Radical Learning for Liberation*, Maynooth Adult and Community Education Occasional Series, No 1. Maynooth: MACE.

Mezirow, J. and Associates, (1990) *Fostering Critical Reflection in Adulthood: A guide to transformative and emancipatory learning*, San Francisco: Jossey Bass.

Michie, H. (1989) 'Not one of the family: the repression of the other woman in feminist theory', in Barr, M. S. and Feldstein, R. (eds) *Discontented Discourses: Feminism/Textual Intervention/Psychoanalysis*, Urbana and Chicago: University of Chicago Press.

Middleton, S. (1993) *Educating Feminists: life history and pedagogy*, New York: Teachers College Press.

Mies, M. and Shiva, V. (1993) *Ecofeminism*, London: Zed Books.

Mies, M. and Shiva, V. (1997) 'Ecofeminism', in Kemp, S. and Squires, J. (eds) *Feminisms*, Oxford: Oxford University Press.

Millett, K. (1971) *Sexual Politics*, London: Granada.

Mitchell, J. (1971) *Women's Estate*, Harmondsworth: Penguin.

Mitchell, J. (1975) *Psychoanalysis and Feminism*, Harmondsworth: Penguin.

Mitchell, J. and Rose, J. (1982) (eds) *Feminine Sexuality: Jacques Lacan and the Ecole Freudienne*, London: Macmillan.

Moi, T. (1985) *Sexual/Textual Politics: Feminist Literary Theory*, London: Methuen.

Moi, T. (1990) 'Feminism and postmodernism: recent feminist criticism in the United States', in Lovell, T. (ed.) *British Feminist Thought: A Reader*, Oxford: Blackwell.

Morrow, R. A. (1994) with Brown, D. B. *Critical Theory and Methodology*, Contemporary Social Theory Vol. Three, London: Sage.

Mulvey, C. (1991) *Evaluation Report on the Allen Lane Foundation's Funding Programme in Ireland 1989–1991*, Dublin: Allen Lane.

Mulvey, C. (1995) *Women's Power ... for a Change: A Report on a Conference of Women's Networks in Ireland, 'Women, Leadership and Change'*, Dublin: AONTAS.

Nicholson, L. (1999) *The Play of Reason: From the modern to the postmodern*, Buckingham: Open University Press.

Norris, C. (1982) *Deconstruction: Theory and Practice,* London: Methuen.

Oakley, A. (1998) 'Gender, methodology and people's ways of knowing: some problems with feminism and the paradigm debate in social science', *Sociology* 32 (4): 707–32.

O'Donovan, O. and Ward, E. (1996) 'Networks of women's groups and politics: what (some) women think', *UCG Women's Studies Review* 4: 1–20.

O'Donovan, O. and Ward, E. (1999) 'Networks of women's groups in the Republic of Ireland', in Galligan, Y., Ward, E. and Wilford, R. (eds) *Contesting Politics: Women in Ireland, North and South*, Boulder, CO and Oxford: Westview Press.

Owen, R. (1813) *A New View of Society: Or Essays on the Principles of the Formation of the Human Character.*

Perry, W. G. (1970) *Forms of Intellectual and Ethical Development in the College Years*, New York: Holt, Rinehart and Winston.

Petchevsky, R. P. (1988) *Abortion and Women's Choice: the state, sexuality and women's freedom*, London: Verso.

Pleck, J. H. (1977) 'The male sex role: definitions, problems and sources of change', *Journal of Social Issues* 32: 155–64.

Porta, G. (1650) *Magie Naturelle.*

Poster, M. (1989) *Critical Theory and Poststructuralism: In Search of a Context*, Ithaca, New York: Cornell University Press.

Potter, J. (1996) *Representing reality: discourse, rhetoric and social construction*, London: Sage.

Potter, J. and Wetherell, M. (1987) *Discourse and Social Psychology: Beyond Attitudes and Beliefs*, London: Sage.

Potts, T. and Price, J. (1995) '"Out of the blood and spirit of our lives": the place of the body in academic feminism', in Morley, L. and Walsh, V. (eds) *Feminist Academics: Creative Agents for Change*, London: Taylor and Francis.

Pritchard Hughes, K. (1995) 'Feminist pedagogy and feminist epistemology: an overview', *International Journal of Lifelong Education* 14 (5): 214–30.

Quinn, M. (1999) 'Narrow paths and distant horizons: perceptions of schooling among disadvantaged young women', in Connolly, B. and Ryan, A. B. (eds) *Women and Education in Ireland* Vol. One, Maynooth: MACE.

Radtke, H. L. and Stam, H. J. (1994) (eds) *Power/Gender: Social relations in Theory and Practice* (Inquiries in Social Construction Series), London: Sage.

Ramazanoglu, C. (1993) 'Introduction', in Ramazanoglu, C. (ed.) *Up against Foucault: explorations of some tensions between Foucault and feminism*, London: Routledge.

Ransom, J. (1993) 'Feminism, difference and discourse; the limits of discursive analysis for feminism', in Ramazanoglu, C. (ed.) *Up against Foucault: explorations of some tensions between Foucault and feminism*, London: Routledge.

Rath, A. (1999) 'Coming to know in Community: voice, metaphor and epistemology', in Connolly, B. and Ryan, A. B. (eds) *Women and Education in Ireland* Vol.Two, Maynooth: MACE.

Renshaw, P. (1990) 'Self-esteem research and equity programmes for girls: a reassessment', in

Kenway, J. and Willis, S. *Hearts and Minds: Self-esteem and the Schooling of Girls*, Barcombe: The Falmer Press.

Rich, A. (1980) 'Compulsory heterosexuality and lesbian existence', *Signs* 5 (4): 631–60.

Richardson, D. (1996a) 'Representing other feminists', *Feminism and Psychology* 6 (2): 192–6.

Richardson, D. (1996b) (ed.) *Theorizing Heterosexuality: Telling it Straight*, Milton Keynes: Open University Press.

Riley, D. (1978) 'Developmental psychology, biology and Marxism', *Ideology and Consciousness* 4: 73–92.

Riley, D. (1983) *War in the Nursery: Theories of the Child and Mother*, London: Virago.

Rogers, C. R. (1961) *On Becoming a Person*, London: Constable.

Rogers, C. R. (1978) *Carl Rogers on Personal Power: Inner Strength and Its Revolutionary Impact*, London: Constable.

Rose, J. (1990, first published 1983) 'Femininity and its discontents', in Lovell, T. (ed.) *British Feminist Thought: A Reader*, Oxford: Blackwell.

Rose, N. (1979) 'The psychological complex: mental measurement and social administration', *Ideology and Consciousness* 5: 5–68.

Roseneil, S. (1995) 'The coming of age of feminist sociology: some issues of practice and theory for the next twenty years', *British Journal of Sociology* 46 (2): 191–205.

Rowbotham, S. (1981) 'The trouble with "patriarchy"', in Feminist Anthology Collective (ed.) *No turning back: writings from the women's liberation movement, 1975–1980*, London: The Women's Press.

Rowland, R. and Thomas, A. (1996) (eds) 'Mothering sons: a critical feminist challenge', Special Feature, *Feminism and Psychology* 6 (1): 93–142.

Rowland, R. and Klein, R. (1996) 'Radical feminism: history, politics, action', in Bell, D. and Klein, R. (eds) *Radically Speaking: Feminism Reclaimed*, London: Zed Books.

Ruddick, S. (1980) 'Maternal thinking', *Feminist Studies* 6.

Ruddick, S. (1984) 'Preservative love and military destruction: some reflections on mothering and peace', in Trebilcot, J. (ed.) *Mothering: Essays in Feminist Theory*, Totowa, NJ: Rowman and Allanheld.

Ryan, A. B. (1992) *Gender Difference and Discourse in School Social Relations*, Unpublished MA thesis, Centre for Adult and Community Education, St. Patrick's College, Maynooth.

Ryan, A. B. (1995) *A Voyage Round my Feminism*, Unpublished paper.

Ryan, A. B. (1997) 'Gender discourses in school social relations', in Byrne, A. and Leonard, M. (eds) *Women and Irish Society: A Sociological Reader*, Belfast: Beyond the Pale Publications.

Ryan, A. B. (1999) 'Sources for a politicised practice of women's personal development education', in Connolly, B. and Ryan, A. B. (eds) *Women and Education in Ireland*, Maynooth: MACE.

Ryan, A. B. and Connolly, B. (2000) 'Women's community education in Ireland and the need for new directions', in Thompson, J. L. (ed.) *Stretching the Academy*, Leicester: NIACE.

Ryan, J. (1990) 'Psychoanalysis: women loving women', in Lovell, T. (ed.) *British Feminist Thought: A Reader*, Oxford: Blackwell.

Sartre, J. P. (1960) *Critique de la Raison Dialectique,* Paris: Gallimard.

Saussure, F. de (1974, first published 1912) *Course in General Linguistics*, Tr. W. Baskin, London: Fontana.

Schor, N. (1989) 'This essentialism which is not one', *Differences* 1 (2).

Scott, J. W. (1988) 'Deconstructing equality versus difference: or, the uses of poststructuralist theory for feminism', *Feminist Studies* 14: 33–50.

Segal, L. (1987) *Is the Future Female? Troubled thoughts on contemporary feminism*, London: Virago.

Segal, L. (1990) *Slow Motion: Changing Masculinities, Changing Men*, London: Virago.

Segal, L. (1997) 'Generations of feminism', *Radical Philosopher* 83: 6–15.

Segal, L. (1999) *Why Feminism?*, Cambridge: Polity Press.

Selby, J. M. (1984) *Feminine Identity and Contradiction: women research sudents at Cambridge University*. Unpublished PhD thesis. University of Cambridge.

Silverman, D. (1985) *Qualitative Methodology and Sociology*, Aldershot: Gower.

Smith, D. E. (1987) *The Everyday World as Problematic: A Feminist Sociology*, Boston: Northeastern University Press.

Snitow, A. (1990) 'A gender diary', in Hirsch, M. and Fox Keller, E. (eds) *Conflicts in Feminism*, London: Routledge.

Snodgrass, J. (1977) *For Men Against Sexism: A Book of Readings*, Albion, CA: Times Change Press.

Spender, D. (1980) *Manmade Language*, London: Routledge and Kegan Paul.

Spender, D. and Sarah, E. (1980, reprinted 1988) (eds) *Learning to Lose: Sexism and Education*, London: The Women's Press.

Spivak, G. C. (1990) *The Post-Colonial Critic: Interviews, Strategies, Dialogues*, ed. S. Harasym, New York and London: Routledge.

Spray, G. (1997) 'The backlash boys', *Irish Journal of Feminist Studies* 2 (1): 106–16.

Starhawk (1989) 'Feminist Earth-based spirituality and ecofeminism', in Plane, J. (ed.) *Healing the Wounds: the Promise of Ecofeminism*, Toronto: Between the Lines.

Steinem, G. (1993) *Revolution from Within: A Book of Self-esteem*, London: Corgi.

Stephenson, N., Kippax, S. Crawford, J. (1996) 'You and I and she: memory work and the construction of self', in Wilkinson, S. (ed.) *Feminist Social Psychologies: International Perspectives*, Buckingham and Philadelphia: Open University Press.

Stewart, W. A. C. (1972) *Progressives and Radicals in English Education 1750–1970*, London: Macmillan.

Strauss, A. and Corbin, J. (1990) *Basics of Qualitative Research: grounded theory procedures and techniques*, London and California: Sage.

Taylor, J. M., Gilligan, C. and Sullivan, A. (1995) *Between Voice and Silence: Women and Girls, Race and Relationship*, Cambridge, MA: Harvard University Press.

Taylor, S. (1991) 'Skinned alive: towards a postmodern pedagogy of the body', *Education and Society* 9 (1): 61–72.

Tennant, M. and Pogson, P. (1995) *Learning and Change in the Adult Years*, San Francisco: Jossey Bass.

Thom, M. (1981) 'The unconscious structured like a language', in McCabe, C. (ed.) *The Talking Cure: Essays in Psychoanalysis and Language*, London; Macmillan.

Thompson, J. L. (1996) '"Really useful knowledge": linking theory and practice', in Connolly, B., Fleming, T., McCormack, D. and Ryan, A. (eds) *Radical Learning for Liberation*, Maynooth Adult and Community Education Occasional Series, No 1, Maynooth: Centre for Adult and Community Education.

Urwin, C. (1984) 'Power relations and the emergence of language', in Henriques, J., Hollway, W., Urwin, C., Venn, C. and Walkerdine, V. *Changing the Subject: Psychology, social regulation and subjectivity*, London: Methuen.

Urwin, C. (1985) 'Constructing motherhood: the persuasion of norman development', in Steedman, C., Urwin, C. and Walkerdine, V. (eds) *Language, Gender and Childhood*, London: Routledge and Kegan Paul.

Urwin, C., Venn, C. and Walkerdine, V. (1985) 'Constructing motherhood: the persuasion of normal development', in Steedman, C., Urwin, C. and Walkerdine, V. (eds) *Language, Gender and Childhood*, London: Routledge and Kegan Paul.

Venn, C. (1984) 'The subject of psychology', in Henriques, J., Hollway, W., Urwin, C., Venn, C. and Walkerdine, V. *Changing the Subject: Psychology, social regulation and subjectivity*, London: Methuen.

Walby, S. (1990) *Theorizing Patriarchy*, Oxford: Blackwell.

Walicki, A. (1983) 'Marx and freedom', *New York Review of Books*, Nov. 24.

Walkerdine, V. (1984) 'Developmental psychology and the child-centered pedagogy: the insertion of Piaget into early education', in Henriques, J., Hollway, W., Urwin, C., Venn, C. and Walkerdine, V. *Changing the Subject: Psychology, social regulation and subjectivity*, London: Methuen.

Walkerdine, V. (1985) 'On the regulation of speaking and silence; subjectivity, class and gender in contemporary schooling', in Steedman, C., Urwin, C. and Walkerdine, V. (eds) *Language, Gender and Childhood,* London: Routledge and Kegan Paul.

Walkerdine, V. (1987) 'No laughing matter: girls' comics and the preparation for adolescent sexuality', in Broughton, J.M. (1987) *Critical theories of psychological development*, New York: Plenum Press.

Walkerdine, V. (1988) *The Mastery of Reason: Cognitive Development and the Production of Rationality*, London: Routledge.

Walkerdine, V. (1989a) (compiled for the Girls and Mathematics Unit, Institute of Education) *Counting Girls Out*, London: Virago.

Walkerdine, V. (1989b) 'Femininity as performance', *Oxford Review of Education* 15 (3): 267–79.

Walkerdine, V. (1990) *Schoolgirl Fictions*, London: Verso.

Walkerdine, V. (1996) 'Psychology and social aspects of survival', in Wilkinson, S. (ed.) *Feminist Social Psychologies: International Perspectives*, Buckingham: Open University Press.

Walkerdine, V. and Lucey, H. (1989) *Democracy in the Kitchen: Regulating Mothers and Socialising Daughters*, London: Virago.

Walzer, M. (1986) 'The politics of Michel Foucault', in Hoy, D. C. (ed.) *Foucault: A Critical Reader*, New York: Basil Blackwell.

Weedon, C. (1997, second edition, first published, 1987) *Feminist Practice and Poststructuralist Theory*, Oxford: Blackwell.

Weedon, C. (1999) *Feminism, theory and the politics of difference*, Oxford: Blackwell.

Weiler, K. (1988) *Women teaching for change: Gender, class and power*, South Hadley: Bergin and Garvey Publishers.

Weiler, K. (1991) 'Freire and a feminist pedagogy of difference', *Harvard Educational Review* 61: 449–74.

Weinreich, C. (1978) 'Sex-role socialisation', in Chetwynd, J. and Harnett, O. (eds) *The Sex-role System*, London: Routledge and Kegan Paul.

Welton, M. (1990) *Shaking the foundations: critical perspectives on adult development and learning*, Unpublished manuscript.

West, L. (1996) *Beyond Fragments. Adults, Motivation and Higher Education: A Biographical Analysis*, London: Taylor and Francis.

Westwood, S. (1988) 'Domesticity and its discontents: feminism and adult education in past time', in Lovett, T. (ed.) *Radical Approaches to Adult Education: A Reader*, London: Routledge.

Wetherell, M. (1986) 'Linguistic perspectives in literary criticism: new directions for a social psychology of gender', in Wilkinson, S. (ed.) *Feminist Social Psychologies: International Perspectives*, Buckingham: Open University Press. [Reprinted in Crawford and Gergen 1997]

Wetherell, M. (1995) 'Romantic discourse and feminist analysis: interrogating investment, power and desire', in Wilkinson, S. and Kitzinger, C. (eds) *Feminism and Discourse: Psychological Perspectives*, London: Sage.

Wilcox, C. (1991) 'The causes and consequences of feminist consciousness among Western European women', *Comparative Political Studies* 32 (4): 519–45.

Wilkinson, S. (1996) 'Feminist social psychologies: a decade of development', in Wilkinson, S. (ed.) *Feminist Social Psychologies: International Perspectives*, Buckingham: Open University Press.

Wilkinson, S. (1997) 'Feminist psychology', in Fox, D. and Prilleltensky, I. (eds) *Critical Psychology: An Introduction*, London: Thousand Oaks and New Delhi: Sage.

Williamson, J. (1981) 'How does girl number twenty understand ideology?', *Screen Education*, 40: 80–7.

Wilson, E. (1982) *Psychoanalysis and feminism, re-opening the case*, Seminar presentation, London.

Winnicott, D. W. (1956) 'Primary maternal preoccupation', in *Collected Papers. Through Paediatrics to Psychoanalysis*, London: Tavistock.

Winnicott, D. W. (1957) *Mother and Child*, New York: Basic Books.

Young, I. M. (1987) 'Impartiality and the civic public: some implications of feminist critiques of moral and political theory', in Benhabib, S. and Cornell, D. (eds) *Feminism as Critique*, Cambridge: Polity Press.

Young, S. (1998) *Changing the Wor(l)d: Discourse, Politics and the Feminist Movement*, London: Routledge.

Index

Also published by NIACE

Stretching the academy: the politics and practice of widening participation in HE
Edited by Jane Thompson
ISBN 1 86201 091 9, November 2000, 188pp, £15.95

A major new intervention in the Widening Participation debate by academics active in radical politics. This collection of essays brings together critical analyses and inspirational prose, rooted in the authority of experience and practice. Essential reading for all those concerned with the part played by Higher Education in widening participation.

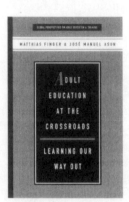

Adult education at the crossroads: learning our way out
Matthias Finger and Jose Manuel Asun
ISBN 1 86201 108 7, January 2001, 228pp, £15.95

An assessment of where adult education now stands: the traditions out of which it came, its current problems, and possible futures.

The authors remind adult educationists of their traditional commitment to social action by surveying the ideas of seminal adult education thinkers as they developed historically in Europe, North America and later the Third World. They show how today's very different context has eroded that original vision and purpose.

Powerful literacies
Edited by Jim Crowther, Mary Hamilton and Lyn Tett
ISBN 1 86201 094 3, March 2001, 200pp, £15.95

The growth of a knowledge-based economy and an information society has meant that literacy increasingly mediates our lives and activities. This evolution can be both liberating and limiting. Through the outcomes of literacy programmes internationally, *Powerful Literacies* explores the interventions and practices which attempt to enhance the autonomy of learners and communities, and their control over their environment.

With adult literacy at the forefront of an agenda of social inclusion, participation and active citizenship, this title will have relevance not only to academics, researchers, practitioners and students in adult, basic and community education, but also to policymakers in central and local government.